Build Your
Own PC

12
18
27
69
84
116
122

Other Computer Titles

by

Robert Penfold

BP470   Linux for Windows users
BP484   Easy PC Troubleshooting
BP495   Easy Windows Troubleshooting
BP503   Using Dreamweaver 4
BP504   Using Flash 5
BP507   Easy Internet Troubleshooting
BP518   Easy PC Peripherals Troubleshooting
BP521   Easy Windows XP Troubleshooting
BP523   Easy PC Interfacing
BP527   Using Flash MX
BP530   Using Dreamweaver MX
BP531   Easy PC Upgrading
BP536   Using Photoshop 7
BP537   Digital Photogrphy with Your Computer
BP539   Easy PC Web Site Construction
BP540   Easy PC Security and Safety
BP541   Boost Your PC's Performance
BP542   Easy PC Case Modding

Build Your Own PC

Robert Penfold

Bernard Babani (publishing) Ltd
The Grampians
Shepherds Bush Road
London W6 7NF
England
www.babanibooks.com

Please note

Although every care has been taken with the production of this book to ensure that any projects, designs, modifications, and/or programs, etc., contained herewith, operate in a correct and safe manner and also that any components specified are normally available in Great Britain, the Publisher and Author do not accept responsibility in any way for the failure (including fault in design) of any projects, design, modification, or program to work correctly or to cause damage to any equipment that it may be connected to or used in conjunction with, or in respect of any other damage or injury that may be caused, nor do the Publishers accept responsibility in any way for the failure to obtain specified components.

Notice is also given that if any equipment that is still under warranty is modified in any way or used or connected with home-built equipment then that warranty may be void.

© 2003 BERNARD BABANI (publishing) LTD

First published - February 2003
Reprinted - June 2003
Reprinted - September 2003
Reprinted - December 2003
Reprinted - February 2004
Reprinted - May 2004

British Library Cataloguing in Publication Data

A catalogue record for this book is available from the British Library

ISBN   0 85934 534 3

Cover Design by Gregor Arthur

Printed and bound in Great Britain by Cox and Wyman

Preface

Although assembling a PC might seem to be something that is only suitable for experts, it is really much easier than most people realise. All the parts required are available from computer shops, mail order warehouses, and computer fairs. Whether you wish to build the most budget of budget PCs, an up-market PC using the latest high-tech components, or anything in between, all the parts required are readily available.

Although one might reasonably expect building a PC to be extremely difficult, it does not require any special skills. In fact the assembly job is pretty straightforward, and it is just a matter of bolting things in place and plugging in a few cables. A crosshead screwdriver might be the only tool required, and it is unlikely that anything else apart from a pair of pliers will be needed. No soldering iron is required, and neither is any experience of electronics construction methods.

All this does not mean that PC building can be undertaken by absolutely anyone. Some experience of using and dealing with PCs is essential, and you need to be reasonably practical. Obviously some technical knowledge is needed in order to buy the right components and get everything put together properly. This book explains in simple terms exactly what components are required and how to assemble them to produce a working PC.

Having built your first PC it then requires more technical knowledge to get everything set up correctly and the operating system installed. Again, this book explains in simple terms, how to get the BIOS set up correctly. The complexity of a modern BIOS Setup program can be a bit intimidating, but in most cases it will set suitable defaults. The user just has to do little more than some "fine tuning". Separate chapters explain in detail how to install and set up Windows 98/ME, and Windows XP. The finished PC is unlikely to give any problems, but the final chapter deals with simple troubleshooting techniques.

A home produced PC should have a comparable level of performance to a ready made equivalent. With wise buying it will probably cost somewhat less than a ready built PC of similar specification, although any savings are not likely to be large. However, by "rolling your own" it is possible to produce a computer that exactly meets your requirements, and you will learn a great deal in the process. It is also good fun and should impress your friends!

Robert Penfold

Trademarks

Contents

1

Fundamentals 1

What's involved? 1
The real thing? 1
Will it work? 2
Will I save money? 3
Can I do it? 4
Why bother? 4
Getting started 5
Integrated audio 7
Right price? 8
Assembly 9
Small hardware 12
Cables 16
Cable confusion 18
Static 18
Setting Up 20
Disc formatting 22
Operating system 22
Driver installation 24
Points to remember 25

2

Components 27

Processor 27
Extra cache 29
Pentium 4 30
Celeron 30
Athlon 32
Duron 33
Processor advice 34
Future proof 35
Heatsink and fan 35
Motherboard 37

Integrated functions 41
Case and PSU 42
Chipsets 45
Memory 46
SIMMs and DIMMs 47
DDR memory 48
RIMMs 50
Keyboard and mouse 51
Floppy disc 52
CD-ROM 53
Hard drives 53
Drive modes 54
PIO mode 54
Master mode 54
DMA 54
UDMA33 to 133 55
SCSI 57
Other drives 57
Video cards 59
AGP 59
Monitor 61
Screen adjustments 62
Soundcards 63
Joystick and MIDI 65
Points to remember 67

3

Assembly 69

Protection racket 69
Anti-static equipment 71
Improvising 73
Anti-static packing 74
Case 74
Knockout panels 76
Stand-offs 77

Different types **79**
Configuration **81**
Clock rates **82**
Core voltage **83**
Clear CMOS **84**
Setting up **85**
Processor **87**
Installation **90**
Heatsink **92**
Socket 478 .... **94**
Fan **96**
Fitting memories **97**
Drives **99**
Drive access **102**
Cabling **104**
IDE connectors **105**
Drive configuration **106**
RAID controller **108**
Floppy drive **108**
Floppy cabling **110**
Strange twist **111**
Termination resistors **113**
Ports **114**
Power supply **116**
Connector block **120**
Power LED **120**
IDE activity LED **121**
Reset switch **121**
Loudspeaker **121**
Power switch **121**
Keylock **121**
Temperature warning **122**
Suspend switch **122**
On the cards **122**
AGP cards **124**
Audio cable **126**
Tidying up **129**

Testing 130
Over-clocking 131
Points to remember 133

4

The BIOS 135

Essentials 135
BIOS basics 135
Entry 137
Standard CMOS 140
Drive settings 141
Non-standard IDE 143
Auto-only 144
Floppy drives 144
Chipset 146
Cache 149
Power Management 149
Monitoring 151
CPU settings 153
PNP/PCI 154
Integrated Peripherals 156
Onboard Device 159
BIOS Features Setup 160
Floppyless 163
The Rest 163
Flash upgrade 163
Write protection 164
Risk factor 165
Boot disc 166
Switches 168
Points to remember 169

5

Installing
Windows 95/98/ME 171

Operating system 171
Formatting 172
Large drives 172
Using FDISK 174
Formatting 177
Windows 178
Windows Setup 181
Installation 183
Time zone 187
Main installation 190
Hardware drivers 193
Device Manager 194
Awkward hardware 195
Screen settings 201
Disc-free ME 202
Points to remember 203

6

Installing Windows XP 205

Boot from CD-ROM 205
XP repair 208
XP compatible? 212
Language settings 213
From scratch 221
Hardware drivers 222
Video settings 226
Scan rate 230
Correct channels 233
Language problems 237
User accounts 239
Registering 243

Anti-piracy 247
WPA problems 249
WPA file 251
Disc cloning.. 253
XP second drive 254
Formatting 259
Points to remember 262

7

Troubleshooting 265

Prevention 265
Blank expression 265
Leads 266
AMD approved 267
On the cards 268
On the level 269
Substitution 271
Partial failure 273
Lead checking 274
Error messages 278
Anomalies 279
Memory 280
DIMM capacities 281
Processor 282
Discs 283
Floppy problems 284
Late problems 285
Right leads 287
Down to earth 288
Minor problems 290
Be meticulous 291
Check-up 293
Memory testing 295
Points to remember 298

Index 301

Fundamentals

What's involved?

Constructing your own PC may seem a daunting prospect, but it is actually much easier than most people realise. It has to be emphasised that we are not talking here in terms of getting out a soldering iron and making your own motherboard, video card, etc., or even in terms of doing some metalwork to produce your own case. Due to the predominance of specialist electronic components in the PC world, most of which are not generally available, this approach is probably not viable even for those prepared to put in the massive time and effort involved. Also, by the time your completely home-made PC was finished it would probably be well and truly out of date!

What we are really talking about here is a home assembled PC based on a set of ready-made boards and housed in a commercially produced case. Everything you need to make a PC is readily available, and the tools needed to assemble one are minimal. In fact one medium size cross-point screwdriver is quite possibly the only tool you will require. Depending on your opinion of these things, building your own PC is as easy or as difficult as putting together your own self-assembly furniture. Inevitably there are some questions that anyone contemplating PC assembly will need answered. We will consider some of the more common questions before taking a look at the basic steps involved in making your own PC. Subsequent chapters consider each of these steps in detail.

The real thing?

Having put together your PC will it work as well as the ready-made "real thing", or will you end up with a low specification PC that is incapable of running high-end software? Provided you compare like with like there is no reason for any difference in performance and capabilities between a ready-made PC and a home-made machine. It pays to bear in mind that most PC manufacturers do not actually make their own motherboards, sound cards, etc., but instead put together PCs from "off the shelf" components.

In other words, most ready-made PCs are put together in the same way as a home-made PC, and apart from the nameplate a ready-made PC is no different to a home produced equivalent. The larger PC manufacturers often make PC components themselves or have them made to their own specification, but the underlying technology is much the same as that used in "off the shelf" components. Of course, if you put together a PC from all the cheapest parts you can lay your hands on it would be naive to expect it to equal the latest thing in commercially produced PC technology. It works the other way, and a homemade PC built using the latest upmarket components will cost more than a readymade budget PC, but it will easily outperform the budget PC. With PCs, as with most things in life, you tend to get what you pay for.

Will it work?

Whether you buy a PC ready-made or make it yourself it is impossible to guarantee that it will work first time and that it will continue to work flawlessly for many years. Neither is it possible to guarantee that there will not be the odd incompatibility problem with a certain piece of hardware refusing to peacefully coexist with a certain piece of software. Provided the PC is built using good quality components and you are not tempted to cut corners it should work first time.

Once it is "up and running", with average luck it should be at least a few years before a major breakdown occurs. Obviously some constructors will have worse than average luck, and will have to deal with a fault or faults. Others will fare better than average, and will not have to fix any faults during the working life of the PC, even if it is used for many years.

Home-made and ready-made PCs should both be covered by manufacturers' warranties, but these operate in very different ways with the two types of PC. With a ready-made PC the manufacturer's guarantee should cover the PC as a whole. If anything goes wrong the manufacturer should locate the fault and fix it for you. There may be a return to base warranty, or some form of on-site maintenance agreement. The latter is clearly preferable to the former, but is likely to be reflected in a higher price tag for the PC, or it will be an expensive optional extra. In either case, unless you buy a lemon the time taken getting things put right should be reasonably short, and no technical skills will be required on your part.

With a home assembled PC you should have individual guarantees for every component in the system, but there is no manufacturer to provide an overall guarantee for the complete PC. If something goes wrong it is up to you to find out just what has gone awry and get the faulty component exchanged under warranty. Locating the faulty component is not usually too difficult, but getting it replaced quickly is not always possible.

If the faulty component was ordered by mail order you will have to send it back, it is likely that it will then go through some sort of testing, and then the replacement will be sent. This could leave the PC out of action for several days. Of course, if you buy a ready-made PC by mail order and it has a return to base warranty, you have the same problem. In fact matters are worse because the whole PC often has to be returned, not just the faulty component.

This lack of speed in getting things fixed may or may not matter. Where it is important to get a PC working straight away, and to keep it working, a ready-made PC with an on-site maintenance agreement with a reputable company is the safest option. You have no absolute guarantee of quick fixes, but there is a good chance of keeping any downtimes to a minimum. You may find a company prepared to offer on-site maintenance on a home constructed PC, but this is by no means certain.

The odd incompatibility problem is likely to be difficult to solve whether you buy a ready-made PC or build one yourself. Whoever you complain to, it is always the other company's fault! Fortunately, this type of thing is much rarer than it used to be, and it is probably not a major issue any more. These incompatibility problems are usually the result of faults in one of the device drivers, rather than a problem with the hardware itself. Improved drivers usually appear on the manufacturer's web site before too long.

Will I save money?

Many people try their hand at DIY PC construction in an attempt to save money. Provided you purchase the individual components wisely it is likely that there will be a small cost saving. However, do not expect to get a half price PC by building it yourself. A saving of around 10 percent is certainly quite possible, and with careful buying of "special offers" you may even achieve a saving of as much as 20 percent or so. On the other hand, with imprudent buying you could easily end up paying 10 or 20 percent more for your PC. Assembling a PC takes no more than a very few hours work, and it would be unrealistic to expect the DIY approach to produce massive cost savings.

It is probably not the assembly costs that account for the majority of the savings anyway. When you by a new PC it generally comes complete with some form of support package such as a one-year onsite maintenance contract and some sort of telephone support system. With a home produced PC you have to be more self-sufficient. There may well be telephone or Email support for some of the components, but in general it is up to you to sort things out when problems arise. If you are able to sort out these problems yourself it makes sense to do so rather than pay for support that you do not really need, and will probably never use.

Can I do it?

As pointed out previously, actually putting the computer together does not require a great deal of skill. Someone who is completely impractical would be well advised not to attempt building a PC, or anything else for that matter. Provided you are not a DIY disaster waiting to happen, you should be able to physically put the PC together. This is not to say that anyone who can use a screwdriver is properly qualified to build a PC. When dealing with computers odd little problems tend to develop, particularly when dealing with device drivers and software installation.

Someone with a few years experience of using PCs should be able to sort out these problems without too much difficulty. For "old hands" at computing this sort of thing is just part of the fun. For a newcomer to PCs it could be difficult and time consuming to get the finished product set up and really working well. In fact it could be difficult to get the PC set up and working at all. Consequently, I would only recommend PC assembly if you have had a few years experience with PCs and are not going to panic if minor problems occur.

Why bother?

If constructing your own PC is not going to save large amounts of money, and you will have to sort out any minor problems yourself, why bother? Although any savings in cost are not likely to be huge, a worthwhile saving can still be made. Alternatively, for the same money it should be possible to produce a PC with a higher specification by doing it yourself. Also, many people find that making their own PC is a fun and interesting experience. If you like making things, having built one PC it is unlikely that you will return to the world of ready-made PCs. I suppose that for many people the kudos of building your own PC is another plus point. It is a good way to impress your friends.

For most PC builders the main advantage is that you can build a PC having the exact specification you require. Many PC companies will to some extent customise one of their standard PCs to suit your requirements, but few will build one to your exact specification. By doing it yourself you can have the video and soundcards you deem the best, the most suitable monitor for your requirements, and so on. If you only need a small hard disc drive but need an advanced 3D-video card and large monitor, then that is what you buy. The time you save in searching for a PC with the right specification at the right price should be more than enough to build the PC yourself. Financial constraints may force a few compromises, but you should end up with the best possible PC for your requirements, or something as near to it as the available money permits.

Another potential advantage of building your own is that it may be possible to use parts from your previous PC. Being realistic about it, there will probably be few (if any) original parts from an old PC that will be suitable for a new one. A few items such as the mouse, keyboard, and floppy disc drive will probably be usable if they are in good condition, but little else is likely to be of much use. However, most PCs get a certain amount of upgrading over the years, and any recent additions to the old PC will probably be useable in the new one. For example, a recently added DVD or CD-RW drive, sound card, or loudspeaker system is usually suitable for transplanting into a new PC. Again, the saving in cost is not likely to be huge, but the cost of the new PC can be significantly reduced without severely compromising its performance.

One final point that is worth making is that you will learn a great deal about PCs by building your own. Constructing a PC will not turn you into a computer expert overnight, but you will certainly learn a great deal about the way everything functions. If any problems arise in the future or you wish to upgrade a PC it should be much easier to sort things out once you have some experience of PC construction.

Getting started

Having decided to "take the plunge" and build your own PC the first task is to make a list of all the components required, complete with brief notes detailing any special requirements. You may already have a fair idea of what you require, but otherwise it is a matter of studying reviews in computer magazines and looking through magazine advertisements in order to find the best components at a price you can afford.

If your aim is merely to produce a PC at a "rock bottom" price it becomes more a matter of scanning the advertisements for "special offers" and touring the local computer fairs for the best deals you can obtain. Before buying any "bargain" components make sure that they are compatible with the other items in the system, and are not totally out of date. Be particularly wary of very cheap motherboards, as these often require obsolete processors and memory modules that can cost a great deal and give relatively poor performance. If components are offered at very low prices there is usually a catch somewhere.

This list represents the minimum you will require in order to produce a working PC.

Case with PSU, set of fixing screws, etc.

Motherboard with cables, etc.

Memory modules to suit the motherboard

Microprocessor with matching heatsink and fan

Keyboard and mouse

Video card

Monitor

3.5-inch floppy disc drive

Hard disc drive

CD-ROM drive

A CD-ROM drive used to be considered something of a luxury, but as most software is now supplied on CD-ROMs you will probably not get far without one. The storage capacity of a floppy disc is very low compared to the amount of data produced by most applications, so a CD-RW drive is well worth the additional cost. In fact many users currently opt for a CD-RW drive plus a DVD type. This enables the PC to produce and read most types of disc, with the obvious exception that DVD discs can not be produced. DVD writers remain quite expensive, as are the discs they use, so these are only a worthwhile proposition if you really need to produce DVDs or require the higher storage capacity per disc.

Integrated audio

For multimedia applications, voice recognition, etc. you will also require a sound card and speakers plus (possibly) a headset and microphone. For most purposes one of the budget audio cards will suffice. A fair proportion of current motherboards have built-in audio circuits that offer a reasonable range of features and performance. In fact some of these integral sound facilities are quite sophisticated. Integrated audio is probably the best option unless a top-notch audio system is required for some reason. There seems to be little difference in the cost of a motherboard having built-in audio and one having similar features but no integral audio. Integrated audio is therefore very cost-effective.

These days a fair proportion of motherboards have integrated video circuits. Whether integrated video is worthwhile depends on the way in which the PC will be used. It is unlikely that the performance of integrated video will satisfy dedicated computer gamers. In order to get the best results from the latest games it is necessary to have a high quality 3D video card that has all the latest tricks. For those not primarily interested in games it is quite possible that the integrated approach will be perfectly adequate. The built-in video circuits have some 3D capability, incidentally, but obviously they do not rival expensive video cards costing a few hundred pounds. Integrated video is generally regarded as more than adequate for a PC that will only be used to run business applications and the like.

Integrated video, like integrated audio, is very cost effective. It is therefore a good choice when building a budget PC. Bear in mind that most built-in video circuits share the main system memory. If (say) 64 megabytes of memory are used for the video generator, there are 64 megabytes less for everything else. This can slow down the PC slightly unless extra memory is fitted. As memory is now relatively cheap and most new PCs are equipped with large amounts of it, this is perhaps less of a problem than it was a few years ago.

The list given previously omits some items that most PC users will require, such as a printer and a modem, but here we will only consider the main constituent parts of the PC itself. It is advisable to put together a basic PC and get it working, and then add peripherals such as scanners, printers, and modems. Most people who build their own PC already have many of these peripherals anyway.

Fig.1.1 The case has bays for two sizes of drive

Right price?

Having selected the components for your new PC it is time to add up the cost. This tends to be higher than you would expect, so it may be necessary to come up with some extra money or compromise slightly and choose some cheaper components. It is also worth looking through some catalogues and magazine adverts to see if you can find better deals on some of the components. It is essential to make sure that the components will actually fit together to produce a working PC. There are more options available than in days gone by, which means that there are also more opportunities for hardware incompatibility to creep in.

Chapter 2 covers each component in detail, and should help you to avoid buying parts that do not properly match up. Many of the motherboard manufacturers have downloadable versions of the instruction manuals on their sites. It is a good idea to look through the manual for your selected motherboard before buying any components. This should avoid any misunderstandings about the type or types of

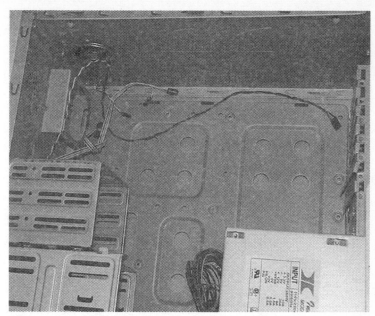

Fig.1.2 The empty area in the case is for the motherboard

memory it can use, the processors it can accommodate, and so on. Checking the manual should avoid any costly mistakes.

Assembly

Having obtained a complete set of parts it is then time to assemble the PC. Before starting to build the PC, look at the various components, including minor items such as cables and small pieces of hardware, and try to get a mental picture of how everything fits together. If you have a ready-made PC it is a good idea to open it up and look inside so that you can see how it fits together. It is best for those with limited experience of computer hardware to adopt a "look but you mustn't touch" approach, so that there is no risk of accidentally damaging anything.

The case you have bought should have two sizes of drive bays (Figure 1.1). The smaller bays take 3.5-inch drives such as a 3.5-inch floppy disc drive and most hard drives. The larger bays are the 5.25-inch variety and take CD-ROM drives, CD-ROM writers, etc. Usually one or two of

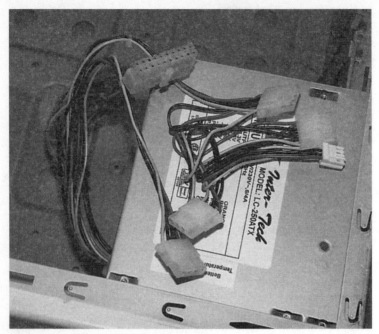

Fig.1.3 The power supply has upwards of six output cables

the 3.5-inch drive bays do not have cutouts in the front panel. These are used for hard disc drives, which do not have to be externally accessible.

There should be a large empty compartment in the case, and this is where the motherboard is mounted (Figure 1.2). The large box mounted on the rear panel of the case, usually in the top right-hand corner (as viewed from the front), is the power supply unit. This has mains input and (possibly) output connectors on the rear, and a selection of power leads for the motherboard and the drives (Figure 1.3). The original PC power supplies had a mains outlet that was intended for use with the monitor. Switching the PC on or off also resulted in the monitor being turned on or off.

In later power supplies the mains outlet was still included (Figure 1.4), but it was not switched. However, the monitor still switched on and off in sympathy with the PC. This automatic switching was provided by the energy saving facility of the monitor causing it to go into standby mode when the video signal from the PC ceased and power-up again when the signal started again. This is the method that is still used today.

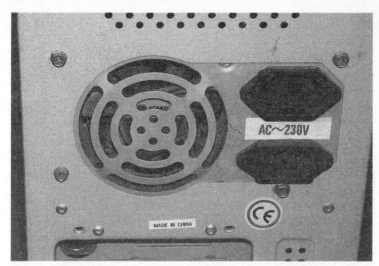

Fig.1.4 This power supply has a mains output for a monitor

Fig.1.5 A modern power supply usually has an on/off switch

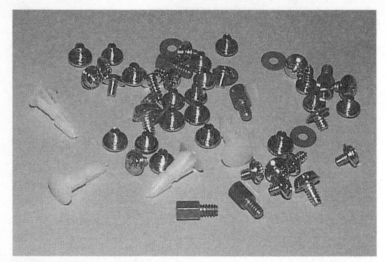

Fig.1.6 Small items of hardware should be included with the case

In the past it was common for a PC power supply to have a voltage selector switch on the rear panel, but this is usually absent on modern supply units. Instead, there is a conventional on/off switch (Figure 1.5) that will always switch off the PC, even in situations where the switch on the front panels will not. Of course, make sure that voltage selector switch is set to the right voltage (230/240 volts for the UK) if the supply unit you obtain does have this feature. Do not worry about the absence of this switch. Most modern PC supply units automatically adjust to suit any mains supply voltage from about 90 to 250 volts. Others are designed specifically for operation with the 240 volt UK mains supply.

Small hardware

The case should be supplied complete with various small items of hardware (Figure 1.6), and it is bordering on the useless without them, so make sure it has the all-important polythene bag of odds and ends. These small items of hardware include the screws that are used to fix the various drives into their cages, although suitable screws may be included with some of the drives as well. In days gone by it was often quite awkward fitting the drives into the case, with plastic guide rails being fitted to the drives before they were slid into place. The rails were then bolted to the case.

Fig.1.7 A plastic guide-rail clipped to a 3.5-inch drive

This system now seems to be totally obsolete, and with most cases the drives are bolted direct to the inner structure of the case. However, some recent PC cases use an updated version of the guide rail idea. The general scheme of things is to have a guide rail fitted to one side of the drive (Figure 1.7), and it is usually held in place via a wire clip. This side of the drive is not bolted into place and is only supported by the guide rail. The other side is held in place by two screws in the normal fashion.

As viewed from the front of the PC, it is the right-hand side of the drive that is fitted with the guide rail. I assume that the idea is to avoid using fixing screws on the right-hand side of the drive, which is usually less accessible than the left-hand side. In fact I have encountered PCs where it is only possible to access these screws by removing the motherboard. Anyway, any case that uses this system should be supplied with one guide rail per drive bay. Where this method of fixing is used it is not possible to fit a drive properly without a suitable guide rail. Note that the guide rails are normally used only for the 3.5-inch bays, with the 5.25-inch types having mounting screws both sides, but there could be some exceptions.

The motherboard has a socket for the processor, and two or more for the memory modules (Figure 1.8). In this example there are two memory

Fig.1.8 This motherboard has two memory sockets

Fig.1.9 A heatsink and fan for a Socket A processor

sockets near the bottom edge of the board on the right-hand side. The socket for the processor is above and to the right of these. Modern processors require a heatsink (a piece of finned metal) and a fan to prevent overheating. The heatsink and fan are normally sold as a single unit (Figure 1.9). Most processors are sold complete with a matching heatsink and fan in a boxed

premiering

retail version. The OEM (original equipment manufacturer) versions are cheaper but do not include the heatsink, fan, or any fitting instructions.

Where possible it is better to fit the processor, heatsink and fan, and the memory modules to the motherboard before it is mounted inside the case. Even with the largest and best designed cases there is relatively poor access to

Fig.1.10 A bank of eight DIP-switches

the motherboard once it is inside the case, so it makes sense to do as much work as possible while the motherboard is still freely accessible. Unfortunately, with some cases it might be difficult or impossible to slide the motherboard into the case with everything preinstalled, but where possible you should certainly do so.

There may be some DIP-switches (Figure 1.10) or jumpers (Figure 1.11) on the motherboard that have to be given the correct settings for the particular microprocessor you are using. These set the clock frequencies, processor operating voltage and possibly one or two other things as well. These should be set before the board is installed in the case because it is then much easier to see exactly what you are doing, and mistakes are much less likely to occur. It can be very fiddly indeed to set the miniature switches or jumpers once the board is fitted in the case.

Not all motherboards are configured using switches or jumpers, and there is a strong trend towards so-called "jumperless" motherboards. These probe the processor to determine its type, and then set themselves

up correctly without any guidance from the user. It is usually possible to override all or some of the settings manually if you do not agree with the default settings. This is done via the BIOS Setup program though, and not using switches or jumpers. Few motherboards are genuinely "jumperless", so always check to see if there are one or two jumpers or switches that might need adjustment.

Fig.1.11 Some configuration jumpers

Fig.1.12 The blanking plates at the rear of the case

When the motherboard is finally installed in the case it must be held clear of the metal casing by mounting it on some form of stand-off. Without the stand-offs the connections on the underside of the board would simply short-circuit through the metal casing. The stand-offs might be moulded into the case or already installed, but they are usually in the bag of bits and pieces supplied with the case.

Cables

With the drives and motherboard in place it is time to start adding the cables. There are cables that connect the motherboard to the disc drives, and there will also be some leads sprouting from the front section of the case that connect to the motherboard. These provide functions such as the hard disc activity light and on/off switching. Depending on the type of power supply in use there will be one, two, or three power leads to connect to the motherboard. AT cases, motherboards, and power supplies are now more or less obsolete, so the power supply will almost certainly be an ATX type. These have one power lead for motherboards that use AMD processors and three for those that use Intel chips. The power lead on the processor's fan is connected to the motherboard, as is the fan for the case if there is one. The disc drives are not powered via the cable that connects to the motherboard, and each one must be connected to one of the power supply's power leads.

Fig.1.13 The three types of expansion slot

With an ATX motherboard and case there is no need to bother with wiring up the standard ports. The motherboard is fitted with standard connectors that can be accessed via cutouts in the rear of the case. The situation is different with an AT motherboard, whether it is fitted in an AT or ATX style case. The connectors for the two serial ports, parallel port, mouse port, and USB ports are mounted on the rear of the case, and then their flying leads are connected to the motherboard. As pointed out previously, AT components are now largely obsolete. Consequently, this complication will probably be avoided. However, there may be additional USB ports or other ports that use this method. These are usually mounted on a bracket that is fitted in place of a blanking plate for an empty expansion slot.

Next the expansion cards are slotted into place on the motherboard and their mounting brackets are bolted to the rear section of the case. The appropriate blanking plates at the rear of the case (Figure 1.12) must first be removed to clear the way for the expansion cards. With more and more features being handled by the motherboard the number of expansion cards is often quite low on a modern computer. With the sound and graphics integrated with the motherboard it is not essential to have any at all, but most PCs utilize two or three cards.

There are three types of expansion card, and therefore three types of expansion slots to accommodate them (Figure 1.13). The largest slots are the old ISA variety, which are now virtually obsolete, and not included on all motherboards. In fact there are very few motherboards that now support this feature. Most modern expansion cards are for the smaller PCI slots. The vast majority of modern motherboards have one AGP slot, which is used for graphics cards. However, PCI graphics cards are still available. The AGP slot in Figure 1.13 is the one on the left, set well into the board. Conventionally the ISA slots are black, the PCI slots are white, and the AGP type is brown. However, there are some multicoloured motherboards that do not adhere to this convention.

To complete the PC any final cabling is added. In most cases this just means adding the cable which connects the audio output of the CD-ROM drive to the appropriate input connector on the sound card.

Cable confusion

People contemplating building a PC for the first time are often worried about getting the cables connected incorrectly. In most cases this is simply not possible, because the cables are fitted with connectors that will only fit in the correct sockets the right way round. There are some cables where it is possible to make mistakes, but the instruction manual provided with the motherboard together with markings on the cables and connectors make it easy to get everything connected correctly.

Provided due care and attention is used when fitting the cables there should be no problems. Do not simply connect things together more in hope that expectation. Take the time and make the effort so that, as far as possible, things are right the first time. It is not a good idea to make a mistake, but if the worst should happen there is little risk of any damage occurring.

Static

Another common worry is that of damaging some of the components by "zapping" them with static electricity. It is true that most of the components in a PC are vulnerable to static voltages, and that these voltages are quite common in normal environments. It is also true that there are numerous items of anti-static equipment available, which can virtually eliminate the possibility of components being damaged by static charges. Some of these anti-static devices are quite cheap, but many are quite costly.

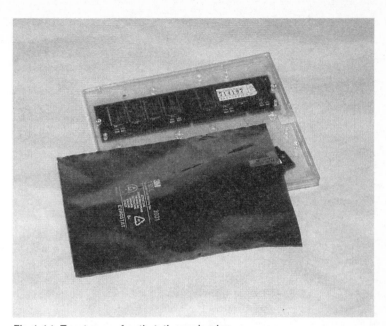

Fig.1.14 Two types of anti-static packaging

For professional PC builders and service engineers it is probably worthwhile spending a fair amount of money on static precautions, as over a period they will be handling computer equipment worth many thousands of pounds. For the do-it-yourself PC builder it is not worth spending much money on this type of thing because the safety equipment could easily cost more than the components it is protecting. On the hand, few amateur PC builders can afford to take no precautions and simply replace anything that is accidentally "zapped".

Fortunately, it is not necessary to spend large amounts of money in order to protect the components. Some low cost equipment and (or) some improvised safety devices are adequate to ensure that your PC components will not be damaged while the PC is being built. Computer components that are vulnerable to static damage are normally supplied in some form of anti-static packing. A couple of examples are shown in Figure 1.14. These either insulate the components from the outside world or encapsulate them in a conductive material. This leaves the components safe from damage by static charges, but only if you leave

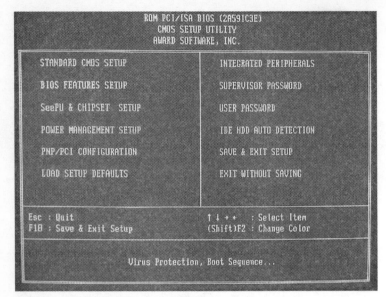

Fig.1.15 A typical menu for a BIOS Setup program

them inside the packing until it is time for installation. Avoid the temptation to remove components from the packing to have a look at them.

Setting up

On the face of it, having built your PC it is just a matter of connecting the peripherals such as the monitor and mouse, and then switching on to see if it works. Unfortunately, it is not quite as simple as that. When you buy a new computer it is normally supplied fully configured with the operating system installed, and possibly even with some applications software already installed. It is then just a matter of connecting everything together, switching on, and computing away merrily. When you build a PC yourself it is necessary to configure it and install all the software yourself.

The configuration is done using the Setup program built into the PC as part of its BIOS (Figure 1.15). The BIOS is the basic input/output system, and it is a program contained in a chip on the motherboard. It is sometimes referred to as the "ROM BIOS", because the chip that contains the program is a ROM (read only memory). A computer must always be running a valid program or it will crash, and the BIOS is the program that runs when you first switch on the computer. Its function is to do some basic checks on the hardware to ensure that the memory and processor are functioning properly, and to then run the operating system. The BIOS can be used by the operating system as an aid to handling the hardware.

Fig.1.16 A lithium backup battery

A PC has some memory that does not lose its contents when the computer is switched off. This is normally in the form of CMOS RAM, which has a very low current consumption. As a result, a back-up battery is adequate to power this memory when the PC is switched off. In days gone by this battery was in the form of an ordinary battery pack that had to be changed periodically, or rechargeable cells that were charged up when the PC was switched on.

These days the battery is usually a long-life lithium type that will last about 10 years and does not need to be replaced. It generally outlives the rest of the PC! It is usually easy to locate on the motherboard (Figure 1.16), and is a sort of giant size version of a "button" cell, as used in older cameras. The battery can actually be replaced in the unlikely event of it running flat or leaking. Incidentally, this battery also runs a clock/calendar circuit that enables the operating system to determine the time and date.

Originally the BIOS used the CMOS RAM to store some basic information about the hardware, such as the amount of memory available, the main parameters for the hard disc drive, and the types of floppy drives installed. It still stores this information in the CMOS RAM, but it also uses it to hold numerous other facts and figures about the hardware. When your new PC is first switched on it is necessary to go into the BIOS Setup program to provide information about the drive types, to set the time and date, etc.

There are also numerous other facts and figures that need to be set. A modern BIOS requires a large amount of information, and there is no denying that much of this information is highly technical. On the other hand, a modern BIOS is semi-intelligent, and it will set sensible defaults for most of the settings. It can also use probing techniques to obtain facts and figures about the amount of memory, the hard drive parameters, etc. In order to get the PC working it does not require a great deal of input from the user, and neither is a vast technical knowledge required.

Disc formatting

In days gone by it was necessary to do low-level formatting of the hard disc drive, and then do high level formatting to suit the selected operating system. These days hard discs are supplied with the low level formatting already done, so it is only necessary to do the high level formatting. Whatever operating system you intend to use, it should have a formatting program that can handle hard disc drives.

Actually there is a step needed ahead of formatting the hard drive, and this is to set up the partitions. By partitioning the disc it can be used as if it was two or more smaller discs. Even if you wish to allocate all the capacity to one partition, the drive still has to be processed using the partitioning software to produce this single partition. Again, the operating system should be supplied with a utility program for partitioning the hard disc. With Windows XP and modern versions of Linux the partitioning and formatting is done as part of the installation process, so there is no need to do either prior to commencing the installation process.

Operating system

Just how difficult or easy it is to install the operating system depends on the particular operating system you select, and to some extent on the hardware in the PC. Getting a simple operating system like MS/DOS installed is quite quick and easy, but with a more modern operating system like Windows ME or Linux it will take longer and is a little more difficult. Modern operating systems have quite sophisticated installer programs though, and to a large extent the installation is automatic. Installing an operating system on a PC is not quite as simple as loading a word processor or accounts program onto the hard drive, but it is not that much more difficult either.

With some operating systems and a modern PC you can boot from the installation CD-ROM. The programs on the CD-ROM may even handle things like partitioning and formatting the hard disc, leaving the user little to do apart from sitting back and watching what happens. With

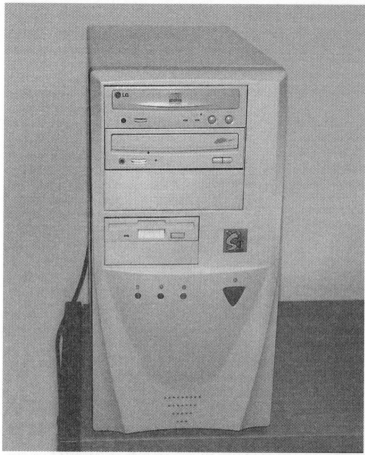

Fig.1.17 The finished article. This home constructed PC has an Athlon XP2000+ processor

other operating systems, notably Windows 98 and ME, it is necessary to make a boot disc and boot from the floppy drive. The boot disc must include support for the CD-ROM drive so that you can run the Setup program on the installation disc once the computer has booted. It is then largely a matter of sitting back while the operating system installs itself on the hard drive.

Driver installation

There is usually a certain amount of work to do once the operating system has completed the automatic installation process. Some of the driver software for the hardware will not have been installed at all, and in other cases there will only be generic drivers. The motherboard, video card, etc., should all be supplied with driver software for the popular operating systems, and with this installed the computer should be fully working. The required screen resolution can then be set, and hardware such as the sound generator can be checked.

Once the operating system is fully "up and running" it is time to install the applications programs and start using the new computer. Installing all this software and getting it set up correctly can be very time consuming. Where you have an old PC with the operating system and applications installed there are possible shortcuts to getting the new computer set up correctly. One of these is to simply use the old hard disc in the new computer, but it is likely that you will wish to use a disc having a much higher capacity than the old drive.

One way around this is to use the old drive as the boot drive, with a new drive being used as well to provide the extra storage capacity. This might not be as straightforward as you might think, because the new PC will have different hardware to the old one, and the operating system will require a substantial amount of reconfiguration before it will run in the new computer. It is possible to copy everything from the old drive to the new drive, but again, the operating system will have to be reconfigured before it will boot and run properly. This is not necessarily too difficult to achieve, and it is quite a popular option.

My preference would be to install everything "from scratch" even if it is very time consuming. When a PC has been in use for some time it tends to get cluttered up with all sorts of files that are no longer used, and the boot-up process often seems to slow down quite noticeably as a computer ages. Having built a new PC it is good practice to make a fresh start and only install those programs and files that you still need. This removes unwanted clutter from the hard disc drive and ensures that your new PC runs as quickly and smoothly as possible.

Points to remember

If you build your own PC to save money you can probably do so with careful buying, but do not expect to get a half price PC. If you do not shop around for the best buys it could actually cost substantially more to build your own PC.

The manual skills involved in building a PC are not great, and no special tools are required. A medium size crosshead screwdriver and pair of pliers are all you should need, and no soldering is involved. Even so, PC construction is not for those who are completely impractical.

Provided you go about things slowly and meticulously the finished PC should work, and work well. There should be no significant difference in performance between a home constructed PC and a ready built PC of equivalent specification.

By building your own PC, funds permitting, you can have a PC that exactly meets you perfect specification. You should also learn a great deal about PCs and have plenty of fun as well.

The completed PC will require a certain amount of setting up before it is ready for the operating system to be installed. There is a trend towards having the PC automatically detect the processor type and adjust itself accordingly, so the amount of manual setting up may be minimal. Otherwise it is just a matter of setting a few switches or placing jumpers on the correct sets of terminals.

Some adjustments will be required to the BIOS, and these are performed via the built-in Setup program. The BIOS is admittedly highly technical, but to a large extent you can just leave the default settings. The user normally has to do little more than set the time and date, and provide some drive information.

Installing the operating system is not quite as easy as installing applications programs. On the other hand, modern operating systems have Setup programs that do most of the installation for you. It is necessary to provide some information when prompted, but little else is required.

With some operating systems it is necessary for the user to set up partitions on the hard disc and perform the high level formatting. This is not too difficult, and the operating system should be supplied with the necessary software to perform both the partitioning and the formatting.

No low level formatting is required with modern disc drives. The low level formatting is performed at the factory, and conventional low level formatting programs do not work properly will modern drives anyway.

There is no overall guarantee for the system if you build your own PC. If a component is faulty it is up to you to locate it and get it exchanged under the guarantee for that individual component. Locating faulty components is not usually too difficult, and in many cases the location of the fault is self-evident.

2

Components

Processor

All modern PCs are based on an Intel Pentium processor, or a compatible processor from another manufacturer. These days the only real competition to Intel is provided by AMD with their Duron and Athlon processor ranges. Pentium processors have additional instructions, but are basically just faster and more efficient versions of the 80486DX and earlier Intel processors in this series. The original Pentium chips ran at 60MHz and 66MHz, and in most speed tests did not perform significantly better than the faster 80486 chips. Later versions used higher clock rates, fitted into a different socket, and had improved motherboards. This provided a boost in performance that gave much better results than any 80486DX PCs could achieve. The clock frequencies for these "classic" Pentium processors are 75, 90, 100, 120, 133, 150, 166, and 200MHz.

Although relatively recent, these processors are now obsolete and are not used in new PCs any more. Pentium processors with MMX (multimedia extension) technology replaced them. The MMX technology is actually an additional 57 processor instructions that are designed to speed up multimedia applications, but can also be used to good effect in other applications such as voice recognition. There were also some general improvements that produced an increase in performance by around 10 or 15 percent when using non-MMX specific software. These MMX Pentium processors were produced in 166MHz, 200MHz, and 233MHz versions.

These are now obsolete as well, and have been replaced by Pentium II, Pentium III, and Pentium 4 processors. The original Pentium II processors had a clock frequency of 233MHz, but much faster chips were soon produced. The Pentium II is now obsolete, but the PCs that use them remain quite potent. The original Pentium processors were fitted onto the motherboard via a conventional integrated circuit holder known as Socket 4. Those operating at 75MHz and above used an improved

27

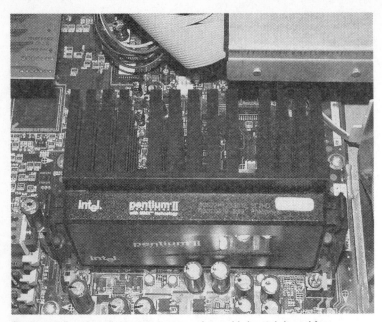

Fig.2.1 A Pentium II processor complete with heatsink and fan

version called Socket 7. Pentium II processors look nothing like conventional processors, and in physical appearance they are like a cross between a videocassette and a memory module (Figure 2.1). They fit into a holder that is more like a PC expansion slot or holder for a memory module than an integrated circuit holder.

One reason for this change in style is that it potentially enables higher clock speeds to be utilized. Another reason for this change in style is that Pentium II chips are so complex that with the technology of the time it was not possible to put the processor and cache memory on the same chip. Cache memory is high-speed memory that is used to store recently processed data. It is likely that this data will need to be accessed again, and having it available in high-speed memory ensures that it can be processed very efficiently when it is needed. In virtually all practical applications this substantially speeds up the rate at which data can be processed.

Extra cache

Previous Pentium processors had some cache memory (typically 32k) on the chip, with a much larger cache of about 256 to 512k on the motherboard. These are known as level 1 and level 2 cache respectively. Level 1 cache is faster, but there are practical limits on the amount of cache memory that can be included in the processor. With the Pentium II chips it had to be omitted altogether, but a "piggy-back" memory chip included in the processor module provides a 512k cache. This memory runs at half the speed of the processor clock and not at the bus speed of the motherboard, which gives a substantial boost in performance. Due to the relatively large size of the level 1 cache no level 2 cache was deemed to be necessary. Hence there is no cache memory on a Pentium II motherboard.

The Pentium II is really a development of the Pentium Pro processor. This relatively unsuccessful processor was an improved version of the "classic" Pentium design, but when running Windows 95 software it often failed to provide much improvement over an ordinary Pentium chip. The Pentium Pro became overshadowed by the MMX Pentium processors, which proved to be an immediate hit with PC buyers. The Pentium Pro is another one that is now long gone.

The Pentium II has the additional MMX instructions, and slightly improved performance compared to an ordinary MMX Pentium processor. The 350, 400, and 450MHz versions are designed to operate on motherboards that operate at a 100MHz clock frequency and use fast memory modules. The earlier Pentium and Pentium II processors operate with 66MHz motherboards and relatively slow RAM. This gives the 350, 400, and 450MHz chips a greater speed advantage over the slower versions than a comparison of the clock frequencies would suggest.

As one might expect, the Pentium II was replaced by the Pentium III, which has SIMD (single-instruction multiple data) technology. This is 70 new instructions designed to speed up certain types of software. These instructions are mainly aimed at high-speed 3D graphics and applications that include voice recognition. They are only of use with software that is written to take advantage of them.

Like the Pentium II processors, the Pentium III has 512k of cache memory running at half the clock speed. However, on the later chips this became 256k of on-chip memory running at the full clock speed. Also, these chips marked a return to socket technology, using a minor variation on the Socket 370 used for the Celeron chips of the period. The original

Pentium III processors used clock frequencies of 450 and 500MHz, but later chips took processor speeds beyond the 1GHz (1000MHz) mark.

The Pentium III has now been largely phased out in favour of the Pentium 4, but at the time of writing this anyway, the faster versions are still available. Some of these have 512k of cache. PCs based on the faster Pentium III processors are suitable for all but the most demanding of applications. However, unless you are putting together a budget PC and Pentium III components are available at the right price, it is probably better to opt for a Pentium 4 based system.

Pentium 4

The Pentium 4 (Figure 2.2) is by no means a new chip, and it has been on offer as an up-market alternative to the Pentium III for some time. The original Pentium 4 processors required Socket 423 motherboards, but

the current ones are of the Socket 478 variety. This processor is basically a faster version of the Pentium III, but the most recent versions have extra instructions and 512k of on-chip cache. With clock frequencies of up to 3GHz (3000MHz), Pentium 4 based PCs are clearly very powerful computers that can handle any

Fig.2.2 A Socket 478 Pentium 4

PC software. In terms of most speed for the money they are probably not the best choice, but many are happy to pay a little extra to get the Intel "real thing".

Celeron

The Intel processor for entry-level PCs is the Celeron, but at the time of writing it seems possible that this will be phased out in the near future. The original Celeron was basically just a Pentium II with the add-on cache

Fig.2.3 A motherboard that takes the original Socket 370 chips

omitted. This saved on manufacturing costs but clearly gave a reduction in performance. The original Celeron did not exactly receive universal praise from the reviewers, and the absence of any on-board cache gave it a tough time keeping up with the latest budget processors from other manufacturers. Its performance was actually quite respectable, being around 15 to 30 percent faster than an Intel 233 megahertz MMX Pentium chip, depending on the type of software being run. This was still well short of full 266 megahertz Pentium II performance though.

Later versions of the Celeron were equipped with 128k of on-chip cache. Although the 128k is only one quarter of the cache fitted to a Pentium II, the fact that it is on the same chip as the processor (and therefore very fast) to some extent makes up for the smaller amount of cache. The Celeron cache runs at the same speed as the processor, while that of the Pentium II runs at half the processor's clock rate. Numerous faster versions of the Celeron were produced, and the original slot design was abandoned in favour of a return to conventional socket design. This was possible with the Celeron as it did not require the so-called "piggy-back" memory chip.

These Celerons use a different socket to the original Pentium chips, and it is called Socket 370 because there are 370 pins on the processor. Confusingly, there are two versions of Socket 370 that are physically much the same but use slightly different methods of connections. Figure 2.3 shows a Socket 370 motherboard which takes the original socket 370 chips. The second type is known as the FC-PGA (flip chip pin grid array) or just plain "flip-chip" version, and the sockets for these look much the same. Celerons around the 500MHz mark were made in both versions.

The latest Celeron processors either fit the FC-PGA version of Socket 370 or the newer 478-pin socket. The FC-PGA chips have been produced with various clock frequencies up to 1.4GHz (1400 megahertz). Faster clock rates of up to 2GHz are available with the 478-pin versions. Clearly the latest versions of the Celeron are very powerful and the PCs that use them can run any current PC software. Unless you need the ultimate in performance one of the current Celeron chips should be more than adequate. If you require a budget PC using an Intel processor, a Celeron is the obvious choice.

Athlon

Over the years various manufacturers have offered Intel compatible processors that can be used in PCs. The only company currently offering real alternatives to the Intel Pentium and Celeron chips is AMD. The AMD chips have their origins back in the days of socket 7 motherboards, and later on there was even a chip that used slot technology (Figure 2.4). This was the original Athlon processor, and it used AMD's own Slot A rather than Intel's Slot 1 technology.

Like the recent Pentiums, modern AMD Athlon chips use conventional sockets (Socket A), and they remain physically and electrically incompatible with the Pentium processors. A modern PC motherboard is designed to take one type of processor or the other, and although the two types of socket may look similar, they are totally incompatible. Fortunately, although the chips and the motherboards are different, they all run the same software and are fully compatible in that respect. The normal Athlon chips have been produced with clock frequencies of up to 1.4 gigahertz, but there are now faster versions. It is the Athlon XP that is normally used in desktop PCs, and the fastest at the time of writing is the Athlon XP2700+. Faster versions are expected in the near future.

Like some earlier processors, the speed ratings of Athlon XP processors refer to their equivalent Pentium speed. An XP1900+ for example, is supposedly slightly faster than a Pentium 4 running at 1.9GHz, and this claim is probably justified. The actual clock frequency of this chip is 1.6GHz. The non-XP Athlons were

Fig.2.4 The Slot A version of the AMD Athlon processor

mostly made in two versions for system frequencies of 200MHz or 266MHz, but there are no 200MHz versions of the Athlon XP. Clearly, PCs based on the faster Athlon XP processors are very powerful and capable of running any current PC software. Where a fast but reasonably priced PC is required, one of the middle ranking Athlon XP processors probably represents the best choice. The fastest Athlon XP is a good choice if the ultimate in PC performance is required.

Duron

The Duron processor is AMD's equivalent to the Celeron, and it is essentially a simplified Athlon with less cache. Although the Duron is less potent that the Athlon, like the Celeron it has achieved good popularity. At one time a PC with a Duron operating at about 800 megahertz was the standard choice for a business PC, and these computers are still more than capable of running standard business applications. In fact speed is not the issue that it once was, and Duron based PCs are still good workhorse PCs that can run most applications.

The latest Durons with clock speeds of a gigahertz and beyond are perhaps less popular than their predecessors, but they have less price advantage over the Athlons at the cheaper end of the range. Speed is less of an issue than was once the case and many business applications in particular do not require the latest high-speed processors. A Duron provides perfectly adequate performance where undemanding software will be used.

Processor advice

The range of processors currently available is a bit bewildering, and it can be difficult to decide which one is the most suitable. Unless money is not an issue it is probably best not to opt for the last word in PC microprocessors. When 66MHz 80486DX microprocessors became available they were only 33MHz faster than the existing 33MHz chips, but that 33MHz represented a doubling in speed. A 3GHz chip is 200MHz faster than a 2.8GHz version, but offers an increase in performance of just a few percent. Even going from a 2.4GHz processor to a 3GHz type only represents a 25 percent increase.

Even with the more demanding applications software an increase in speed of a few percent will be barely noticeable. Programs that run slowly on a 2.8GHz PC will still run slowly on a 3GHz PC. Where there is a minimal difference in cost it might be worthwhile going for the slightly faster processor, particularly if you are running processor intensive applications, but otherwise it does not make economic sense to do so.

The main choice is between Intel and AMD processors, and it pays to bear in mind that these use different motherboards. At one time the motherboards for Intel chips tended to be significantly more expensive than those for AMD processors. These days there is relatively little difference in the prices of the two types, and the facilities offered by the motherboard is the main factor governing the price. When operating on a tight budget it is still a good idea to consider various processor and motherboard options, and to take into account the cost of different types of memory.

Buying a fast processor and then economising on the rest of the system does not usually produce the best system for the money. Many applications programs will run better with a slightly slower processor plus more memory and a better video card. Overall results are likely to be best with a well balanced system that has no major weaknesses.

Even the cheapest of the current budget processors are adequate for most business and general applications. Many of these applications require large amounts of memory though, as does multitasking (running several programs simultaneously). Windows XP tends to require more memory than Windows 98 or ME, and it is important to bear this in mind when building a PC that will run Windows XP. Skimping on the memory to pay for an expensive processor is usually a mistake. Skimping on the processor to fit more memory is often the better strategy.

Future proof

Many people, quite understandably, would like their new PC to be as future proof as possible. In other words, they would like the PC to be easy to upgrade in the future so that it remains reasonably up-to-date at low cost. Unfortunately, the fact that your PC has the right kind of socket does not necessarily mean that it will be able to use all the processors that use that type of socket. Newer and faster processors often need newer and faster motherboards and faster memory as well. New types of socket are likely to be used in the future. Even if future processors use the same type of socket, it is likely that most of the current motherboards will be able to operate at high enough clock speeds to accommodate them.

You can try to choose a set up that can be easily upgraded, but do not be surprised if a future processor upgrade requires the motherboard and memory modules to be upgraded as well. The best future proofing is obtained by using a motherboard that uses a recent chip set. The current processors are unlikely to push the motherboard to anything approaching its limit, and with luck it will be usable with faster processors released a year or two later. Budget motherboards using old chip sets are unlikely to be compatible with future processors. In fact some of these boards can not accommodate the fastest of the current processors.

At the time of writing this piece the cheaper Athlon XP processors seem to be the best choice if a reasonably fast but inexpensive processor is required. The faster Athlon XP and Pentium 4 processors are both good choices if something more potent is required. However, as Harold Wilson almost said, "a week is a long time in computing", and things change rapidly. It has almost become a matter of looking to see how many processor prices have been cut today, and checking to see how many new processors have been announced this week! It is really a matter of deciding on the processing power you require, and then looking for the best bargain at that power level.

Heatsink and fan

The original PC processors managed quite happily without any cooling system, but all modern PC processors are short lived unless they are kept cool by a heatsink and fan. A heatsink is simply a piece of metal having fins that enable it to efficiently transfer excess heat from the

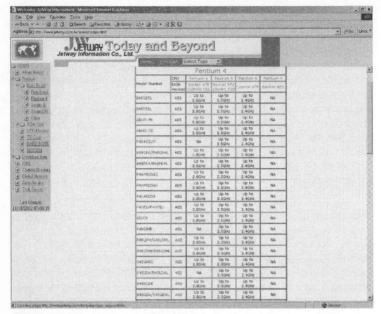

Fig.2.5 The processor compatibility chart on the Jetway web site

processor to the air inside the case. The cooling fan improves the efficiency of the heatsink by ensuring that there is a flow of cool air over it.

These days the heatsink and fan are invariably in the form of a single unit, and you do not buy them as separate entities. In fact processors are sometimes supplied as a sort of boxed set, complete with heatsink, fan, and fitting instructions, so you may not need to buy the heatsink and fan separately. This is the safe way to obtain the heatsink and fan, as they are guaranteed to be a correct match for the processor. Processors offered at "rock bottom" prices are usually the OEM (original equipment manufacturer) versions, which are "bare" processors.

When buying the heatsink and fan it is important to realise that there are different sizes and types. The Socket 478 uses a totally different method of fixing to the Socket A type, and consequently needs a totally different heatsink and fan. Some processors generate more heat than others, and therefore need a larger heatsink. Other than buying them as a boxed set, the safest way to buy the heatsink and fan is to obtain them from the

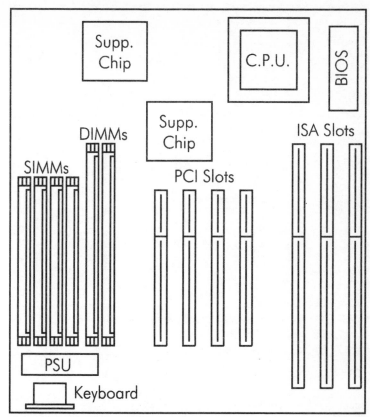

Fig.2.6 A typical AT motherboard layout

same source as the processor and at the same time, preferably getting an assurance that the cooling system is suitable for use with the processor. Any company selling processors should be able to supply a matching heatsink and fan. If anything should go wrong any reputable company should be prepared to make amends for their mistake.

Motherboard

Having selected the processor it is then a matter of finalising the choice of motherboard. As explained previously, AMD and Intel processors use different motherboards, so do not waste time looking at boards that are

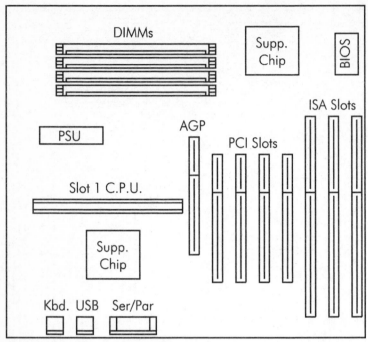

Fig.2.7 Typical layout for an ATX motherboard

not compatible with your chosen processor. When you find some likely looking motherboards it is essential to carefully check their specifications to ascertain whether or not they will accept the processor you intend to use.

It is worthwhile investigating the web sites of some motherboard manufacturers where you will find a lot of technical information on their motherboards. There are often charts to show the processors that are compatible with each board (Figure 2.5), and there may even be the full instruction manuals for the boards in downloadable form. Apart from helping you to select a suitable motherboard, reading through a few of these manuals can teach you a great deal about PC building and setting up the finished unit.

There are two main forms of motherboard, which are the AT and ATX varieties. The AT boards are now largely obsolete and few if any boards

Fig.2.8 An AT motherboard with SIMM and DIMM sockets

of this type are now produced. Even when offered at low prices it is difficult to recommend AT boards for use in new PCs. There are plenty of good ATX boards available at competitive prices, so there is no need to opt for an AT board on cost grounds. One difference between the two is that the power supply connectors are different, although many AT boards have the ATX connectors as well.

The main difference is that the board layout is different, with many of the connectors positioned for better accessibility in the ATX layout. The ATX layout also enables more of the expansion slots to be used with the long cards. With the AT layout the processor's heatsink and fan tend to obscure some of the expansion slots. Figures 2.6 and 2.7 respectively show example AT and ATX motherboard layouts. Photographs of actual AT and ATX motherboards are provided in Figures 2.8 and 2.9 respectively.

AT style boards are primarily designed for use with a power supply that has a conventional on/off switch fitted in the mains supply. An ATX power supply is switched on and off by way of a simple pushbutton switch on

Fig.2.9 An ATX motherboard that takes Socket A processors

the case, which connects to the power supply via the motherboard. The point of this system is that it permits automatic control of the on/off switching. With any modern version of Windows for example, when the system is closed down the power supply switches off automatically. The

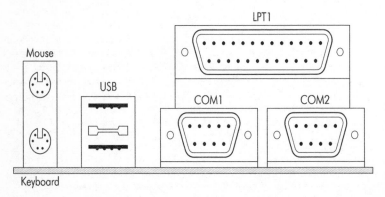

Fig.2.10 The basic set of ports for an ATX motherboard

monitor, assuming it is a reasonably modern type, then goes into its power saving standby mode. This effectively results in the entire computer switching itself off when Windows is shut down.

Fig.2.11 The standard set of ATX ports

Another difference is the on-board serial and parallel port connectors of ATX boards. These are accessible via cut-outs in the rear of the case, rather like the keyboard connector of an AT motherboard. In fact there is more than just the serial and parallel ports included in this group of connectors, and there is usually a minimum of two USB ports, a mouse port, and a PS/2 style keyboard port. Figure 2.11 shows a standard set of connectors, and Figure 2.10 identifies each port in the cluster. An AT motherboard has the larger 5-pin DIN keyboard connector incidentally. There may be other connectors included, such as a connector for a sound/MIDI port. This depends on whether or not the motherboard has any integrated peripherals.

Integrated functions

In recent years there has been a definite trend towards motherboards having integrated functions such as sound and video. Since motherboards that have these features do not cost a great deal more than those that do not, they are an attractive proposition for those requiring a low cost PC. On the other hand, by using a motherboard of this type you might be "painting yourself into a corner". Sometimes any integrated functions can be switched off, but with some motherboards there is no way of disabling them. This could make it difficult or impossible to upgrade to superior sound or graphics should you wish to do so at some later time.

Sometimes the motherboard has no AGP expansion slot, so there is no way of installing the latest AGP wonder video card even if the on-board graphics can be disabled. Also bear in mind that with many of these boards the main system memory is used by the on-board video and (or) sound circuits, so some extra memory has to be fitted in order to compensate for this. This is perhaps less of an issue than it used to be, as some extra memory costs very little these days.

Of course, if you simply require a good low cost PC, and will never need highly sophisticated sound facilities or the latest high speed 3D graphics, one of these integrated motherboards probably represents the best choice. They certainly seem to be gaining in popularity, and even some of the more upmarket motherboards now have integrated sound and (or) graphics.

Case and PSU

Computer cases are normally supplied complete with a power supply unit (PSU). As pointed out in the previous section, there are two distinctly different types of case and power supply, for the two different types of motherboard (AT and ATX). Also as pointed out previously, the ATX is the more modern and versatile option, which is likely to be well worth

any small extra cost. There are four normal styles of case to choose from, and the most suitable style depends on the number of drive bays required and the space available for the finished PC.

A mini tower case is usually the easiest to accommodate in your home or office (Figure 2.12), but there is often provision for just two 5.25-inch drives and three 3.5-inch drives. The one shown in Figure 2.12

Fig.2.12 Mini tower cases are small, but often have few drive bays

does actually have three 5.25-inch drive bays. Two 5.25-inch bays are sufficient for most purposes, since the majority of PCs have one 5.25-inch drive bay occupied by a CD-ROM drive, and two 3.5-inch drive bays taken up by the hard disc drive and a floppy drive. Even if a CD-ROM writer and a second hard disc drive are added, a mini tower will still have sufficient drive bays to accommodate them.

The main problem with mini tower cases for the do-it-yourself PC builder is that they can be difficult to deal with. With a great deal crammed into their limited dimensions it can be difficult to physically get everything reliably fitted into place and connected together. Some mini tower cases are actually quite easy to work on, while others are a constant pain to deal with. Also, some mini tower cases are easy to use with some motherboards, but with others it is difficult to gain access to the memory sockets, the connectors for the disc drive cables, and this type of thing.

Some of the larger motherboards are incompatible with very small cases such as mini tower types. They can accommodate the 5.25-inch drives or the memory modules, but not both. Another potential problem with small cases is that the power supply is often positioned over the processor. This can leave too little space for a tall heatsink and fan assembly. Especially when using a full-size motherboard, a larger case is a safer option.

A midi tower case (Figure 2.13) is slightly higher than the mini type, but a well designed case of this type has plenty of space for the components. A case of this type should have a minimum of three 5.25-inch and three 3.5-inch drive bays, and still has what is usually a less crowded interior than a mini tower case. The same is true of most desktop cases, but be slightly wary of some of the more compact desktop designs. These sometimes use unusual interior layouts that are not well suited to all motherboards. When building your own PC it is safest to opt for a conventional case that should take any standard PC components without difficulty.

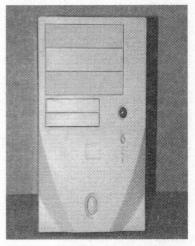

Fig.2.13 A Midi tower case is usually a good choice

The top of the range cases are the full-size towers, and one of these is the best choice if you will be installing a range of drives, or may wish to upgrade the PC by adding more drives in the future. Apart from having more drive bays, full-size tower cases are normally fitted with a slightly larger power supply that is well able to deal with extra drives. With a rating of around 300 watts an ordinary PC power supply should not be found wanting in this respect. However, with a PC that has more drives than usual it is as well to play safe and have a supply with a rating of around 400 watts. Physically the ATX supplies are a standard size and have standard mounting arrangements. There should be no difficulty in upgrading to a more powerful supply if the PC is eventually upgraded to the point where the original can no longer cope.

Most cases have some or all of the drive bays removable, which can make life much easier. The 3.5-inch bays are often well within the area of the case occupied by the motherboard, and to some extent the rear

sections of the 3.5-inch drives will intrude over the top of the motherboard. Particularly with the smaller cases, it can be much easier to fit the motherboard if the 3.5-inch drive bays are temporarily removed from the case (Figure 2.14). It can also be easier to fit the drives into the loose bays first, and then fit this whole subassembly into the case. The bays are much more accessible when they are removed from the

Fig.2.14 The 3.5-inch drive bays are often removable

case. Only choose a case that does not have removable bays if you are sure that it is well designed and enables the motherboard and drives to be fitted reasonably easily.

Virtual all PC cases have provision for a cooling fan on the front panel (Figure 2.15), although many seem to be sold without this component actually fitted. Modern PCs generate significant amounts of heat, due to the large amounts of RAM often used, complex processors that get very hot in operation, complex support chips on the motherboard that get hot, and so on. This tends to produce quite high operating temperatures inside the case, and can result in the over-temperature protection circuits on the motherboard coming into operation. This is most likely to occur on warm summer days when the air temperature inside the case is quite

high even before the
PC is switched on.

If you are building a
fairly high
specification PC I
would certainly
recommend using a
case that is fitted with
a cooling fan, or
adding a fan if it is not
supplied as standard
with the case. The
vast majority of cases
take a standard 80
millimetre cooling fan.
Whenever possible,
obtain the fan
complete with a set of

*Fig.2.15 A fan for the case is often an
optional extra*

fixing screws, or you may have to improvise in order to fix it on the case.
If no other method of fixing can be found, a good adhesive will do the
job well enough.

Chipsets

When looking at the specifications for motherboards you will inevitably
come across references to chipsets. These are the integrated circuits
that provide various essential functions that are not included in the
processor itself. In the original PCs these functions were provided by
dozens of ordinary logic integrated circuits. Even though a modern PC
requires much more help from the supporting electronics, there are
normally just two or three support chips. Some low-cost motherboards
have used a single support chip.

Over the years Intel has manufactured various chipsets to support the
Pentium processors. However, other manufacturers make Pentium
support chips. Similarly, AMD has produced support chips for the Athlon
and Duron processors, but so have other chip manufacturers. In fact
motherboards that use the genuine AMD support chips are probably a
minority.

I suppose that using a motherboard having support chips made by AMD
or Intel is the safe option, but the chip sets from VIA and others have

proved to be reliable. Whether you opt for a board that uses Intel/AMD support chips or chips from another producer, it is advisable to select one that uses a modern chipset. There are usually plenty of bargain motherboards available, but most of these will not take modern processors. Unless the aim is to produce a budget PC with the specification being of little importance, choose a motherboard that is reasonably up to date.

Memory

Probably the most frequently asked of frequently asked PC questions is "how much RAM do I need." This is very much a "how long is a piece of string" style question, and it is entirely dependent on the applications software that you will be running. The software manuals should give details of the minimum requirements, but the minimum is the bare minimum needed to run the software at all. Most programs can run in a relatively small amount of RAM by using the hard disc for temporary storage space.

This usually works quite well, but gives noticeably slower results than when using RAM as the temporary data store. With complex graphics oriented programs the operating speed can be painfully slow unless the PC is equipped with large amounts of RAM. There will probably be a recommended minimum system to run the software, a typical system, or something of this type. I tend to regard the amount of RAM recommended for a typical system as the minimum that will really be usable in practice.

For most software at present, 32 megabytes of RAM is sufficient provided the operating system is Windows 95, 98, or ME. This is the absolute minimum though, and upwards of 64 megabytes is preferable. The story is very different with Windows XP, where 128 megabytes represents a realistic minimum. At least 256 megabytes of memory is preferable. Some applications require much larger amounts of memory, and programs that handle photographic images or other large bitmaps are particularly demanding in this respect. Programs that handle video also require large amounts of memory, and probably hard disc space as well.

As an example, when handling large bitmap images in PhotoShop it is recommended that the amount of RAM in the PC should be at least double the size of the bitmap. In order to handle scanned bitmaps of around 25 to 30 megabytes at least 60 megabytes of RAM would therefore be required. Fitting the PC with 64 megabytes of RAM should therefore give workable results, but 96 or 128 megabytes would probably give noticeably quicker and smoother running. With Windows XP you would probably have to add at least 96 megabytes to these figures.

Bear in mind that large amounts of RAM can be needed in order to run several programs at once. In theory you do not need (say) 48 megabytes of RAM to multitask with two programs that require 16 and 32 megabytes of RAM. Somewhat less than 48 megabytes should suffice, because you are only running one copy of the operating system, and the two programs will share some resources. Practical experience would suggest that 48 megabytes would actually represent a realistic minimum in this situation.

Although memory has been very expensive in the past, it is currently quite cheap and putting large amounts of RAM into a PC is likely to be well worth the modest cost involved. Memory is like you know what and hard disc space: you can never have too much of it. You do not hear people claiming that they have wasted money putting too much memory in their computers, but you do hear people expressing regret for not having specified more RAM when buying their PC.

SIMMs and DIMMs

The original PCs had memory in the form of memory chips mounted directly on the motherboard. Later PCs had the memory in the form of modules that fitted into holders on the motherboard, which made adding or removing the memory much quicker and easier. The original memory modules are called SIMMs (single in-line memory modules). A memory module of this type is a small printed circuit board, which is fitted with miniature DRAM chips of the surface-mount variety. The socket on the motherboard is like a sort of miniature version of the standard expansion slot system. The original SIMMs have 30 pins, and although generally called 30-pin SIMMs, there are no pins and the connections to the device are via copper pads. The 30-pin SIMMs were superseded by the 72-pin type, but both types are now largely obsolete.

SIMMs have been replaced by DIMMs (dual in-line memory modules), which look like outsize SIMMs. The original type of DIMM has 168 terminals (Figure 2.16). Currently there are three speeds of DIMM available, and these are now normally referred to as "PC66", "PC100" and "PC133" DIMMs in catalogues. The PC66 DIMMs are suitable for use in motherboards that operate at 66MHz, whereas the PC100 and PC133 DIMMs are suitable for bus speeds of up to 100MHz and 133MHz respectively.

Fig.2.16 A 168-pin PC133 DIMM

It should perhaps be explained here that current processor technology has moved some way ahead of memory technology, resulting in the necessity to run the main system memory and the processor at different clock rates. This operates on the basis of having the processor operate at so many times the clock frequency of the motherboard. Particularly when an up-to-date processor is matched with older memory technology, the difference between the two operating frequencies can be massive. An Athlon XP2000+ processor actually operates at 1.67GHz, which is some 12.5 times faster than 133MHz memory modules. More modern memory modules can operate at higher frequencies, but still lag the fastest processors by a considerable margin. This is clearly far from ideal, but it is the best solution that the current technology can provide.

DDR memory

A few of the current motherboards can use ordinary DIMMs, but most of these have this type of memory as an alternative to the more recent DDR (double data rate) memory rather than as the only option. With these boards it might seem like a good idea to use some memory from an old PC and top it up with some new DDR memory. However, motherboards that have two types of memory socket normally operate on the basis of using one type or the other. Trying to use a mixture of two memory types is unlikely to give good results, and in most cases the PC would probably not even get past the POST (power-on self-test).

The "double" part of the DDR name refers to the fact that the memory operates at twice the clock frequency of the motherboard. Clock frequencies of 200 megahertz and 266 megahertz are used with the original versions of DDR memory, and these respectively use motherboard

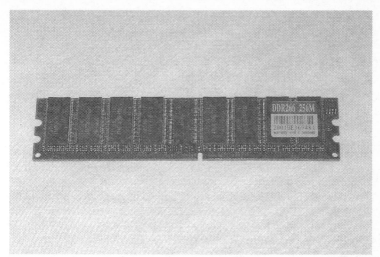

Fig.2.17 A 184-pin DIMM that has 266MHz DDR memory

bus frequencies of 100 and 133 megahertz. I think it is fair to say that DDR memory did not give the sort of speed increase that many had hoped for, but it did give a significant improvement. When the price of DDR memory became comparable to the PC100 and PC133 varieties it was inevitable that it would gradually take over.

DDR memory is sold in the form of 184-pin DIMMs (Figure 2.17). From the physical point of view a DDR DIMM is essentially just a slightly scaled-up version of the 168-pin components. The 200 and 233 megahertz DDR modules are sometimes sold as such, but they are more usually called PC1600 and PC2100 modules respectively. The number in each case refers to the bandwidth in megabits per second. The PC1600 modules seem to be relatively difficult to obtain these days, but the faster PC2100 type can be used instead.

Things move on, and faster (PC2700 and PC3200) DDR modules are now starting to appear. The PC2700 modules are for use at 333 megahertz and the PC3200 modules are for operation at 400 megahertz. Of course, these are the operating frequencies for the memory modules, and in standard DDR fashion the motherboards operate at half these frequencies.

With DDR memory, and possibly with other types, you may encounter a rating such as "CL3" or "CL2.5". This refers to a memory timing parameter in the BIOS Setup program, where it is usually called something like CAS Latency. A low figure here gives higher performance, but there is no guarantee that "bog standard" memory modules will work reliably with so-called "aggressive" memory timing. If you wish to push the system to its limits it is essential to obtain modules that are guaranteed to operate with a low CAS Latency setting.

RIMMs

There is an alternative form of high-speed memory in the form of RIMMs (Figure 2.18), which are memory modules from Rambus Inc. Each Rambus DRAM (RDRAM) can operate at up to 800 megahertz over a 16-bit wide channel. RIMMs are often called PC800 modules, with the 800 being derived from the maximum operating frequency. Note that a PC1600 DDR module is not twice as fast as a PC800 RIMM. The 1600 refers to the bit rate, whereas the figure of 800 is the frequency for a 16-bit bus. The PC800 modules should be something like eight times faster than the PC1600 variety, but the difference in overall performance is, of course, very much less than this. The latest RIMMs (PC1066) operate at up to 1066 megahertz.

RDRAM memory is certainly very fast, and it is used with many Pentium 4 based systems. Its drawback has always been the very high price tag, which in the past added substantially to the cost of the complete computer system. Although RIMM prices have come down over the years, this type of memory remains relatively expensive. This has led to the widespread use of PC133 and DDR memory with Pentium 4 systems.

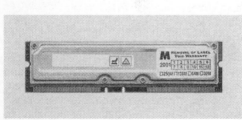

Fig.2.18 A PC800 RIMM

The memory will be relatively expensive if you build a PC that uses RIMMs.

The types of memory detailed previously are the ones that have been in common use over the past few years. It is only fair to point out that there are variations such as 200-pin SODIMS and that some PC manufacturers have gone their own way with so-called proprietary memory. The memory chips on these modules are much the same as those on equivalent types of standard memory, but the modules are physically different to the standard types. Provided you build a PC using a standard motherboard from one of the large manufacturers it should only be necessary to use mainstream memory modules.

I would strongly recommend studying the manual for the motherboard before buying the memory. The manual should make clear which type or types of memory can be used, the maximum amount of memory that can be fitted, and anything else that you need to know. As pointed out previously, many motherboard manufacturers have the manuals freely available for download on their web sites, and it is well worthwhile downloading and reading the manual for any motherboard that you are thinking of buying. You can then see whether or not it is likely to suit your requirements before parting with any money. It is also worthwhile checking through the "fine print" to see if there are any shortcomings that the advertisements for the motherboards have conveniently forgotten to tell you!

Keyboard and mouse

The choice of keyboard and mouse is a personal one, but make sure that you obtain a keyboard that matches the motherboard. AT motherboards are equipped with a 5-way DIN keyboard connector, but the ATX boards have the smaller PS/2 style connector (Figure 2.19). There are plenty of keyboards on sale that are primarily intended for use as replacements for old PCs, and therefore have the AT style DIN connector. If you are using an ATX motherboard make sure that the keyboard you obtain has a PS/2 connector. Some keyboards have both types of connector, or an adapter that enables them to operate with either type of motherboard. In either case the keyboard is obviously usable with AT or ATX motherboards.

Modern computer rodents are for use with either a serial port or a PS/2 mouse port. It will not usually matter which type you buy because an ATX motherboard has a mouse port and two serial ports. I suppose that there is a potential advantage in using the mouse port because this avoids occupying one of the serial ports and leaves the greatest possible scope for expansion. On the other hand, serial ports are utilized rather less than was once the case, so one serial port left free could well be one more than will actually be needed!

At one time the mouse port variety had something of a reputation for causing hardware conflicts, but this mainly occurred where a mouse

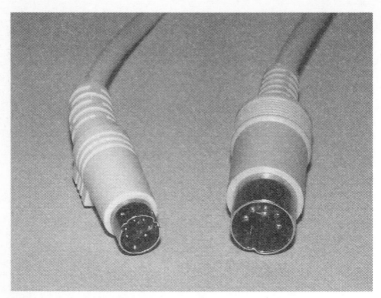

Fig.2.19 The PS/2 (left) and 5-way DIN (right) keyboard plugs

port mouse was used as a replacement for a serial mouse. This would sometimes cause problems with the mouse refusing to work properly. If the mouse was finally installed properly, sometimes another device such as a modem would refuse to work. Problems such as this are relatively rare these days, and do not normally occur anyway if a mouse port mouse is used from the outset.

Floppy disc

In these days of huge data files, software distribution via CD-ROMs, and mass storage devices such as Zip drives and CD-ROM writers, the humble floppy disc drive is rather less important than it once was. It is still an essential part of the PC for most users, and installing the operating system can be impossible on a PC that does not have a floppy disc drive. Modern motherboards usually have support for all the normal types of PC floppy drive from 5.25-inch 360k units through to 2.88MB 3.5-inch drives.

Probably most users will require nothing more than an ordinary 3.5-inch 1.44MB drive, but it should be possible to use something like a 5.25-inch

1.2MB drive if you need compatibility with old 5.25-inch discs. The only problem is that the older style drives tend to be relatively expensive, if you can actually manage to obtain one at all. A motherboard only has one floppy drive interface, but this can be used with one or two drives. There is no problem if you require (say) a 3.5-inch 1.44MB drive and a 5.25-inch 1.2MB type, or two 3.5-inch drives to make disc copying easier.

CD-ROM

In theory a CD-ROM drive is not an essential part of a PC, but in practice the vast majority of software is now supplied on CD-ROMs, including most operating systems. The cost of most CD-ROM drives is such that there is little saving to be made by omitting one anyway. The cheapest and easiest type to deal with are the drives which have a standard IDE interface, or ATAPI interface as it is often called in this context. These days there are few (if any) internal CD-ROM drives that use any other type of interface.

The IDE/ATAPI interface is the same type that is used for most hard disc drives, and a modern motherboard has at least two IDE interfaces. Each of these can handle up to two drives, making it possible to have a maximum of four drives. If you require something like two hard drives, a CD-ROM drive, and a CD-ROM writer, this set-up can be accommodated by the motherboard's built-in IDE interfaces. Note that internal CD-RW and DVD drives also use an IDE/ATAPI interface. They are installed and set up in the same way as ordinary CD-ROM drives, but some additional software is then installed to enable the drive to burn CDs, play DVD movies, or whatever.

Hard drives

As pointed out previously, most hard disc drives have an IDE interface that enables them to be connected direct to the motherboard. Hard and floppy disc controller cards are not needed with modern PCs. As the disc capacities have increased over the years it has been necessary for the operating systems and BIOS programs to be altered in an attempt to keep up with things. How well or otherwise large discs are handled depends on the operating system you are using and the motherboard.

Assuming you are not building new PCs using very old surplus or second hard components there should be no major difficulty in using high capacity drives. Where necessary, very large drives are usually supplied complete with any utility software needed to fully exploit their capacity. In fact hard drives are often supplied complete with quite a range of software designed to make it easy to install them in a new system or as an upgrade in an existing computer.

Drive modes

The IDE interface has received various updates over the years, but it has full compatibility with older drives. Any IDE hard disc drive should therefore work perfectly well with any modern motherboard. When dealing with IDE interfaces and hard drives, etc., you will inevitably come across references to the various IDE operating modes. In most instances you do not have to bother too much about these modes, and you can simply let the system "do its own thing". The BIOS program should correctly determine and use the right mode for any device connected to it. However, it is worth taking a quick look at the various modes and the ways in which they differ.

PIO mode

A PIO (programmed input/output) mode is where the processor has direct control of the hard disc via one of the support chips on the motherboard. In order to place data on the disc or read it from the disc the processor must issue the appropriate commands to transfer the data between the disc and the computer's memory.

Master mode

In a master mode the microprocessor is not in direct control of the hard disc, but instead this task is handed over to one of the support chips. Obviously the processor still has to issue commands to the chipset so that it knows which data to access and where to place it, but the processor has little involvement beyond that. A Master mode is not inherently any quicker at transferring data than a PIO mode. However, it places less of a burden on the processor and can therefore provide a boost in performance in other respects.

DMA

This is direct memory access, and any mode where the chipset moves data between the disc and memory independently of the processor makes use of DMA.

There are five PIO modes numbered from 0 to 4 and the higher the number, the greater the maximum data transfer rate possible. There are three DMA modes numbered from 0 to 2, and again, the higher the mode number the faster the maximum transfer rate. These are the maximum rates for the four PIO modes and three DMA modes, but not all hard discs and PCs are necessarily capable of providing these rates. Also, not all drives can use the faster modes.

PIO Mode 0	3.3MB per second
PIO Mode 1	5.2MB per second
PIO Mode 2	8.3MB per second
PIO Mode 3	11.1MB per second
PIO Mode 4	16.6MB per second
DMA Mode 0	4.16MB per second
DMA Mode 1	13.3MB per second
DMA Mode 2	16.6MB per second

Any reasonably modern hard disc drive should be able to support the faster transfer modes, but other IDE devices such as CD-ROM drives and other interchangeable disc systems may not. Bear in mind that there is no point in using a fast transfer mode with a device that can only accept or supply data at relatively low rates.

UDMA33 to 133

All modern IDE hard disc drives support UDMA33 and some of the more advanced DMA modes (UDMA66/100/133). These are developments that can only be implemented if the IDE interface on the motherboard and the hard drive both support them. They also need support from the operating system, and motherboards are usually supplied complete with drivers for various versions of Windows. As the names suggest, these modes provide transfer rates of up to 33, 66, 100, and 133 megabytes per second. UDMA33 uses the same connectors and cables as a standard IDE interface, but the UDMA66/100/133 interfaces require a different cable. The two types of cable actually look much the same (Figure 2.20), but the original type has 40 connecting wires whereas the new cables have 80.

It is possible to use one of the faster drives with a standard IDE cable, but it will only operate as a UDMA33 device. A UDMA33 or earlier device will work using an 80-way IDE cable, but obviously it will not work in one

*Fig.2.20 These two IDE data cables look similar, but the one on the
right has 80 wires and is suitable for UDMA66 and faster
drives. The one on the left has 40 wires*

of the faster modes. The faster IDE interfaces adjust to suit the slowest
device on the interface, which means that it is not a good idea to use a
fast hard disc drive on the same IDE interface as a slower drive such as
a CD-ROM or DVD type. This would result in the fast hard disc drive
operating in one of the slower modes.

It is therefore advisable to have the hard disc as the sole drive on the
primary IDE interface, and to use an 80-way data cable. This will enable
the drive to operate in the fastest mode that is supported by both the
drive and the motherboard. The CD-ROM drive or drives should be used
on the secondary IDE interface. CD-ROM drives do not usually have
anything beyond a UDMA33 interface, so 40 and 80-way IDE cables are
both suitable. If a second hard disc drive is fitted, this should be used as
the slave device on the primary IDE interface. Note though, that this
could result in the main hard drive operating below maximum speed if
the second hard disc drive is an older type that has a slower version of
the IDE interface.

SCSI

Some up-market hard disc drives and even some CD-ROM drives do not use any form of IDE interface, but instead use a SCSI type. SCSI stands for "small computer systems interface" and is generally pronounced something like "scuzzy". This is really a general-purpose computer interface that can be used with a wide range of internal and external peripherals such as scanners and scientific instruments. It is used with the more expensive drives to provide faster data transfers, but with improvements in the IDE interface over the years SCSI drives perhaps have rather less of an advantage than they once did. If the ultimate in performance is essential, such as for a network server, a SCSI drive might still be the best choice.

However, SCSI drives are not as straightforward to use as the IDE variety. Using a SCSI device has never been particularly easy, and matters have become more complicated over the years as new versions of this interface have evolved. Using a SCSI hard disc drive is certainly not something that could be recommended to first-time PC builders. Using a SCSI drive is not as difficult as it was in days gone by, where it was often necessary to use another drive to boot-up the system, and then use the SCSI drive as the main one once the operating system was set up successfully to recognise it.

Motherboard and operating system support for SCSI devices is now much improved, and some motherboards actually have a built-in SCSI facility. It is worth considering one of these if you will be using the computer with a SCSI drive or other SCSI device. It is unlikely to make any great saving in cost compared to using an ordinary motherboard plus an add-on SCSI expansion card, but it can save a lot of hassle. There should be no problem with hardware conflicts when using a built-in SCSI port.

Other drives

These days it is not uncommon for PCs to have some form of interchangeable mass storage device such as a Zip drive, LS120 drive, or a CD-ROM writer. The internal versions normally use either an IDE or SCSI interface, and the IDE versions are usually much cheaper and easier to deal with. There may be a performance advantage in using a SCSI version, depending on the innate speed of the device in question. In general these devices are handled much like a hard disc or a CD-ROM drive, but for LS120 and Zip drives there is often specific support available from the BIOS. In some cases it might even be possible to boot from

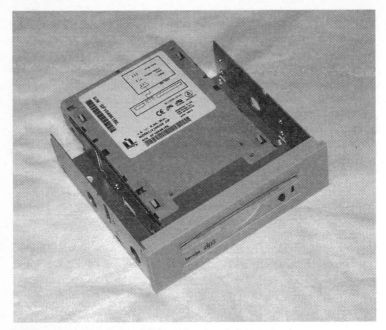

Fig.2.21 A 3.5-inch drive fitted in a 5.25-inch chassis

one of these drives. Where necessary any driver software for operation with Windows should be included with the drive.

There have been problems in the past with interchangeable disc drives that the operating system considered to be fixed drives. The practical consequence of this was that the only way to get the system to use a changed disc was to reboot! Provided you use an up-to-date operating system and motherboard this sort of problem should not occur.

There is a potential problem with drives that require 3.5-inch drive bays. This is simply that many cases have only one 3.5-inch bay with external access. With a 3.5-inch floppy disc drive already installed in this bay there is nowhere for a Zip, LS120, or similar drive to go. The usual solution is to mount the drive in an adapter that enables it to fit into a 5.25-inch drive bay (Figure 2.21). Most cases have at least three 5.25-inch drive bays with external access, so there should be no problem in accommodating the drive once it is fitted in an adapter.

Video cards

One of the great strengths of PCs has always been that the video circuits are not built onto the main circuit board. This gives manufacturers the freedom to produce ever bigger and better video cards and the consumer the freedom to choose the most suitable card. You do not have to spend a large amount of money on the latest super-fast 3D graphics card if all you require is a simple 2D type. Neither are you restricted to simple 2D graphics when you really need advanced 3D capabilities. The video card you choose will obviously depend on the money available and the type of software you will be running.

You may have the choice of a PCI or AGP version of the selected video card. The original PC expansion slots used the ISA (industry standard architecture) interface. This was more or less the raw processor buses with some added wait states when an expansion card was accessed. These wait states were needed to slow things down so that the slower expansion cards could keep up. ISA expansion slots went through a certain amount of development, but are now obsolete and have largely been phased out. It could be difficult to find a new motherboard that has an ISA expansion slot.

As PC technology advanced, the ISA slots proved to be too slow. They also made it awkward to implement new ideas such as "plug-and-play", and made it difficult to accommodate large numbers of expansion cards without hardware conflicts occurring. Eventually the PCI standard was adopted, and this removes many of the restrictions associated with ISA expansion cards. PCI cards use a different connector, and the port itself is totally incompatible with ISA cards anyway. A PCI slot is really a form of input/output port, and it does not operate direct onto the processor's buses like an ISA slot.

AGP

While PCI slots are more than adequate for many purposes, they can limit performance when large amounts of data must be transferred. In practice this mainly means when a video card is producing rapidly changing graphics. Hence the development of AGP slots for video cards. With "run of the mill" 2D video cards there is probably little advantage in using an AGP interface, but for high performance 3D cards there is a substantial gain in performance. Note that PCI and AGP cards are physically incompatible (Figure 2.22), and electrically incompatible as

Fig.2.22 AGP (top) and PCI (bottom) connectors are totally incompatible

well. An AGP video card is only usable with a modern motherboard that has an AGP expansion slot.

When building a new PC it makes sense to opt for the more up-to-date AGP version of a video card when both types of card are on offer. These days there are relatively few PCI video cards available, so there will probably be no choice anyway. There are now faster versions of the AGP interface, and these are the 2x, 4x, and 8x varieties. As the names suggest, these operate at two, four, and eight times faster rates than the original AGP bus. The original specification permits data to be transferred at up to 264 megabytes per second, which is twice the rate provided by the PCI bus. The faster versions offer correspondingly higher transfer rates, with the 4x AGP bus providing transfer rates of up to 1066 megabytes per second for example.

Do not assume that a motherboard having (say) an 8x AGP slot will accommodate slower video cards. For example, some motherboards lack support for 2x AGP cards, which operate at a higher voltage than the faster types. In fact some motherboards have a sticker on the AGP slot warning of dire consequences if it is used with some 2x AGP cards. It is advisable to read the relevant section of the motherboard's instruction manual to determine the AGP compatibility before buying the video card. Also check the modes supported by prospective AGP cards before parting with any money. Few suppliers will give full refunds on components that were bought by mistake.

Of course, some motherboards have integrated graphics adapters, and these are perfectly adequate where the ultimate in 3D graphics is not required. Integrated graphics probably offers the most cost effective method when only 2D graphics is required. Some of these motherboards have an AGP slot and permit the built-it video circuits to be switched off. Any compatible video card can then be used in the AGP slot in the usual way. In some cases there is no way of switching off the built-in graphics adapter, and no AGP slot for a video card. This gives some saving in cost, but clearly gives no upgrade path if a more advanced graphics adapter is needed at some future date.

Monitor

In the past there were various colour and monochrome display cards that required different types of monitor. These old standards such as the MDA and CGA varieties are now obsolete, and the majority of modern PC monitors are incompatible with some or all of these old standards. Modern PC monitors are multi-standard types that can be used in the standard 640 by 480 pixel VGA mode, plus various super-VGA modes. The number of additional modes available varies from monitor to monitor, but at least the 800 by 600 pixel mode should be supported, and most monitors can also handle 1024 by 768 pixels.

The higher resolution modes such as 1280 by 1024 and 1600 x 1200 pixels are not usually available on 14-inch and 15-inch monitors, although few conventional monitors of these sizes are produced. Even if these modes were available, they would be unusable. With the Windows "big fonts" selected, menus, etc., would still be displayed too small to be really usable. In fact most PC monitors are barely usable in their highest resolution mode for this reason. As 17-inch monitors of reasonable quality are now available at low prices there is little point in opting for anything smaller.

For each of the supported resolutions a monitor has a maximum refresh rate. This is simply the maximum number of complete scans of the screen that can be produced in one second. This is an important factor, because a low scan rate will produce a display that flickers quite noticeably. A display of this type is not unusable, but most users find them unpleasant to use for long periods. The minimum acceptable scan rate is a matter of opinion, but anything from about 70Hz upwards should be perfectly usable. I am reasonably happy with a 65Hz refresh rate, but at anything much less than 65Hz the picture flicker becomes very noticeable indeed.

When looking at monitor specifications you will often encounter the term "dot pitch". In theory, the smaller the dot pitch, the higher the display quality is likely to be. In reality matters are not as straightforward as this, and two monitors having the same claimed dot pitch might actually give significantly different display qualities. The only way to judge the quality of a display is to try it out and make a subjective judgement.

The claimed size of the screen is something that is sometimes a bit over optimistic. Thankfully, some of the practices used in the past to inflate monitor sizes in specification sheets have now largely died out. If you buy a 17-inch monitor you should not find that the diagonal measurement of the picture is actually about 14 inches. On the other hand, it will not be 17 inches either. Because the picture tube has rounded corners the usable picture size is somewhat less than the notional size. Some monitors give a larger display than others of the same specified size, but in general the actual diagonal measurement is about an inch or so less than the stated screen size.

Screen adjustments

These days virtually all monitors allow the horizontal and vertical sizes of the display to be adjusted so that it can be made to fill the screen. There should also be controls to enable the display to be accurately centred on the screen. Although you might expect two display cards operating in the same mode to position the display in more or less the same position on the screen, there can actually be quite large differences. Of more importance, the display can shift significantly when switching from one screen mode to another and it can also expand or shrink.

To avoid the need to readjust the controls each time the screen mode is altered, most monitors remember the control settings for each screen mode, and automatically switch to the appropriate settings when the mode is changed. Some video adapters are supplied with a utility that enables the card to be adjusted to suit the monitor for each screen mode. Again, the appropriate settings are used when the screen mode is changed, making it unnecessary to make any manual adjustments. Monitors normally have at least one or two controls that can be adjusted to minimise various forms of distortion, and in the case of larger monitors there are often several controls of this type.

Actually connecting the monitor to the video card should present no problems since all PC video cards and monitors use the same 15-way "D" style connector. The original PC monitors used a nine-way connector, but this became obsolete many years ago. The more upmarket monitors often have four BNC connectors that offer an alternative method of connection to the PC. PC monitors are normally supplied with a suitable video cable, but if in doubt check this point before ordering.

In fact most monitors have so called captive video cables. In other words, the video cable is permanently connected to the monitor and does not unplug at the monitor end. One slight drawback of this system is that the whole monitor has to be returned for serving if the video cable becomes damaged. The chances of this happening are probably quite low though.

In the past there were two ways of powering the monitor. It could be powered from the mains outlet on the PC's power supply unit or direct from an ordinary mains socket. These days the power lead supplied with the monitor will be a standard mains lead that enables the monitor to be powered from an ordinary 13-amp mains socket. Even if the PC has a mains outlet, which is unlikely, it is best to use the ordinary mains lead and plug supplied with the monitor. The monitor will automatically go into standby mode when the PC is switched off or the power management facility comes into operation.

Soundcards

PCs have a built-in loudspeaker, but this is driven by some very basic hardware that is really intended to do nothing more than produce a few simple "beep" sounds. For anything more than this a proper soundcard and a pair of active speakers is needed. In other words, speakers that have built-in power amplifiers. Most soundcards do actually have built-in amplifiers, but they only provide low output powers and generally provide quite modest volume levels when used with passive speakers (i.e. speakers that do not have built-in amplifiers).

The simplest soundcards only offer synthesised sounds, almost invariably produced using FM (frequency modulation) synthesis. FM synthesis gives adequate sound quality for many purposes, but wavetable synthesis is better for music making. This method uses standard analogue synthesis techniques, but the basic sounds are short bursts of recorded instrument sounds rather than simple waveforms from oscillator circuits. Much more realistic results are produced using this method, although all wavetable soundcards seem to produce variable results.

With any type of synthesis there are usually a few hundred different sounds available, and I suppose it is inevitable that some will sound more convincing than others. Modern soundcards can typically produce 32 or 64 different sounds at once, or in some cases much more than this. They are capable of reproducing quite complex music sequences, and in most cases sound reasonably convincing. Even the cheapest cards have the ability to record and play back in high quality stereo, and to play back pre-recorded sound samples (WAV files).

When dealing with soundcards you are likely to encounter frequent references to software and hardware wavetable synthesis. The hardware variety uses sound samples that are stored in a ROM on the soundcard, whereas software wavetable synthesis uses samples that are loaded from disc into the computer's main memory. Obviously the software type takes up some of the main memory, and less obviously it usually requires the processor to do more of the work.

Since modern PCs tend to have plenty of memory and processing power this is less important than was once the case. Software wavetable synthesis has the advantage that it is possible to add or change sounds quite easily. This is normally only possible with hardware wavetable soundcards if they have some added memory, effectively making them a form of software wavetable card. Some soundcards offer the best of both worlds by having a mixture of software and hardware wavetable sounds. These can usually provide a huge range of sounds operating on a large number of channels.

In theory the hardware wavetable and simple FM synthesiser cards should be the easiest to install and use. In practice the software wavetable cards have drivers that largely hide the differences between the two types of card. Soundcards in general have a reputation for being awkward to install, and likely to uninstall themselves given half a chance. Certainly in my experience the most likely troublesome component in a newly constructed PC is the soundcard. Fortunately, the new PCI soundcards seem rather better than the old ISA variety.

A substantial percentage of current motherboards have a built-in sound generator. This can usually be switched off so that a soundcard can be added into a PCI slot, but the built-in sound generators are adequate for most needs. Actually, some motherboards have quite advanced integral sound circuits having facilities that will satisfy all but the most demanding users. Unless you genuinely need the facilities of a top-notch soundcard, integrated audio is the easiest and best option.

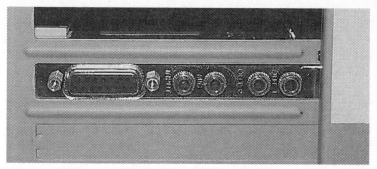

Fig.2.23 Soundcards normally have a joystick/MIDI port

Joystick and MIDI

Apart from three or four audio input and output sockets, soundcards normally have a 15-way connector that is a combined MIDI port and game port (Figure 2.23). When used as a game port it takes standard PC joysticks and similar devices. Most new games controllers connect to a USB port, so the game port is now little used in this role.

When used as a MIDI port it enables music programs to operate with MIDI synthesisers, keyboards, sound modules, etc. However, note that standard MIDI cables have 5-way (180 degree) DIN plugs at both ends, and are therefore incompatible with the 15-way D connector of a PC soundcard. A special MIDI cable is needed to connect a PC soundcard to MIDI devices. Actually, it is rather more than a cable, and it includes a small amount of electronics. It is consequently more expensive than most other PC cables.

MIDI tends to cause a certain amount of confusion because most soundcards have two or three MIDI drivers. One of these is the MIDI port driver, and it will produce a Roland MPU-401 compatible port. This is the device you use in order to communicate with MIDI synthesisers, keyboards, etc., but it does not get the soundcard itself to produce any sound. There will be one or two other drivers that produce virtual MIDI synthesisers. These can be used with software that has the ability to drive a MIDI device, and they get the soundcard to operate as a MIDI synthesiser. If the card has wavetable and FM synthesis there will probably be a separate driver for each type of synthesis. Additionally, there will be a driver for the joystick port. It is probably this proliferation of drivers that makes soundcards relatively difficult to install.

In the past PC soundcards were often equipped with an interface for a CD-ROM drive. The reason for this is simply that many people added a CD-ROM drive to their PC at the same time as they added a soundcard, since both of these items are required in order to run multimedia applications. Several CD-ROM interfaces have been used in the past, but only the ATAPI (IDE) and SCSI interfaces are currently in use on new drives. A few soundcards might still have a CD-ROM port so that they can be used as replacements or upgrades in an existing computer that requires an interface on the soundcard. Any port of this type is of no use with a new PC, so if possible switch it off, or simply ignore the port if it can not be deactivated.

Points to remember

You can not simply buy any motherboard and stick any processor on it. You must choose a processor and then look for a motherboard that supports the selected chip and has the features you require. Make sure the motherboard can handle a processor of the exact type and clock frequency you will be using.

Buy a matching heatsink and fan when you buy the processor. Some processors are actually supplied complete with a suitable cooling system, but most are not.

There are differences in the performance of similar motherboards from different manufacturers, but with modern boards these differences seem to be too small to worry about. Choose a board on the basis of cost, quality, and features.

No-name generic motherboards are significantly cheaper than those from well-known manufacturers. On the other hand, there is generally little or no support from the manufacturer with these boards, and it might be impossible to obtain BIOS upgrades. For the beginner at PC construction a board from a well-known manufacturer is the safer option.

If you buy an ATX motherboard you must use an ATX case and power supply. If you use an AT motherboard you can use an AT case or an ATX type. AT cases and motherboards are now more or less obsolete and are probably best avoided.

Make sure the case is supplied complete with small items of hardware. It is of little use without them. It is cheaper and easier if the case and power supply are bought as a single item rather than separately. When using a Pentium 4 motherboard, make sure the power supply is a type that has the additional power leads for this type of board.

A case that has removable drive bays is much easier to use than one where they are fixed. Small cases often give very restricted access to the interior, and medium or large cases are generally easier to deal with. In general they also have more drive bays.

Integrated video is fine for most software, but games devotees will require a PC having the latest 3D video card. It is preferable to use a motherboard that has an AGP slot and permits the built-in graphics adapter to be switched off. This leaves the option of upgrading to an expensive 3D video card.

The old ISA expansion slots are gradually being phased out. If you have an old ISA card that you wish to use in the new PC, the new motherboard must be one of the few that has an ISA expansion slot to accommodate it. In fact it might be impossible to obtain a new motherboard that has an ISA slot, and the ISA card will then have to be replaced.

The motherboard should be supplied with a basic set of leads for the drives. It can be expensive to buy these leads separately, so a budget board sold without leads might not be such a good bargain after all.

Beginners would be well advised to buy hard drives and CD-ROM drives having an ordinary IDE (ATAPI) interface, and not SCSI types. IDE drives are much easier to use and these days they have more than respectable levels of performance.

Integrated audio is more than adequate for most purposes. Many integrated audio systems are now quite sophisticated, offering surround-sound and other advanced features.

Assembly

Protection racket

Those readers who are used to dealing with electronic components will no doubt be aware that most computer components are vulnerable to damage by static electricity. They will also be used to handling static-sensitive components and taking the necessary precautions to protect them from damage. Probably most readers are not familiar with these precautions, and I will therefore outline the basic steps necessary to ensure that no components are accidentally "zapped".

I think it is worth making the point that it does not take a large static charge complete with sparks and "cracking" sounds to damage sensitive electronic components. Large static discharges of that type are sufficient to damage most semiconductor components, and not just the more sensitive ones. Many of the components used in computing are so sensitive to static charges that they can be damaged by relatively small voltages.

In this context "small" still means a potential of a hundred volts or so, but by static standards this is not particularly large. Charges of this order will not generate noticeable sparks or make your hair stand on end, but they are nevertheless harmful to many electronic components. Hence you can "zap" these components simply by touching them, and in most cases would not be aware that anything had happened.

I think it is also worth making the point that it is not just the processor and memory modules that are vulnerable. Completed circuit boards such as video and soundcards are often vulnerable to static damage, as is the motherboard itself. In fact most modern expansion cards and all motherboards are vulnerable to damage from static charges. Even components such as the hard disc drive and CD-ROM drive can be damaged by static charges. The case and power supply assembly plus any heatsinks and cooling fans represent the only major components that you can assume to be zap-proof. Everything else should be regarded as potentially at risk and handled accordingly.

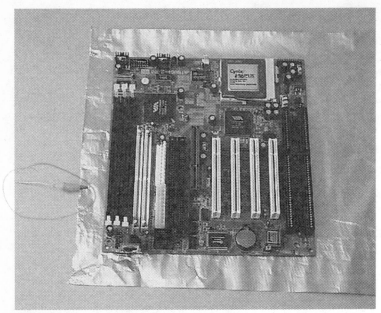

Fig.3.1 An improvised conductive work surface

When handling any vulnerable computer components you should always keep well away from any known or likely sources of static electricity. These includes such things as computer monitors, television sets, any carpets or furnishings that are known to be prone to static generation, and even any pets that are known to get charged-up fur coats. In general, objects that are wholly or partly made from metal are safer than those that are made entirely from plastic.

Avoid wearing any clothes that are known to give problems with static charges. This seems to be less of a problem than it once was, because few clothes these days are made from a cloth that consists entirely of man-made fibres. There is normally a significant content of natural fibres, and this seems to be sufficient to prevent any significant build-up of static charges. However, if you should have any garments that might give problems, make sure that you do not wear them when handling any computer equipment or components.

Anti-static equipment

Electronics and computing professionals often use quite expensive equipment to ensure that static charges are kept at bay. Most of these are not practical propositions for amateur computer enthusiasts or those who only deal with computers professionally on a very part-time basis. If you will only be working on computers from time to time, some very simple anti-static equipment is all that you need to ensure that there are no expensive accidents.

When working on a motherboard it is essential to have some form of conductive worktop that is earthed. These can be purchased from the larger electronic component suppliers, but something as basic as a large sheet of aluminium cooking foil laid out on the workbench will do the job very well (Figure 3.1). The only slight problem is that some way of earthing the foil must be devised.

The method I generally adopt is to connect the foil to the metal chassis of a computer using a crocodile clip lead (Figure 3.2). Crocodile clips are available from electronic component suppliers, as are sets of made-up leads. The ready-made leads are often quite short, but several can be clipped together to make up a longer lead. The computer that acts as

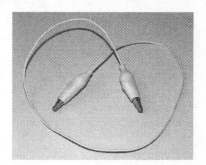

Fig.3.2 A crocodile clip lead

the earth must be plugged into the mains supply so that it is earthed via the mains earth lead. The computer should be switched off, and the supply should also be switched off at the mains socket. The earth lead is never switched, and the case will remain earthed even when it is switched off.

If you wish to make quite sure that your body remains static-free, you can earth yourself to the computer by way of a proper earthing wristband. This is basically just a wristband made from electrically conductive material that connects to the earth via a lead and a high value resistor. The resistor does not prevent any static build-up in your body from leaking away to earth, but it will protect you from a significant shock if a fault should result in the earthing point becoming "live".

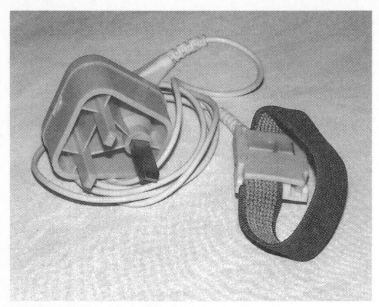

Fig.3.3 An anti-static wristband, lead, and earthing plug

There are two ways of earthing the wristband. One of these is to have a crocodile clip on the end of the earthing lead, and this can be connected to any piece of earthed metal that happens to be handy. In a PC context this usually means the chassis of a PC, but there might be other electrical gadgets having earthed chassis that could be used. The easier method is to have a sort of dummy mains plug on the earthing lead (Figure 3.3). This enables the wristband to be earthed via any mains socket.

Of course, only the earth pin of the plug connects to the wristband, and the rest of the plug is normally plastic so that there is no risk of a fault causing the wristband to be connected to a "live" pin. The resistor is included in the lead, so there is no danger of receiving a strong electric shock if, for instance, the mains socket's wiring is faulty.

Note that anti-static wrist-bands are sometimes sold as a complete kit with everything you need, but they are also sold as individual items (wristband, lead, and earthing plug or clip). Make sure that you know exactly what you are buying before parting with any money. If you are intending to do more than very occasional PC building, upgrading, or servicing, it is certainly worthwhile buying a good quality wristband kit.

It will ensure that you can handle computer components safely for many years.

Improvising

If you do not want to go to the expense of buying a wristband, a simple but effective alternative is to touch the conductive worktop or the metal chassis of the computer from time to time. This will leak away any gradual build-up of static electricity in your body before it has time to reach dangerous proportions. Again, the computer must be connected to the mains supply, but it should be switched off and the mains supply should be switched off at the mains outlet.

That is really all there is to it. Simply having a large chunk of earthed metal (in the form of the computer case) near the work area helps to discourage the build-up of any static charges in the first place. The few simple precautions outlined previously are then sufficient to ensure that there is no significant risk to the components.

Do not be tempted to simply ignore the dangers of static electricity when

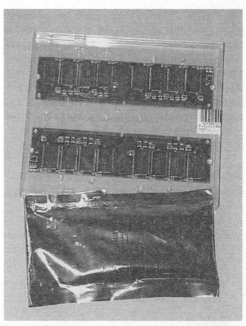

Fig.3.4 Two forms of anti-static packing that work in different ways but achieve the same thing

handling computer components. When building electronic gadgets I often ignore static precautions, but I am dealing with components that cost a matter of pence each. If one or two of the components should be zapped by a static charge, no great harm is done. The same is not true when dealing with computer components, some of which could cost in excess of a hundred pounds.

Anti-static packing

One final point is that any static sensitive components will be supplied in some form of anti-static packaging. This is usually nothing more than a plastic bag that is made from a special plastic that is slightly conductive. Processors and memory modules are often supplied in something more elaborate, such as conductive plastic clips and boxes. There is quite a range of anti-static packaging currently in use, and Figure 3.4 shows a couple of examples.

Although it is tempting to remove the components from the packing to have a good look at them, try to keep this type of thing to a minimum. When you do remove the components from the bags make sure that you and the bags are earthed first. Simply touching the earthed chassis of a computer while holding the component in its bag should ensure that everything is charge-free. Make sure that you always handle the components in an environment that is free from any likely sources of static charges. There will then be a minimal risk of any damage occurring.

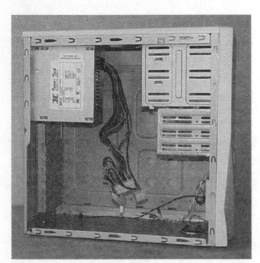

Fig.3.5 Removing one side panel gives good access to an ATX case

Case

Having set up any necessary anti-static precautions the next task is to get the case ready for assembly to begin. Unless you obtain one of the more exotic cases there should be no difficulty in opening the case. Removing four or six screws at the rear of the case should release the two side panels of a tower case, or the top and bottom panels of a desktop type. Look

Fig.3.6 Alternative plates for the ATX port cluster

carefully to see which screws actually hold the outer casing in position, or you will probably find that you have removed the power supply instead! Figure 3.5 shows an ATX case with one side panel removed.

With some ATX cases you only need to remove the left-hand side panel (as viewed from the front) in order to assemble the PC. With most it is necessary to remove the other panel in order to get the drives properly fixed into the bays, and it might also be necessary in order to get the motherboard installed. It is a good idea to remove both panels anyway as this makes it easier to see what you are doing, and to see how the case fits together.

Inside the case there should be various accessories, including a mains lead fitted with suitable connectors at both ends. The end that connects to the computer normally has a standard IEC plug, as used for most mains powered gadgets these days. There will also be various items of hardware such as screws, and there might also be two or three metal plates with various holes stamped in them (Figure 3.6). These fit on the rear of the case and accommodate various port configurations.

As pointed out in the previous chapters, an ATX motherboard has the standard ports actually fitted on the board, and the connectors for these ports are accessed via a cut-out in the case. However, as supplied most

PC cases do not have the necessary cut-outs in the rear of the case. The upper plate in Figure 3.6 suits boards that have the standard port cluster. The lower square towards the left of the plate is pressed out if the motherboard has built-in USB ports, and the one above is removed if it has addition USB ports or LAN types. The removable plates on the right are pressed out to accommodate boards that have an integrated sound generator. The lower plate is for use with boards that have a built-in graphics adapter.

Knockout panels

If you look at the area of the case where the cutouts should be you will probably find that there is a metal panel instead. This panel will be largely cut from the case, and will only be held in place by two or three thin pieces of metal. This approach to things is used a great deal with modern

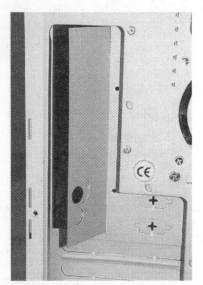

computer cases, and it is a simple way of having optional cut-outs. It is the same system that is used for the optional ports in the plates of Figure 3.6. Removing an unwanted panel is not difficult, and it is just a matter of pressing it with your finger to break one side free from the case (Figure 3.7). Then the panel is waggled backwards and forwards a few times until the fingers of metal securing it to the case fatigue and break.

There may be some rough edges produced where the metal fatigues and breaks. It is tempting to use a miniature file to rectify this, but filing or cutting a PC case using a saw is not something to be recommended. The problem is simply that the small metal fragments produced are difficult to thoroughly clean from the case, and they are also good at producing short-circuits if they get onto any of the circuit boards. If there are any dangerously sharp edges they must be removed, but otherwise do not

Fig.3.7 Removing a port cover plate from an ATX case

bother. If you do have to file away any sharp edges try to thoroughly clean away any swarf. A damp rag does the job quite well, but the sticky side of adhesive tape or some Bostik Blu-Tack are probably the most effective ways of mopping up the swarf.

Having removed the panel you can simply leave a large hole in the rear panel, but one of the plates supplied with the case should match up properly with the connectors on the motherboard. Much neater results will be produced if this is bolted in place on the rear panel (Figure 3.8). As pointed out previously, you may have to press out one or two small pieces of metal from the panel to make it match the connectors on the motherboard. Obviously this should be done before the

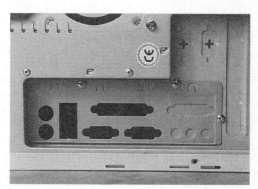

Fig.3.8 The new port cover plate installed on an ATX case

motherboard is fitted in the case, and it is usually easier if it is done prior to fitting the plate on the case.

Stand-offs

The next task is to install the stand-offs on which the motherboard will be mounted. It is possible that these will be built into the chassis, or that they will already be fitted to the chassis. This is unlikely though, and the first part of the assembly process is to fit the stand-offs to the chassis. If you look at the mounting holes in the motherboard and those in the chassis you will find that there are many more in the chassis. This is simply because the case is normally designed to take various types of motherboard, old and new. Some of the holes in the chassis probably have no relevance to any modern motherboards, and others will probably not be relevant to the particular board you are using.

The only sure way of telling which holes in the chassis should be fitted with stand-offs is to place the motherboard in position inside the case.

With most cases it should be possible to fit the motherboard in place without any difficulty, but with some of the smaller cases it will be necessary to remove the 3.5-inch drive bay and (or) the power supply unit. Do not flex the board or use force to get it into position, as this could easily damage it beyond repair.

Methods of fixing the drive bay cages vary somewhat, but it usually involves nothing more than undoing one or two screws and sliding the

Fig.3.9 Two plastic stand-offs

cage out from the main assembly. It often takes a fair amount of force to get the cage free. With some cases the drive cages are not removable, but with these it should be possible to fit the motherboard with the cages in place. Once the motherboard is inside the case it can be moved around until all the holes in the board match up with holes in the case. Make a careful note of

which holes in the case should be fitted with stand-offs, making a quick sketch if necessary.

It is possible that there will be some holes in the motherboard that have no counterparts in the case. This was quite normal with an AT motherboards, but it is less likely to occur with the ATX variety. The extra holes can simply be left unused, and provided there are at least four mounting points spread well across the board it should be held in place adequately.

A check through odds and ends of hardware supplied with the board will probably throw up a few plastic stand-offs that can be fitted into the underside of the motherboard, but have no provision for fixing to the chassis (Figure 3.9). These stand-offs are simply pushed into a mounting hole on the underside of the motherboard, and they can be used in any holes that have no counterparts in the case. They will avoid any tendency for the board to droop and possible short circuit to the case. They will also effectively stiffen the board, reducing the risk of any damage occurring when fitting any expansion cards that need firm pushes to slot them into place.

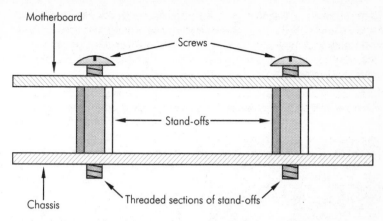

Fig.3.10 The most common form of stand-off for motherboards

Different types

There are several types of stand-off used with motherboards. Probably the most common stand-off at present is the hexagonal type that has a threaded section at the base which screws into the threaded holes in the chassis. The motherboard is then bolted to the stand-offs (Figure 3.10). These should be screwed quite firmly into the chassis, but with computers

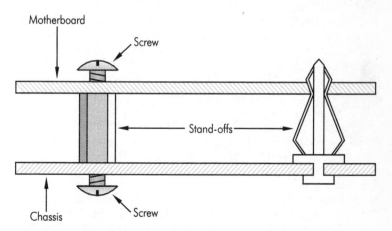

Fig.3.11 These two types of stand-off are quite common

it is not a matter of tightening everything as hard as you can. In order to avoid sheared threads you should tighten things enough to prevent them from easily coming apart again, but no more. In the absence of a suitable nut-driver for the stand-offs a pair of pliers should enable them to be tightened properly.

A similar type of stand-off is fixed in place by a screw, as in Figure 3.11. There are also plastic types that clip into the motherboard and then slide

into cutouts in the chassis, and this type is also depicted in Figure 3.11. These operate in conjunction with one or two metal stand-offs that enable the board to be bolted in place, and provide an electrical connection from the earth rail of the motherboard to the case. The slide-in approach can be a bit awkward in practice with some of the stand-offs tending to buckle under the board rather than sliding nicely into place. If necessary, slide the motherboard back out again and

Fig.3.12 Two types of metal clip-in stand-off

try again, and do not simply leave the board supported by buckled stand-offs. They may fall out of position and permit the board to short-circuit to the case.

Another type of stand-off clips into the case and the motherboard is then bolted to the stand-offs. A variation on this clip-in method has the motherboard slide into place under hooks on top of each stand-off. The hooked stand-offs have to be used in conjunction with one or two screw types so that the motherboard is reliably fixed in place. Both types are shown in Figure 3.12. There are other types of stand-off in use, but they are mostly variations on the types described here. It should not be too difficult to work out how other types of stand-off are used.

Be careful not to fit metal stand-offs to the chassis at any points where there are no matching mounting holes in the motherboard. Doing so could result in connections on the underside of the board being short-circuited to the case. Once the stand-offs are in place the motherboard should be mounted inside the case to ensure that everything fits correctly. When you have established that everything is all right the motherboard should be removed so that the processor and memory can be installed, and (where appropriate) the motherboard can be configured via the DIP-switches and jumpers.

Configuration

Some motherboards do not require any configuration at this stage of the proceedings, but are instead configured using the BIOS Setup program. In fact most of these boards configure themselves using probing techniques to determine what processor is fitted, and manual configuration is only needed if you do not agree with the default settings for some reason. If you are not using one these "jumperless" boards it will be necessary to use DIP-switches or jumpers to set up the board to suit the processor.

In some cases there is the option of configuring the board using jumpers or the BIOS. Selection is unusually via a jumper on the motherboard, but the default setting is usually for configuration via the BIOS. The option of manual configuration is mainly included for those wishing to over-clock the processor. If it works, over-clocking provides extra speed, but it takes the processor beyond its rated limits. In most cases it also takes other components beyond their normal working limits, including the memory, support chips, and probably the graphics adapter as well. Whether it is worth the effort and risk to the affected components depends on your need for processing speed, but over-clocking is certainly not the place to start. Where there is the option of automatic configuration it is best to use it.

Manuals for pieces of electronic equipment and computer software tend to get ignored, and are only read as a last resort. This is not an option when dealing with motherboards, and it is essential to read through the manual and constantly refer to it for vital pieces of information. You will certainly need to study the instruction manual for details of how to set it up to suit the particular processor you are using.

The parameters that are set via the jumpers or switches depend on the type of motherboard in use. The processor and motherboard clock speeds will certainly have be set, and the two are linked. The correct clock rate for the motherboard is set, and then a multiplier is used to produce the required clock frequency. As a couple of examples, an Athlon XP2000+ processor actually operates at about 1.66GHz, and with the motherboard operating at 133MHz (0.133GHz) a multiplier value of 12.5 (133 x 12.5 = 166.25). A Pentium 4 operating at 2.4GHz with a 133MHz bus frequency would require a multiplier value of 18 (133 x 18 = 2394).

As will be apparent from the first of these examples, the mathematics is not always perfect. In most cases the actual processor clock frequency will be slightly lower than its nominal value, or the motherboard bus speed will be fractionally higher (133.33MHz instead of 133MHz for example). It does not really matter which, and there will be no noticeable difference in performance between clock rates of (say) 2.394GHz and 2.4GHz. Matters can be confused slightly by different parts of the system operating at different frequencies. For example, the memory often operates at double or more the basic frequency of the motherboard. The processor's clock multiplier is relative to the basic motherboard frequency, and not any higher frequencies such as those used by memory or the graphics adapter.

Clock rates

As pointed out previously, there is a slight complication with the processor frequency for the AMD Athlon XP chips in that their actual clock frequencies are lower than the name of the processor would suggest. This is not a new phenomenon, and some of the Cyrix chips use the same system, where a figure in the name gives the speed in terms of an

Fig.3.13 An IBM/Cyrix processor marked with the system frequency and multiplier

equivalent Pentium processor. Matters were complicated by the fact that there was more than one version of some Cyrix chips, with each version requiring a different clock frequency. Fortunately, there is only one version of each AMD processor.

An automatic detection system should correctly identify any processor and set the correct multiplier, etc. The only proviso is that the BIOS must be sufficiently up to date to recognise the processor. Using the very latest processor with a motherboard that has been in the retailer's warehouse for some months runs a slight risk of the BIOS not being sufficiently up to date. When using a recently introduced processor always make sure that the motherboard you are using is fully compatible with it. Updating the BIOS of a modern motherboard is not difficult, but it requires the board to be in a fully working PC.

At one time it was common for processors to have the bus frequency and multiplier marked on the top of the chip, and the correct core voltage was usually indicated as well (Figure 3.13). This information is not usually included on modern processors (Figure 3.14), but it should be included in the instruction booklet provided with the chip. Also, the instruction manual for the motherboard will probably have a chart showing the correct

Fig.3.14 Modern processors are usually devoid of information such as operating frequencies and voltages

settings for the compatible processors. Wherever possible it is best to make life easier and simply opt for automatic detection. This also removes the slight risk of getting things wrong and damaging the processor.

Core voltage

Conventionally, logic circuits operate from a 5-volt supply, but in order to get the highest possible performance it is common practice for other supply voltages to be used in parts of the computer. Memory circuits and some sections of the processor often operate at 3.3 volts, and the main processor circuits often work at a somewhat lower voltage. A supply voltage as low as 1.5 volts is often used for modern processors. It is this core voltage that might have to be set via jumpers or DIP-switches. The instruction manual for the motherboard should give the correct settings for all the usable processors, and this information should be supplied with the processor. Again, it is best to use automatic detection and setting whenever possible.

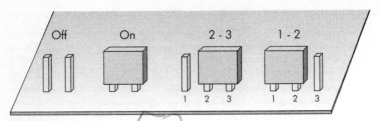

Fig.3.15 The two types of jumper normally used on motherboards

Clear CMOS

There may be other settings to make, but these additional parameters vary a lot from one motherboard to another. One virtually standard feature is a jumper that enables the CMOS memory to be disconnected from the backup battery. By default this should be set so the board functions normally, with the backup battery ensuring that the BIOS is free from amnesia, with the correct drive parameters, etc., being used each time the computer is switched on. Setting this jumper to the "off" position for a few minutes wipes the CMOS memory of all its contents. With the jumper restored to the "on" setting the computer is able to function again, but it is a matter of starting "from scratch" with the CMOS memory settings.

In effect, this jumper provides a means of resetting the CMOS memory. This would be probably only be necessary if someone started to use the password facility and then forgot his or her password. The only way of getting the computer to boot if this happens is to clear the current set-up from memory. The next time the computer is started it uses the default settings, which means that it starts up without implementing the password facility. Unless there is a good reason to do so, it is best not to use any BIOS password facility.

Note that it is not necessary to clear the CMOS memory in this way if you manage to make a complete mess of the BIOS settings. From within the BIOS Setup program it is usually possible to revert to one or two sets of default settings, and then do any necessary "fine tuning". Provided the computer can be persuaded to get as far as the initial testing routine, it should be possible to enter the BIOS and select the Standard Defaults option. It is not necessary to clear the CMOS memory before using the motherboard for the first time.

There can be other jumpers or DIP-switches to set such things as the motherboard's bus frequency, to disable the built-in audio system, and this type of thing. You really have to read the manual for the motherboard to determine what jumpers or DIP-switches have to be set up correctly, if any. The modern trend is towards as much as possible being set using auto-detection methods, or via the BIOS Setup program. Many motherboards only have one switch or jumper that can be used to power-down the CMOS memory. Boards of this type are certainly preferable for those building their first PC.

Setting up

Actually setting any jumpers or switches should not give any major problems. There are two types of jumper, which are the straightforward on/off type and the two-way variety. The on/off type has two pins and you fit the jumper over the pins to connect them together ("on") or do not fit the jumper at all ("off"). This simple scheme of things is shown in the left-hand section of Figure 3.15. It is common practice to fit

Fig.3.16 The "ON" marking on a DIP-switch

the jumper on one of the pins to provide the "off" setting. If you should need to change the setting at a later time you then know exactly where to find a jumper. The jumpers are minute and are likely to get lost if you store them somewhere other than on the motherboard.

The second type of jumper block has three pins, and the jumper is used to connect the middle pin to one of the outer pins, as shown in the right-

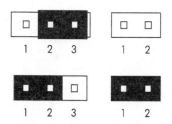

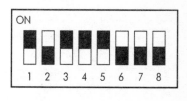

Fig.3.17 Some switch and jumper diagrams are clearer than others

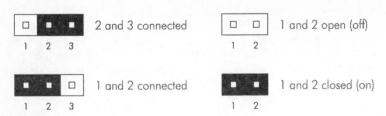

Fig.3.18 An explanatory diagram for jumper settings

hand section of Figure 3.15. The jumper is connecting together two pins, as before, and the jumpers are exactly the same whether they are used on a two-pin block or a three-pin type.

DIP-switches are normally in blocks of four or eight switches, but not all the switches in a block will necessarily be utilized. They are a form of slider switch, and are more or less a miniature version of the switches often used in small electronic gadgets such as cassette recorders and personal stereo units. The block of switches is marked with "on" and (or) "off" legends (Figure 3.16) to make it clear which setting is which.

The motherboard's instruction manual normally includes a diagram showing the correct switch or jumper settings for a given processor. There is a slight problem here in that these diagrams are open to misinterpretation. In the two examples of Figure 3.17, which pins do the jumpers connect and which switches are in the "on" position. My guess would be that the black blocks represent the jumpers and the control knobs on the switches, but there is no way of telling for sure without some further assistance. The manual should provide this assistance in the form of another diagram showing exactly how the switch or jumper setting diagrams should be interpreted. These diagrams will be

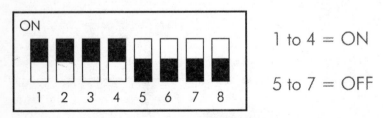

Fig.3.19 An explanatory diagram for DIP-switches

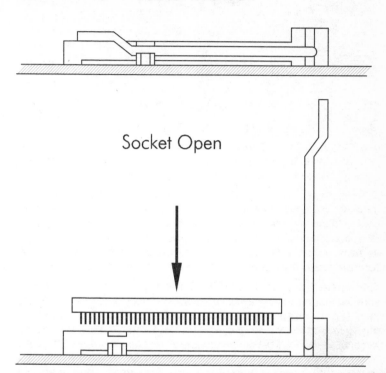

Socket Locked

Socket Open

Fig.3.20 The ZIF socket is opened by raising the lever

something like Figure 3.18 and 3.19. Never rely on guesswork when setting jumpers and DIP-switches. Mistakes are unlikely to result in any damage, but it is not worth taking the risk. Carefully study the instruction manual for the motherboard and get things right first time.

Processor

Once any necessary configuring of the board has been completed the processor can be fitted into its socket. This is much the same for AMD and Intel processors. Both types of processor fit into a ZIF (zero insertion force) socket on the motherboard. Conventional integrated circuit

Fig.3.21 The socket is polarised by having a "missing" hole in one corner

holders, even when used with integrated circuits that have only a few pins, are something less than easy to use. It is often quite difficult to squeeze the integrated circuits into them. The AMD and Intel chips have literally hundreds of pins. The Intel chips, for instance, use Socket 478 motherboards, and the Socket 478 name refers to the number of pins.

Getting a chip of this size into a holder could be bordering on the impossible, but the situation is greatly eased by the use of ZIF sockets. The holder has a lever that is raised to the vertical position in order to open the socket (Figure 3.20). The lever normally has to be pulled outwards slightly in order to unlock it before it can be raised. With the socket open the processor should simply drop into place without any difficulty. Returning the lever to its original position then locks the processor in place.

The processor must be fitted with the correct orientation, and with modern socket processors it impossible to fit a processor the wrong way round. If you look at the socket you will find that there are three corners that have provision for a pin on the processor, and one that does not (Figure

Fig.3.22 The "missing" pin is marked on the top surface of the chip

3.21). It is this missing hole in the socket that prevents the processor from fitting into it unless the processor has the correct orientation. If you look at the upper surface of the processor you will find a dot in one corner, and that corner of the casing will probably be chamfered as well (Figure 3.22). If you match that corner of the chip with the missing hole in the socket, the processor should drop easily into place.

Socket A, as used for AMD Athlon and Duron processors, does

things slightly differently. There are two corner holes "missing" from the socket and the corresponding pins of the processors are also absent. Figure 3.23 shows one of these sockets and it is the top and bottom left-hand corners that have the two "missing" holes. Confusingly perhaps, the processor itself still has only one proper corner marker,

Fig.3.23 Things are done differently with AMD's Socket A

Fig.3.24 An AMD XP2000+ processor fitted in its socket

Fig.3.25 Socket 478 is rather different to previous processor sockets

but there might be a smaller mark near the other corner. The main marker corresponds to the top left-hand corner of the socket as viewed in Figure 3.23. In other words, you have to look for the "missing" hole next to the lever of the ZIF socket. Alternatively, just look at the underside of the processor to see which two corners do not have a pin.

Installation

The processor should simply fall into place but it might take a certain amount of manoeuvring to get it into just the right position. Make sure that the locking lever is fully raised prior to fitting the processor, and move it right back to its original position once the processor is in position. If the processor will not fall into place, check that its orientation is correct. If it still fails to drop into place it is likely that one of the pins has become

Fig.3.26 A 2.4GHz Pentium 4 processor fitted in its socket

bent out of position. Look closely at all the pins and if necessary use the blade of a small screwdriver to carefully straighten any that are seriously bent out of place. Proceed very careful and gently, because the processor will be a write-off if one of the pins is broken off.

Fortunately, the pins on modern processors are quite short and strong, so there should be no problems with bent pins unless the device has been seriously mistreated. Figure 3.24 shows an AMD XP2000+ processor in place in its socket.

The Socket 478, as used for most Intel processors, looks rather different to a conventional processor socket (Figure 3.35). The socket is somewhat smaller, reflecting the small size of the Intel processors. It is surrounded by black plastic "fence" which is used to fit the heatsink and fan assembly in place. The processor is fitted and locked into place in standard fashion though. Figure 3.26 shows a Pentium 4 processor fitted in its socket.

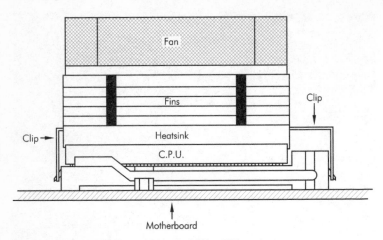

Fig.3.27 The heatsink and fan clip to the ZIF socket

Heatsink

With the processor in place the heatsink and fan are then fitted. With socket A and 370 chips, fitting the heatsink and fan can be rather fiddly and in some cases you may find that the heatsink does not clip securely in place. The side-on view of Figure 3.27 shows the simple method of fixing that seems to be used for all Socket A and 370 heatsinks. Fitting the heatsink is just a matter of fitting one end of the spring clip on the heatsink under one of the plastic retaining clips on the socket. Without letting this end slip out of position, the other end of the clip is then secured on the other side of the socket. With some combinations of heatsink and processor it is a rather tight fit, but once the heatsink is actually in place it should stay there and work efficiently.

If the heatsink is a loose fit it may not work very well, and there is a real risk that before long it will become dislodged. If you look carefully at the clip that secures the heatsink to the motherboard you will probably find that part of the clip can be removed and repositioned further up the main section of the clip. Using this second position should result in the heatsink and fan being held in place much more securely.

With the heatsinks for modern processors, particularly the faster types, there may be a pad of a rather sticky rubber-like material on the underside of the heatsink. At one time this was often included on top of the processor, but these days it is only included on the heatsink. The pad is usually protected by a tear off strip of paper (Figure 3.28), and this should be removed just before the heatsink is fitted on the processor. Figure 3.29 shows the pad on the underside of the heatsink, and Figure 3.30 shows the heatsink and fan safely installed on an AMD XP2000+ processor.

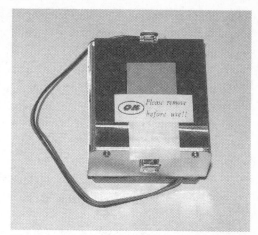

Fig.3.28 There is usually a protective covering on the pad of heatsink compound

The purpose of the pad is to ensure that there is a good thermal connection between the processor and the heatsink. Some processors consume quite high power levels and could overheat if there is an inefficient thermal contact with the heatsink. Do not remove the pad and be careful not to damage it. Doing either of these could seriously reduce the efficiency of the heatsink, and could even result in the processor overheating. If it becomes necessary to remove the heatsink at some time in the future, use a fresh pad or a smear of heatsink compound to ensure a good thermal contact when the heatsink is replaced.

Fig.3.29 The pad of heatsink compound

Fig.3.30 The heatsink and fan clipped into place

Socket 478

The method of mounting the heatsink described previously is the one used for Socket 370, and Socket A boards, but the Pentium 4 and Socket 478 boards use a different type of heatsink. The heatsink does not clip onto the socket. Around the processor there is a black plastic mounting bracket with a post in each corner, and the heatsink clips onto this. Refer back to the photographs of Figures 3.25 and 3.26 where the bracket can be clearly seen. The heatsink itself (Figure 3.31) is relatively large, and dwarfs the processor, but Pentium 4 processors run relatively cool because of this. The heatsink has two locking levers, one at each end.

Fitting the heatsink onto the motherboard is very easy, and it simply presses down into place on the black plastic mounting bracket. If it is reluctant to fit into place you probably have one or both of the levers in the locked position, and correcting this should enable it to be pressed down into place. The levers are set to the locked position once the heatsink has properly clipped into place. The levers operate a cam

Fig.3.31 A heatsink and fan for a Pentium 4 processor

Fig.3.32 The heatsink clipped onto the plastic holder

Fig.3.33 One of the cams can be seen in this side-on view of the heatsink in position

mechanism that forces the heatsink down onto the processor. Figure 3.32 shows the heatsink locked into place, and one of the cams can be seen in the side-on view of Figure 3.33.

Fan

The cooling fan will require a 12-volt supply, and there are two normal ways of obtaining this. In the past the most common method was to obtain power from one of the 5.25-in. disc drive supply outputs of the power supply unit. There will not always be a spare output of this type, but the fan will almost certainly be fitted with a lead that has two connectors (Figure 3.34). One of these connects to the output of the power supply and other connects to a 5.25-in. drive. This enables a single output of the power supply to provide power to both the cooling fan and one of the drives. If you use this method of powering the fan it is obviously not connected to the power supply until the motherboard has been finally installed in the case.

The alternative method, and by far the most common one these days, is to power the fan from the motherboard. Virtually all modern motherboards have a small three-pin connector that can supply 12 volts to the cooling fan, and most processor cooling fans are now fitted with this type of connector. There is no need to worry about getting this

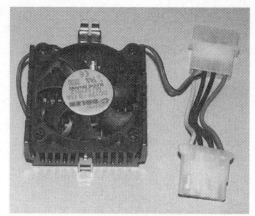

Fig.3.34 This fan taps off power from a 5.25-inch drive's power lead

connector fitted the right way round, because it will only fit with the correct orientation. If the fan is powered in this way it should be connected to the motherboard as soon as it has been fitted on the processor.

Modern motherboards often have more than one power supply output for a fan. If this should be the case the motherboard's instruction manual should indicate which output to use for the processor's fan. Although it might appear that any suitable power output will do, there is a potential problem. Some motherboards will sense that there is not an operating fan connected on the processor fan's output. This can cause warning alarms to sound or could even result in the PC failing to get through the initial start-up routine. The same problem can arise if the fan is powered from a 5.25-inch drive supply. The safest option is to power the fan from the correct output on the motherboard.

Fitting memories

The next stage is to install the memory on the motherboard. Modern motherboards mostly use some form of DIMM, but RIMMs are used in some Pentium 4 motherboards. Fitting DIMMs is very easy, and it is impossible to fit them the wrong way round because the DIMM's circuit board has a polarising "key". This is just an off-centre notch cut in the circuit board that matches a bar in the DIMM socket. Refer back to Figure 2.17 in chapter 2 for a photograph of a DDR DIMM. The key is

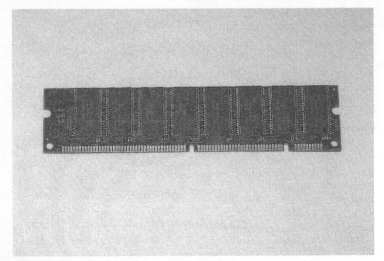

Fig.3.35 A 256 megabyte non-DDR DIMM

apparently in slightly different position depending on the supply voltage
of the module and the type of RAM fitted, and there are two keys in some
DIMMs. Figure 3.35 shows a non-DDR DIMM that has a second notch.
These differences should make it impossible to fit a DIMM of the wrong
type.

Because one notch and bar are well off-centre it is easy to determine
which way around the module should go. The module simply drops into
place vertically and as it is pressed down into position the plastic lever at
each end of the socket should start to close up. Pressing both levers
into a fully vertical position should securely lock the module in place, if
the levers do not snap into this position anyway. Make sure the levers
are pulled fully outwards before you try to fit the DIMM. Figures 3.36 and
3.37 respectively show a DIMM that is ready to be pushed down into
place, and one that is locked in place. To remove a DIMM, simply press
the two levers outwards as far as they will go. This should unlock the
memory module so that it can be lifted free of the socket.

Installing RIMMs is much the same as fitting DIMMs, and the same basic
method of locking and unlocking is used. With DIMMs it is permissible
to have unused memory holders, and a single DIMM can be used even if
the motherboard has three of four memory sockets. With RIMMs it is
necessary to have all the sockets occupied, so a Continuity Module has

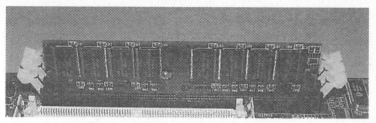

Fig.3.36 Here the DIMM is only partially slotted into place

to be used in any holders that are not fitted with RIMMs. It is essential to read the appropriate section of the motherboard's instruction manual when dealing with the memory, but it is especially important when RIMMs

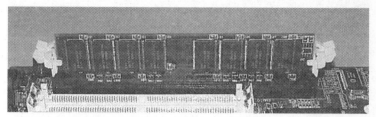

Fig.3.37 The DIMM pushed into the holder and locked in place

are used. Make sure that everything it strictly in accordance with the recommendations of the motherboard's manufacturer.

Drives

Once the memory modules have been fitted and the motherboard is installed in the case, the next step is to install the drives in the drive bays. There are plastic covers over the external drive bays, and these must be removed at the positions where drives are to be fitted. These are easily pushed out from the rear, but there will probably be a slight snag here in the form of a metal plate behind each plastic cover. These plates are partially cut from the case, and must be removed from any bays where externally accessible drives will be fitted. They can usually be left in place where other drives, such as the hard drive or drives, will be fitted.

They are removed in the same way as other blanking plates in the case. Remove the plastic cover first. There are usually a couple of holes in the

Fig.3.38 The metal plate and plastic cover removed from a drive bay

metal plate so that you can push out the plastic cover from the rear by poking a screwdriver through one of these holes. With a bit of pushing and shoving it should be possible to turn the plate through about 30 degrees or so, although it can take a while to get the blanking plate completely free. You can then get hold of one edge, and with a bit of waggling the plate should soon break away from the case.

With the plate and plastic cover removed (Figure 3.38) the bay is ready for the drive to be fitted. Note that with some of the more expensive cases the metal plates are held in place by two or four screws, so check for these before trying to break the plates free.

It is likely that there will be more drive bays than drives, leaving some of the bays unused. It does not really matter too much which bays you leave unused, but where possible it is probably better to arrange things so that there is an unused bay between drives. Spacing out the drives often makes installation slightly less fiddly, and it can also make them easier to use. Another factor is that many modern drives get quite hot when they have been in use for a while. Spacing them out as much as possible makes it easier for the air to circulate and should help to keep the drives cool.

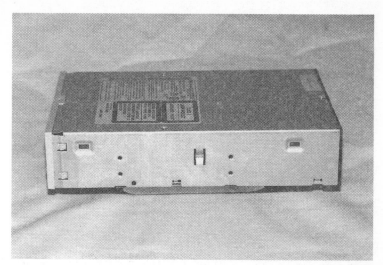

Fig.3.39 There are four mounting holes in each side of a 5.25-inch drive

With modern cases there should be no difficulty in fitting the drives since they mostly slot direct into the bays. Suitable fixing screws should be supplied with the case, and will probably be included with some of the drives as well. It is best to only use the screws supplied with the drive or case, as they are suitably short. Screws even slightly longer might penetrate too far into the drive and cause severe damage. Where appropriate, the fixing screws that are supplied with a drive should always

be used, since they will presumably be a perfect fit for the drive. Some of the screws supplied with the case should do the job perfectly well though.

There are usually four mounting holes in each side of 5.25-inch drives (Figure 3.39), but it is only necessary to use two fixing screws in each

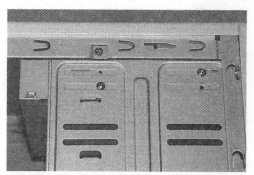

Fig.3.40 Two fixing screws per side will hold a drive in place

Fig.3.41 The enclosed side of a hard disc drive is usually the top

side (Figure 3.40). Initially leave the screws slightly loose, and then manoeuvre the drive precisely into the right position so that its front panel is flush with the case's front panel. Then tighten the screws, being careful not shift the drive out of position.

Drive access

Depending on the design of the case you are using, it may or may not be possible to gain adequate access to both sides of the 3.5-inch drive bays. If necessary, remove the 3.5-inch bays from the case, fit the drives, and then replace the drive bays complete with the drives. With most cases, extricating the 3.5-inch bays only requires one or two screws to be removed, and then the bay can be slid away from the main casing. If this proves to be impossible it may be necessary to have the drives only secured to the bays on one side. This is not a desirable state of affairs, but it should hold the drives in place adequately.

Some cases give better access to the underside of the 3.5-inch bays when the motherboard is not in the case, but you may then find it difficult to install the motherboard with the 3.5-inch drives fitted. You have to use your initiative when dealing with this type of thing, or you will simply end

Fig.3.42 A circuit board is usually visible on the underside of the drive

up going round in circles. Try to avoid the embarrassing mistake of fitting one or more of the externally accessible drives up side down.

3.5-inch hard disc drives usually have a metal covering on one of the large surfaces (Figure 3.41) and a circuit board visible on the opposite surface (Figure 3.42). The metal covering is on what is usually the top of the drive. There is usually a minimum of three mounting holes in each side of the drive, but when the drive is fitted in the drive bay it is likely that only two holes will match up with the holes or slits in the bay (Figure 3.43). However, two mounting bolts per side are more than adequate.

It might be necessary to move the drive backward and forward to get the mounting holes in the drive to match up with those in the drive bay. It is more likely that there will be a range of positions where a match is obtained. Where there is a choice, always mount the drive as far forward as possible. The 3.5-inch drives tend to obscure the motherboard to some extent, but mounting them as far forward as possible minimises this problem.

The more upmarket cases are sometimes designed to have the 3.5-inch drives only bolted in place on one side. Any case of this type should be

Fig.3.43 Only two mounting holes per side will match up with holes in the drive bay

supplied complete with one mounting rail per 3.5-inch drive bay. It is unusual for the guide-rails to have provision for fixing screws, and most of them simply clip onto the side of the drive. The drive and guide-rail assembly is then slid into the drive bay and held in place by two screws that fit into place on the side that does not have the guide-rail. The other side of the drive is supported by the guide-rail, which clips into the case reasonably securely.

I think it is as well to repeat the warning that mounting bolts should not be tightened using the maximum force you can muster. Obviously the bolts need to be tightened sufficiently to reliably hold the drives in place for several years, but the "hammer and tongs" approach can result in screw threads being sheared. It is best to err on the side of caution. If a screw should eventually work loose it only takes a few seconds to tighten it again.

Cabling

It is best to complete the cabling next, prior to installing the expansion cards (which tend to get in the way and make it difficult to fit the cables). The motherboard should be supplied complete with a basic set of connecting cables. For an ATX board this will probably just be a data cable for the floppy disc drive and another one for the IDE drives. Both of these cables will support two drives, but in the case of the IDE drives you may prefer to buy a second cable so that the hard disc and the CD-ROM drive can be operated from separate IDE ports.

In fact it is definitely a good idea to do so. As pointed out previously, this should give faster data transfers from the hard disc which will be free to operate in the fastest mode that both the drive and the motherboard support. Using some form of CD-ROM drive on the same interface would probably result in the hard disc drive operating in a more basic mode such as UDMA33, with a consequent slow-down in transfer rates. Also, transfers between the CD-ROM drive and the hard disc are likely to be faster with the two drives on different IDE interfaces. If you should settle for a single cable, the drives can normally be connected to the IDE1 or the IDE2 interface, but the convention is to use the IDE1 port. Some motherboards will only boot from devices on IDE1, so this is the safe option.

The hard disc drive will presumably operate in a "turbo" mode such as UDMA133, and it will need the special cable that supports UDMA66 operation and beyond. The IDE cable supplied with the motherboard will almost certainly be of this type. A second IDE cable might be supplied with the motherboard, but this is by no means certain. If there are two IDE cables, the one having 80 connecting wires is used with the hard disc drive, and the one having 40 thicker wires is used with the CD-ROM drive, etc. If you have to buy an IDE cable for use with CD-ROM drives, etc., on the second IDE interface, a 40-way cable will suffice, but an 80-way type should work perfectly well.

When using two modern hard disc drives they can both be connected to IDE1, and they should both provide fast data transfers. If one of the hard disc drives is an older and slower unit it is better to connect it on IDE2. It is otherwise likely that the old drive will result in the faster hard disc drive being reduced to a slower operating mode by the presence of the older drive.

IDE connectors

In theory the IDE connectors are polarised and can only be fitted the right way round. In practice some of the connectors, especially on motherboards, are rather basic and are not properly polarised. The plugs on the motherboards and drives should each have a cutout in the plastic surround, and this should match up with a protrusion on each plug. Figure 3.44 shows an IDE socket (top) and a matching plug (bottom), and the polarising keys are clearly visible.

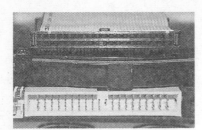

Fig.3.44 IDE and floppy drive connectors are polarised

Some manufacturers take a "belt and braces" approach, and there may also be a missing pin on the plug and a blocked hole in the socket. If you look carefully at Figure 3.44 you will see that the connectors have the missing pin and blocked hole. Cables that have this method of polarisation are only suitable for use with motherboards that have the missing pin. This will not be a problem when using the cables supplied with the motherboard or if you buy standard IDE cables. It could be a problem if you try to use a cable removed from a defunct PC. However, it is usually quite easy to drill out the blocked hole using a very small drill bit.

If you find that it is possible to fit the connectors either way round it is still quite easy to determine the correct method of connection. Computer data cables are made from a ribbon-like cable, which, unsurprisingly, is actually called ribbon cable. This is grey in colour, but there is a red mark or pattern running along one edge of the cable. This is the lead that connects pin one on one connector to pin one on the other connector.

The instruction manuals for the motherboard and drive should have diagrams that show the position of pin 1 on each connector. In fact pin one is usually marked on the actual components, although you will probably have to look carefully to find these markings. Make sure that the red lead always matches up with pin one on the drives and motherboard, and the drives will be connected correctly. These days some of the more upmarket motherboards are supplied with "round" IDE cables that use conventional multi-way cable rather than the ribbon variety. Pin one of each connector should still be clearly marked though.

Drive configuration

The two devices on an IDE port are called the "master" and "slave" devices. It does not matter which drive you connect to which connector on the IDE cable. Jumpers on the device itself control the role of an IDE device. If there is only one device on an IDE port it is normally set up as the master, but the system should work just as well if it is set as the slave device. The hard disc drive used to boot the system is normally the master device on IDE1.

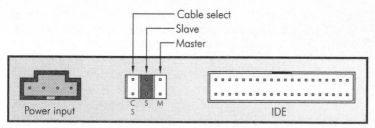

Fig.3.45 The configuration jumpers for a CD-ROM drive are buried in
        the connectors at the rear of the unit

The more or less standard arrangement for the jumpers on a CD-ROM
drive is shown in Figure 3.45. The jumper is used to bridge the two "S"
terminals if it is to be the slave device or the "M" terminals if it is to be the
"master" drive. The "CS" (cable select) terminals and any others are not
needed and are left unconnected, as are any other terminals in the block.

Hard disc drives normally operate using a similar arrangement, but when
used as a master device some drives are not quite as straightforward as
this. A different jumper configuration can be needed depending on
whether or not there is a slave device on that IDE port. The Master
setting is then only used if there is a slave device on the same IDE interface
as the hard drive. The alternative setting, which will be called something
like the Sole setting, is used if the hard disc is the only drive on that IDE
interface.

You should always
check the instruction
manuals of IDE drives
to see if there are any
unusual aspects to
the configuration, and
then   proceed
accordingly. Retail
boxed drives are
usually supplied with
a detailed instruction
manual, but the OEM
units are usually
"bare"   drives.
Instruction manuals
for hard disc drives
are usually available

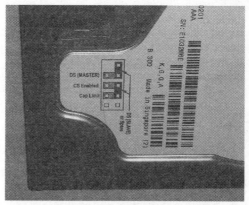

Fig.3.46 There is a jumper setting diagram on
        most hard disc drives

from the manufacturer's web site. The vast majority of modern drives have a configuration diagram or chart marked on the actual drive (Figure 3.46), and this is usually the only installation information you will require.

RAID controller

It has been assumed here that the motherboard has two IDE interfaces. Some motherboards have a built-in RAID (Redundant Array of Inexpensive Discs) controller, giving two additional IDE interfaces. This used to be an expensive addition to a motherboard, but it is increasingly common for mid-price and even budget motherboards to sport this feature. It is not essential to use the two additional IDE ports, and they can simply be ignored. The section of the BIOS that handles the input and output circuits usually has a setting that permits the RAID controller to be switched off.

There are various RAID operating modes that enable additional hard disc drives to be used in various ways. Apparently the basic idea is to permit two or more hard disc drives of relatively low capacity to operate as one huge disc drive. This has potential advantages, but "small" hard drives currently offer capacities of 20 to 40 gigabytes, which is more than adequate for most purposes. Another operating mode (RAID 1) has data written to two hard disc drives simultaneously, and it can then be read from either drive. If one drive fails, the other effectively becomes a backup device that should still have perfect copies of all your files.

Using a RAID controller really goes beyond the scope of this book, and it is probably something that is best avoided when building your first PC. If you use a motherboard that has a RAID controller it is probably best to switch it off or ignore it initially. Once the PC has been built and tested you can always add an extra disc or two and try out the RAID controller. Unfortunately, the RAID documentation provided with motherboards is often limited or even absent, but there is plenty of information on this subject available on the Internet.

Floppy drive

Like CD-ROM and DVD drives, a 3.5-inch floppy drive requires a drive bay that has external access. Many cases only have one 3.5-inch drive bay with external access, which is usually the top one, so there may be no choice but to use this bay for the floppy drive. Where appropriate, the plastic cover and metal plate covering the front of the drive bay must be removed. The conventional way of fitting a floppy disc drive is to have the front of the drive flush with the front panel of the case, as in Figure 3.47.

It is increasingly common for modern cases to use the alternative method of having a sort of plastic facia on the front of the case, with the drive fitted behind it (Figure 3.48). The drive's disc eject button is operated via

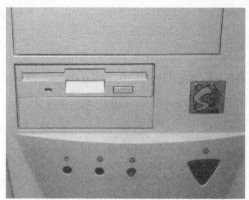

Fig.3.47 The conventional method of fitting a 3.5-inch floppy disc drive

a button built into the front of the case. Most cases will take ordinary 3.5-inch floppy drives, but some require a drive having a somewhat simplified front section. It is probably best to avoid this type of case unless you are sure that a matching floppy drive can be obtained, or a suitable drive is supplied with the case.

A 3.5-inch floppy disc drive usually has three mounting holes per side (Figure 3.49). The one nearest the front is a bit difficult to spot in Figure 3.49, but it is unlikely that there will be matching hole for this in the drive bay. The other two are used to hold the drive in place, and the drive bays usually have slits (Figure 3.50) that permit the drive to be positioned

Fig.3.48 This case hides the floppy drive behind a facia

so that its front panel is flush with the front of the case. If the case is a type that has a plastic facia, simply mount the drive as far forward as it will go.

Fig.3.49 There are three mounting holes in each side of a 3.5-inch floppy disc drive

Floppy cabling

Connecting the floppy disc drive tends to cause a certain amount of confusion due to the unusual method of cabling used. The standard PC floppy disc drive cable consists of a length of 34-way ribbon cable, which is fitted with 34 way edge connectors and IDC connectors at the floppy drive end. 3.5-inch floppy drives require the IDC connectors, and 5.25-inch types connect to the edge connectors. The connector at the motherboard end is a 34-way IDC connector. Most cables are for twin drives, and therefore have two sets of drive connectors, which is some four in total. The maximum number of floppy drives that can be used is two and not four.

In a standard floppy drive set-up, the two connectors would be wired in exactly the same way. Pin 1 at the controller would connect to pin 1 of both drives, pin 2 would connect to both of the pin 2s, and so on. On the face of it, the two drives will try to operate in unison, with both trying to operate as drive A. In practice this does not happen, because there are jumpers on the drives which are set to make one operate as drive A, and

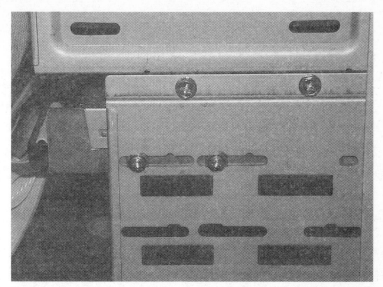

Fig.3.50 Two mounting bolts per side will hold a floppy drive in place

the other as drive B. This is essentially the same as the master and slave system used for drives connected to an IDE interface.

The jumper blocks are normally in the form of four pairs of terminals marked something like "DS0", "DS1", "DS2", and "DS3" (or possibly something like "DS1" to "DS4"). The instruction manual for the disc drive (in the unlikely event of you being able to obtain it) will make it clear which of the many jumper blocks are the ones for drive selection. Drive A has the jumper on "DS0", while drive B has it on "DS1".

Strange twist

Things could actually be set up in this fashion in a PC, but it is not the standard way of doing things. Instead, both drives are set as drive B by having the jumper lead placed on "DS1". The so-called "twist" in the cable between the two drive connectors then reverses some of the connections to one drive, making it operate as drive B. This may seem to be a strange way of doing things, but there is apparently a good reason for it. If you obtain a PC disc drive, whether for use as drive A or B, the same drive configured in exactly the same way will do the job. This

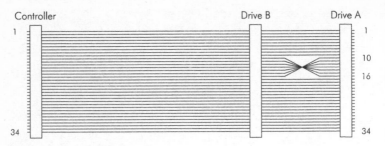

Fig.3.51 The arrangement used for a PC floppy disc data cable

avoids the need for dealers to stock two different types of drive, which in reality is exactly the same type of drive with a slightly different configuration. In fact these days most drives sold for use in PCs do not have the jumper blocks, and a hard-wired to act as drive B.

The computer will still work if you get the connections to two floppy drives swapped over, but the one you required as drive A will be drive B, and vice versa. The connector at the end of the cable couples to drive A, while the other one connects to drive B. Figure 3.51 shows this general scheme of things, and Figure 3.52 shows a floppy disc cable that has two pairs of drive connectors. Getting the floppy drive cable connected to the new drive should be straightforward, because the connectors should be polarised, so that they can not be fitted the wrong way round. In reality matters are not always as straightforward as this.

The connectors used for 3.5-inch drives are much the same as the ones used for IDE drives, but with 34 pins instead of 40. Like the IDE connectors, they are not always properly polarised. Some floppy drives unhelpfully have two polarising keys so that the data lead can be connected either way round. Floppy drive cables use the same system as the IDE variety, with pin 1 indicated by a red lead. If the connectors are not properly polarised, check the pin numbering on the drive and the motherboard and make sure that the red lead connects to pin 1 at both ends of the cable. It can be difficult to locate the pin numbering on floppy drives, but there are usually at least a couple of numbers marked to show which end of the connector has pin 1.

5.25-inch floppy drives have a different connector to the 3.5-inch variety. A simple edge connector system is used, and this is similar to an expansion card and an expansion slot. The connector on the drive is just part of its main printed circuit board, and the connector on the lead is a bit like a miniature expansion slot. These connectors are properly

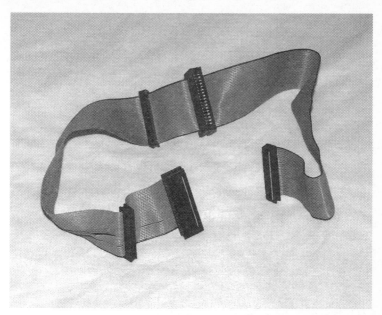

Fig.3.52 A floppy disc cable having two sets of drive connectors

polarised, and the necessary "key" is just a small metal rod on the edge connector, which fits into a slot in the connector on the drive. Note that many modern floppy disc cables do not have the connectors for 5.25-inch drives. It may be necessary to do some searching for a suitable lead in the unlikely event that you wish to include a 5.25-inch drive in a PC.

Termination resistors

Floppy disc drives used to be supplied with a block of removable resistors, or resistors that could be switched out of circuit. The idea was to have these termination resistors connected into circuit on the drive at the end of the cable, but not on any drives along the way. Modern floppy disc drives for use in PCs do not seem to have these resistors, or if they do there is no way of cutting them out of circuit. Consequently you will not have to bother with these resistors unless you are using an old floppy drive in your new PC. The resistors should then be switched out or removed if the drive is used as drive B (the one connected to the middle of the cable).

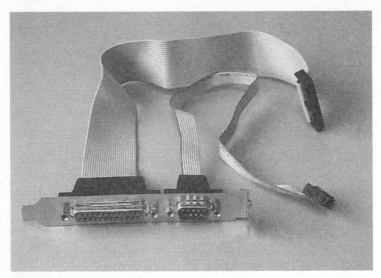

Fig.3.53 Parallel and serial port connectors fitted to a blanking plate

Without an instruction manual for the disc drive it could be difficult to deactivate the resistors. A search of the drive's circuit board will probably bring to light a small component mounted in a socket so that it can be removed easily, and this will probably be the termination resistors. Alternatively there might be a switch or a jumper with markings that suggest it is for deactivating the termination resistors. If not, the drive probably does not have these resistors and it can then be used as is.

Ports

AT motherboards do not have "proper" on-board connectors for the serial and parallel ports. Instead, the basic connectors on the board are wired to sockets mounted on the rear of the case, or in banking plates that are fitted behind any vacant expansion slots. The boards were normally supplied with connectors and leads for the serial and parallel ports, and possibly connectors and leads for the mouse port as well. Figure 3.53 shows a blanking plate fitted with connectors for one serial and one parallel port.

As explained previously, ATX motherboards make things much easier by, as far as possible, having the connectors for the ports mounted on the motherboard and accessible through cut-outs in the rear of the case.

In most instances there is no need for any connectors mounted on blanking plates. However, some ATX motherboards have provision for extra ports that do require connectors provided in this fashion. For example, additional USB ports are sometimes provided in this way, as are infrared (IrDA) ports.

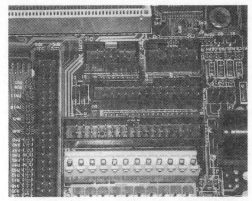

Fig.3.54 The port connectors are often like smaller versions of IDE connectors

At the motherboard end of the cables the connectors are usually small IDC types, like the disc drive connectors. In Figure 3.54 the three smaller connectors near the top are for off-board ports, and the one below them is a floppy drive port. The connectors should be polarised, but if not you will have to use the red lead to pin 1 method. Pin 1 might be indicated on the motherboard itself, but if not there should be a diagram in the instruction manual that shows pin 1 of every connector on the board. It is worth remembering that the motherboard's instruction manual gives concise connection information for all the onboard connectors, and should be able to solve problems when connecting anything to the motherboard.

Note that the connectors and leads needed to implement additional ports are sometimes optional extras. If you wish to use these facilities and suitable leads are not supplied with the motherboard you must be sure to obtain the correct lead and connector set. There are often minor differences from one manufacturer to another, and in some cases the connectors at the motherboard end are completely different. In others they are the same but wired differently. Buy leads that are specifically designed for use with the particular motherboard you are using, and connected them in accordance with the instructions in the motherboard's instruction manual.

Some motherboards have connectors for additional USB ports and (or) a second set of audio connectors, but they are not intended for use with brackets mounted at the rear of the PC. Instead, they are intended for

Fig.3.55 An ATX power connector fitted on a motherboard

use with cases that have provision for USB and (or) audio sockets mounted on the front panel. Front panel audio and USB sockets are very useful, and it is well worth implementing this facility. Unfortunately, even if you are using a case and motherboard that support this feature, in practice it can be difficult to get all the hardware to implement it. It is certainly worth giving it a try if you have the necessary leads, etc.

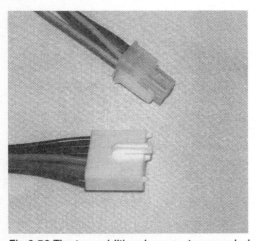

Fig.3.56 The two additional connectors needed for a Pentium 4 motherboard

Power supply

Connecting an ATX power supply to the motherboard should present no major difficulties since there is normally just one connector (Figure 3.55) and it will only fit the right way round. Some of these connectors can be reluctant to fit into place, but with firm pressure it should do so. The power connector is a locking type, and the lever mechanism on the connector must be operated in order to pull it free of the motherboard.

Power supplies for Pentium 4 motherboards have two additional connectors (Figure 5.56). If you are building a PC based on a motherboard that requires the additional power sources it is clearly essential to buy a case that has a suitably equipped power supply. Both the additional power connectors are properly polarised so there is no risk of

Fig.3.57 An AT power supply has two power leads for the motherboard

connecting them the wrong way round. The two extra power connectors on the motherboard will not necessarily be close to the main power input, but they should be easy to spot. As far as I am aware, motherboards for use with AMD processors only require the main power connector.

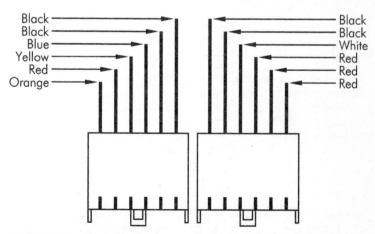

Black
Black
Blue
Yellow
Red
Orange

Black
Black
White
Red
Red
Red

Fig.3.58 With AT power leads connected correctly the black leads are grouped together

Fig.3.59 The 5.25-inch power connectors are polarised

An AT power supply has two leads that connect to the motherboard (Figure 3.57). The connectors are polarised, but there is nothing to stop you from getting them swapped over. The convention is for the black leads to be grouped together in the middle, as in Figure 3.58, and not at the ends of the row of connections. This type of power connector is a bit fiddly, and you need to be careful not to get everything shifted along by one connection point. Like an ATX power connector, the AT variety locks into place and the lever mechanism must be operated to release each one.

With a modern power supply there should be more than ample power leads for the disc drives. The larger connectors are the ones for the 5.25-inch drives and 3.5-inch hard drives. Figure 3.59 shows the power port of a 5.25-inch drive or hard drive together with a matching connector of the power supply. Getting this type of connector into place can require a substantial amount of force. It can require even more effort to remove one again, so be prepared to use a certain amount of brute force with this type of connector. It is impossible to fit these connectors the wrong way round.

The smaller connectors for the 3.5-inch drives are also polarised, and it should need relatively little force to connect them to the drives. Figure 3.60 shows a 3.5-inch power connector fitted to a floppy drive. If you find it difficult to fit these plugs into the drives you either have them up side down or out of alignment with the connectors in the drive. The concave side of the connector faces downward and the convex surface faces upwards.

Fig.3.60   The power lead connected correctly to a 3.5-inch floppy drive

There can be problems with the terminals on the floppy drive's connector getting bent slightly upwards, making it impossible to fit the power connector on the supply lead. Pressing the terminals down slightly should permit the supply to be connected. Make sure that you get the floppy power connected fitted just right. Mistakes here can have dire consequences for the power supply and (or) the floppy drive. Figure 3.61 shows the connector on the drive, and the connector on the power lead the right way up, ready to be fitted to the drive.

Fig.3.61   The 3.5-inch floppy disc power connectors

Connector block

The motherboard will have a connector block that accepts leads from various items on the case (Figure 3.62). This block is a common cause of confusion for newcomers to PC building because the facilities of the

Fig.3.62 A typical connector block

case never seem to perfectly match up with those of the motherboard. A typical set of connectors for an ATX case is shown in Figure 3.63. There may be some features of the case that are not supported by the motherboard, and there will almost certainly be several motherboard features that the case is unable to accommodate.

This is something where you have to take a down to earth attitude, and provided a few basic features are implemented on both, which they will be, that is all that is needed to get your new PC operating successfully. These are the functions that you should be able to implement:

Power LED

This connects to what is usually a green LED on the front of the case that switches on whenever the computer is operating. Note that an LED, unlike an ordinary light bulb, will only work if it is connected with the

Fig.3.63 A typical set of connectors for an ATX case

right polarity. The instruction manual for the motherboard will have a diagram showing the functions of the various pins in the block, and this with have a "+" sign on one of the pins that connects to the power LED. The connectors on the leads that connect to the LEDs, etc., will be marked with their functions, and the connector for the power LED might have its polarity marked. If

not, it is usually the white lead that is the "–" connection and the coloured lead that is the "+" one. There is little risk of a LED being damaged if it is connected with the wrong polarity, so you can use trial and error if necessary.

IDE activity LED

This is sometimes called the hard disc light, and in days gone by it would probably only switch on when the hard disc was active. However, this light actually switches on when any IDE device is active, and these days there will normally be other IDE devices such as CD-ROM drives and CD writers. This LED must be connected with the right polarity. Again, trial and error can be used if necessary.

Reset switch

This is the switch on the front panel that can be used to reset the computer if it hangs up. Its lead can be connected either way round. Some users prefer not to connect this switch, so that it is not possible to accidentally reset the computer. However, without the reset switch the only means of providing a hardware reset is to switch the computer off, wait at least a couple of seconds, and then switch on again.

Loudspeaker

This is the lead for the computer's internal loudspeaker, which is little used in modern computers. This loudspeaker is normally used to produce one or two beeps at start-up to indicate that all is well or a different set of beeps if there is a fault. The leads on this connector will probably be red and black, but it can actually be connected either way round and it is not polarised.

Power switch

This facility is not used with an AT power supply, which is switched on and off by way of an ordinary mains power switch. With an ATX power supply the on/off switching is controlled via a signal from the motherboard. The on/off switch connects to the power supply via the motherboard and the supply's main power output lead. Pressing the power switch turns on the computer, pressing it again switches off the computer, and so on. This switch appears to operate like a normal power switch, but note that the computer will be in the off state if the mains supply is removed and then reinstated. This lead can be connected either way round.

These are some of the functions that might be implemented on the motherboard, but they are non-essential:

Keylock

It used to be standard practice for PCs to have a key that could be used to operate a special type of switch fitted on the front panel. This switch enabled the keyboard to be switched off, thus preventing anyone from tampering with the PC while you were not looking. This feature was never very popular, and when control of PCs was partially handed over to the mouse it failed to fulfil its intended task anyway. It is probably not worth implementing even if this feature is supported by the case.

Temperature warning

Because modern PCs contain a lot of components that get quite hot it is now very common for some sort of temperature monitoring and warning feature to be included on motherboards. Exactly what happens when something in the PC starts to get too hot varies from one motherboard to another, but the internal loudspeaker will probably start to "beep", a warning LED might start flashing, or the PC might even switch itself off. If there is an output for a temperature warning LED and the case has a spare LED indicator, I would recommend implementing this feature. Note that the LED will only work if it is connected the right way round. Most facilities of this type have the LED normally switched on, and it flashes when an excessive temperature is detected.

Suspend switch

This switch can be used to enable and disable the power management function. This is probably something you can live without, which is just as well since few cases have the necessary switch. There is sometimes an output for a LED which operates in conjunction with this feature.

There may well be other functions available, and it is a matter of consulting the motherboard's instruction manual for details of any additional features. However, unless the case has some spare switches and (or) LEDs any "extras" will only be of academic interest.

On the cards

By this stage the PC is nearly complete, and the only major task remaining is to fit the various expansion cards. Some advocate having only the essential cards installed initially, with others being added once the PC has been completed and the operating system has been installed. Windows 95 was notorious for installation difficulties with several expansion cards installed. The installation process tended to go round in circles with the drivers being installed, the computer resetting, the drivers being installed again, and so on. This does not seem to be a major problem with Windows 98 and beyond, and I have no qualms about fully completing the PC before installing the operating system.

Fig.3.64 The expansion cards are bolted to the rear of the case

Before the cards can be fitted it is necessary to remove the blanking plates in the rear of the case for the particular slots you will be using. Cases used to be supplied with blanking plates that were held in place by screws, but only a few up-market cases still use this method. The more usual method is for the blanking plates to be partially cut out. Those that are not required are simply broken away from the main case. Some cases have blanking plates that can be unclipped. Provided this is done carefully, it is usually possible to clip them back in place again, should the expansion card be removed at some time in the future.

The expansion cards should fit into place without having to push too hard. If a moderate amount of force fails to get one or more of the cards into position it is likely that the motherboard is slightly out of alignment with the case. Try slackening the motherboard's mounting screws slightly, fitting a couple of expansion cards, and then tightening the mounting screws again. It should then be easy to fit any remaining expansion cards, remembering to bolt the metal bracket of each card to the rear of the case (Figure 3.64).

Fig.3.65 The brackets on the expansion cards should fit into holders in the rear of the case

If it is still difficult to fit one or two of the expansion cards the most likely cause of the problem is the metal bracket at the rear of the offending card or cards. If you look at the rear of the case you will notice that there are receptacles to take the bottom sections of the mounting brackets (Figure 3.65). With some expansion cards it is necessary to carefully bend the lower section of the mounting bracket backwards so that it engages with the receptacle in the case. Everything should then slot nicely into position.

AGP cards

Unless the motherboard has integrated video circuits, an AGP video card will presumably be used. Fitting an AGP card is slightly different to fitting a PCI or ISA type. There is a locking lever at the front of the expansion slot, and the locking mechanism is much like the one used on memory sockets. Unlike a memory socket, the locking mechanism is only included at one end of the connector. It is quite common for expansion cards to ride up slightly at the front when the mounting bolt is tightened. The connector of an AGP card has so many terminals in such a small space that even a small degree of tilt can prevent it from connecting to the motherboard properly. The purpose of the locking mechanism is to ensure that the card can not ride up slightly at the front.

Fig.3.66 A notch in the front of an ADP card enables it to be locked in place

Any modern AGP card should have a cut-out in the front edge of the connector to take the locking mechanism (Figure 3.66). Initially the locking lever on the AGP slot should be in the open (down) position, as in Figure 3.67. When the

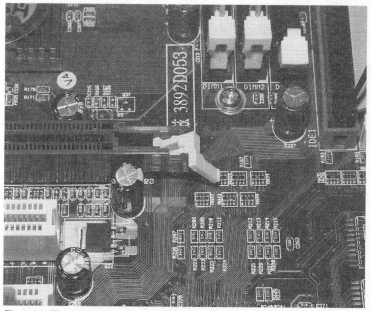

Fig.3.67 The locking lever on an AGP expansion slot

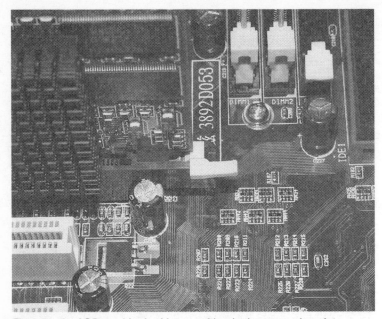

Fig.3.68 An AGP card locked into position in the expansion slot

card is pushed into its expansion slot the lever should automatically move up and into place (Figure 6.68), but if necessary it can be given a little manual assistance.

Note that some motherboards can be rather fussy about the video cards that they will work with reliably. In particular, some motherboards lack proper compatibility with some 2x/4x AGP boards. The problem seems to stem from the fact that 2x operation uses higher signal voltages than 4x operation, but some video boards do not adjust to low voltage operation in the 4x mode. If you are using a motherboard of this type there will probably be a warning sticker on the AGP slot itself as well as warnings in the instruction manual. Make sure that the video card is a compatible type if you use one of these boards, since a mistake could result in damage to the motherboard.

Audio cable

These days most CD-ROM drives are supplied complete with an audio cable that can connect the audio output at the rear of the drive to the

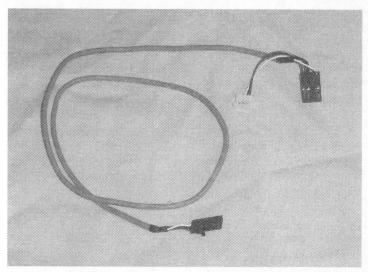

Fig.3.69 A CD-ROM audio lead having two types of connector

audio input of the soundcard. This enables audio CDs in the CD-ROM drive to be played through the computer's speakers. This lead is not needed if you will only play audio CDs through headphones connected direct to the CD-ROM drive, or if you are not interested in playing audio CDs at all. On the other hand, you may as well fit it anyway just in case you need to use this facility at some future time.

The connector at the soundcard end of the cable will almost certainly be a type that is compatible with SoundBlaster cards. Most other soundcards now use the same type of connector, or have two audio input connectors including one SoundBlaster compatible type. There is still a slight risk that the cable will not be compatible with your soundcard, and you will then have to seek out a cable of the correct type. Some PC audio cables have both types of soundcard connector (Figure 3.69), guaranteeing compatibility with the soundcard. There should be at least one audio input on the motherboard if it is a type that has integrated audio. The connector will almost certainly be a standard SoundBlaster type.

These days it is quite normal for a PC to have two CD-ROM drives of some kind, such as a CD-RW drive and a DVD type. Two audio inputs are needed in order to permit both drives to play CDs via the computer's

Fig.3.70 An interior view of the completed Athlon XP2000+ PC

sound system. Modern soundcards often have several audio inputs, and should be able to accommodate two CD-ROM drives. Integrated audio systems sometimes have two or three audio inputs, but many have only one audio input port. Unfortunately, only one CD-ROM drive can be used with the PC's sound system if there is only one audio input available.

You then have what is basically a complete PC base unit. There may be one or two other leads that need to be connected, such as cables from the soundcard or modem to the motherboard, but this is dependent on both items of equipment supporting some extra features, and you wishing to implement them. Where necessary, add any extra cables in accordance with the instructions in manuals for the items of equipment concerned. The motherboard will probably have a power output for a fan fitted at the front of the case. Practically every PC case has provision

Fig.3.71 An interior view of the Pentium 4 PC, which is a little more cluttered than the Athlon PC

for a fan, but they are not often fitted as standard. If no fan is supplied with the case it is advisable to fit one.

Tidying up

The interior of the finished PC can look a bit untidy, but things are not as bad as they used to be. ATX motherboards have helped to reduce the amount of cabling and this greatly reduces the amount of clutter inside the PC. I made two PCs while producing this book. One is a budget but quite fast PC based on an Athlon XP2000+, and the other is a slightly more upmarket PC based on a 2.4GHz Pentium 4. Interior views of these PCs are shown in Figure 3.70 and 3.71 respectively.

Results can certainly be made much neater by fixing the cables to convenient points on the case rather than just leaving them dangling. It is definitely a good idea to secure each cable in at least one place if the PC will be transported several miles or more. It is otherwise of relatively little importance. Double-sided adhesive pads represent the easiest way of fixing the cables to the case, drive bays, or whatever.

It is best not to get carried away with this sort of thing. I once bought a PC that had received a glowing review in a magazine, and it had been particularly complemented for the tidiness of its cables. The interior of the PC was indeed very neat, but there were major problems each time I tried to upgrade any of the hardware. The very neat cabling was effectively barring access to the drives, memory, expansion cards, and just about everything else inside the PC. It was necessary to carefully cut one or two cables free each time a change was made to the hardware. Tidy up the cabling by all means, but do not get carried away.

Testing

With the minor cabling completed the base unit of the computer is finished. Before connecting the mouse, keyboard, and monitor it is definitely a good idea to thoroughly check everything, making sure that all the cables are connected correctly and that none have been accidentally dislodged when working on the unit. None of the connectors lock into place, and it is very easy to dislodge one connector while fitting another. Also check that the expansion cards are fitted into their slots properly.

It is not possible to boot from the hard disc until it has been properly prepared, so initially try booting from something like an MS-DOS boot disc. Better still, use a Windows 98 start-up disc as this can provide CD-ROM support, and it will enable you to check that the CD-ROM drive is working properly. When the computer is switched on it should go through the normal BIOS start-up routine. By default it will probably be set to auto-detect the IDE devices, and it will probably list the drives that are detected.

If nothing happens, or there is any sign of a malfunction, switch off at once and recheck the entire wiring, etc. Assuming all is well, let the computer go through its boot-up routine so that you can check that it is more or less working correctly. If it is, the next step is to go into the ROM BIOS Setup program and configure the CMOS memory correctly. This is covered in the next chapter. Tips on getting troublesome PCs sorted out are provided in chapter 5.

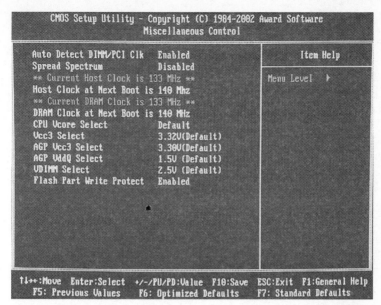

CMOS Setup Utility - Copyright (C) 1984-2002 Award Software
Miscellaneous Control

Auto Detect DIMM/PCI Clk	Enabled	Item Help
Spread Spectrum	Disabled	
** Current Host Clock is 133 MHz **		Menu Level ▶
Host Clock at Next Boot is 140 Mhz		
** Current DRAM Clock is 133 MHz **		
DRAM Clock at Next Boot is 140 MHz		
CPU Vcore Select	Default	
Vcc3 Select	3.32V(Default)	
AGP Vcc3 Select	3.30V(Default)	
AGP VddQ Select	1.5V (Default)	
VDIMM Select	2.5V (Default)	
Flash Part Write Protect	Enabled	

↑↓→←:Move Enter:Select +/-/PU/PD:Value F10:Save ESC:Exit F1:General Help
F5: Previous Values   F6: Optimized Defaults   F7: Standard Defaults

Fig.3.72 This section of the BIOS permits over-clocking to be used

Over-clocking

Over-clocking is sometimes referred to as the "free upgrade", and it is the practice of using electronic components beyond their maximum speed rating. By no means all motherboards support any form of over-clocking. With those that do, the motherboard's instruction manual usually contained one or two disclaimers, saying something along the lines that the board has the ability to use over-clocking, but the manufacturer does not condone this practice. This may seem rather two-faced, but the manufacturer is basically saying that the board has the overclocking facility, but you use it at your own risk.

Modern processors seem to invariably have the clock multiplier locked, and the motherboard is unlikely to provide any means of altering this setting. Consequently, the only way of using over-clocking is to increase the basic clock frequency of the system. This boosts the operating frequency of the memory, AGP card, etc., and not just the processor. While this gives a greater increase in speed than simply boosting the clock frequency of the processor, it reduces the chances of over-clocking being usable. If any component in the system is unable to support the

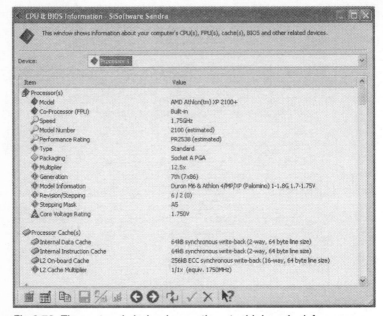

Fig.3.73 The system is indeed operating at a higher clock frequency

higher frequency caused by over-clocking, then the PC will fail to operate reliably.

Over-clocking the motherboard's chipset is unlikely to damage anything, but good reliability can not be guaranteed. The same is true of the memory modules. Over-clocking the processor is a bit more dubious since it increases its power consumption and causes it to operate at a higher temperature. This might necessitate the use of a bigger heatsink, and even with a larger heatsink it is a dubious practice with a processor that runs quite hot at its normal operating frequency.

Where over-clocking is supported, it is usually possible to increase the basic clock frequency in one megahertz increments via the BIOS Setup program. Figure 3.72 shows the relevant section of the BIOS Setup program for the Athlon XP2000+-based PC. As an experiment I tried overclocking the Athlon XP2000+-based PC by raising the system bus frequency from 133MHz to 140MHz. I also tried the same thing with the PC based on a 2.4GHz Pentium 4. In both cases no reliability problems were apparent, and the components all ran quite cool.

Figure 3.73 shows a diagnostics program running on the Athlon XP2000+ PC, and it correctly shows the increased processor clock frequency. In fact the higher clock frequency has caused the program to identify the processor as an Athlon XP2100+. Although this method of over-clocking will usually provide some increase in speed, it will not turn a slow PC into a fast one. In this example the increase in clock frequency is a very modest five percent or so, giving only a very minor boost in speed. Trying for a much more significant increase in speed gives little chance of success.

Bear in mind that if you should damage a processor by over-clocking it, or if it should fail for any reason while it is not being used within its normal operating parameters, it will almost certainly not be covered by the guarantee. If you experiment with over-clocking techniques you do so entirely at your own risk. New PC builders would be well advised to do everything "by the book", and not risk problems trying to stretch any item of hardware beyond its normal limits.

Points to remember

Try to get a mental picture of how everything fits together before you actually start assembling the PC. Also make sure that you have everything you need including small items such as bolts and stand-offs.

Although most people only refer to instruction manuals as a last resort, this is not an option with the manual for the motherboard. Read it through carefully so that you can determine what configuration is needed for the particular processor you are using. It should also explain any special features that the board supports.

Do not rush construction of the PC. Proceed carefully, double-checking everything as you go, and the completed PC should work first time.

Unless the case limits access and makes it impossible, fit the processor, the processor's heatsink and fan, and the memory modules before fitting the motherboard in the case. Any configuration switches or jumpers should always be set up before fitting the motherboard in the case. Working on the motherboard is much easier before it is fitted in the case, because it is much more accessible. With smaller cases, fitting the motherboard is often easier if the 3.5-inch drive bay assembly is removed from the case first.

The motherboard must be mounted on stand-offs so that the connections on the underside of the board are held well clear of the case. Otherwise short-circuits will occur and the motherboard could be damaged. There will probably be more mounting points on the case than the motherboard can handle, but there should still be sufficient mounting holes in the board to enable it to be properly supported over its entire area.

It is usually easier to mount the 3.5-inch drives if the drive bay is removed, the drives are fitted in the bay and then the whole drive and bay assembly is fitted in the case. Two mounting bolts per side are sufficient to securely fix the drives in place.

Most of the cables are properly polarised and will only fit the right way round. If one of the data cables is not properly polarised, refer to the instruction manuals to find pin 1 of the connector on the motherboard and the connector on the drive. The red lead of the data cable carries the pin 1 to pin 1 connection. The end of the cable having the "twist" connects to the floppy disc drive, and the other end connects to the motherboard.

The functions provided on the motherboard's connector block will probably not match up exactly with the functions supported by the case. The reset switch, IDE activity LED, and power LED are the only ones that are really needed. With an ATX case and power supply the on/off switch must also be connected to the motherboard. An AT power supply and case have a conventional on/off switch in the mains supply. Note that the front panel LEDs will only operate if they are connected the right way around.

To complete the PC fit the expansion cards, followed by any cables that connect to these cards. There will usually be an audio cable to connect the CD-ROM drive to the soundcard, but in most cases no other cables will be needed.

Have a final and thorough check of the completed PC before it is switched on and tested. Check that you have not accidentally dislodged one lead while fitting another.

4

The BIOS

Essentials

Before you can go on to install the operating system and applications it is essential to set up the BIOS correctly. A modern BIOS Setup program enables dozens of parameters to be controlled, many of which are highly technical. This tends to make the BIOS intimidating for those who are new to PC building, and even those who have some experience of PC construction.

However, it is not necessary to go through the BIOS setting dozens of parameters in order to get the PC to perform satisfactorily. The BIOS should be customised to suit the particular motherboard it is fitted to, and it should set sensible defaults. In order to get the PC running well it is usually necessary to do nothing more than set a few basic parameters such as the time, date, and some drive details. Some "fine tuning" of a few other parameter might bring benefits, but is not essential.

We will therefore start by considering the BIOS essentials before moving on to consider some of the other features that can be controlled via the BIOS. A detailed description of all the BIOS features would require a large book in itself, so here we will concentrate on those that are of most importance.

BIOS basics

Before looking at the BIOS Setup program, it would perhaps be as well to consider the function of the BIOS. BIOS is a acronym and it stands for basic input/out system. Its basic function is to help the operating system handle the input and output devices, such as the drives, and ports, and also the memory circuits. It is a program that is stored in a ROM on the motherboard. These days the chip is usually quite small and sports a holographic label to prove that it is the genuine article (Figure 4.1). The old style ROM is a standard ROM chip, as in Figure 4.2. Either way its function is the same.

Fig.4.1 The BIOS is a program stored in a ROM chip

Because the BIOS program is in a ROM on the motherboard it can be run immediately at start-up without the need for any form of booting process. It is the BIOS that runs the test routines at switch-on, or the POST (power on self test) as it is known. With these tests completed successfully the BIOS then looks for an operating system to load from disc. The operating system appears to load itself from disc, which is a bit like pulling oneself up by ones bootlaces. It is said to be from this that the term "boot" is derived. Of course, in reality the operating system is not loading itself initially, and it is reliant on the BIOS getting things started.

Another role of the BIOS is to provide software routines that help the operating system to utilize the hardware effectively. It can also store information about the hardware for use by the operating system, and possibly other software. It is this second role that makes it necessary to have the Setup program. The BIOS can actually detect much of the system hardware and store the relevant technical information in memory.

However, some parameters have to be set manually, such as the time and date, and the user may wish to override some of the default settings. The Setup program enables the user to control the settings that the BIOS

Fig.4.2 An older style ROM BIOS chip

stores away in its memory. A battery powers this memory when the PC is switched off, so its contents are available each time the PC is turned on. Once you have set the correct parameters you will probably not need to deal with the BIOS Setup program again unless you do some drastic upgrading.

Entry

In the past there have been several common means of getting into the BIOS Setup program, but with the motherboards available to amateur builders at present there is only one method in common use. This is to press the Delete key at the appropriate point during the initial testing phase just after switch-on. The BIOS will display a message, usually in the bottom left-hand corner of the screen, telling you to press the "Del" key to enter the Setup program. The instruction manual should provide details if the motherboard you are using has a different method of entering the Setup program.

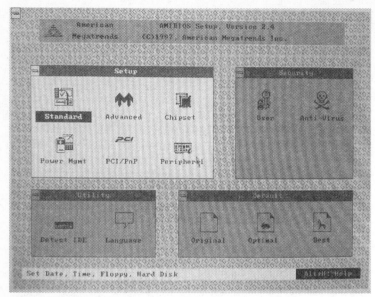

Fig.4.3 The AMI BIOS has a form of WIMP environment

The manual should also have a section dealing with the BIOS. It is worth looking through this section to determine which features can be controlled via the BIOS. Unfortunately, most motherboard instruction manuals assume the user is familiar with all the BIOS features, and there will be few detailed explanations. In fact there will probably just be a list of the available options and no real explanations at all. However, a quick read through this section of the manual will give you a good idea of what the BIOS is all about. A surprisingly large number of PC users who are quite expert in other aspects of PC operation have no real idea what the BIOS and the BIOS Setup program actually do. If you fall into this category the section of the manual that deals with the BIOS should definitely be given at least a quick read through.

There are several BIOS manufacturers and their BIOS Setup programs each work in a slightly different fashion. The Award BIOS and AMI BIOS are probably the most common ones fitted to the motherboards available to the do-it-yourself builder. The AMI BIOS has a Setup program that will detect any reasonably standard mouse connected to the PC, and offers a simple form of WIMP environment (Figure 4.3). It can still be controlled via the keyboard if preferred, or if the BIOS does not operate with the

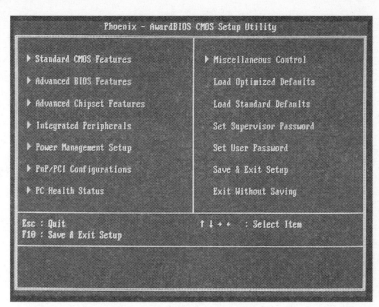

Fig.4.4 The main menu of a Phoenix-Award BIOS

mouse you are using. The Award BIOS, or the Phoenix-Award BIOS as it now seems to be, is probably the most common and as far as I am aware it only uses keyboard control. Figure 4.4 shows the main menu for a modern Phoenix-Award BIOS.

Apart from variations in the BIOS due to different manufacturers, the BIOS will vary slightly from one motherboard to another. This is simply due to the fact that features available on one motherboard may be absent or different on another motherboard. Also, the world of PCs in general is developing at an amazing rate, and this is reflected in frequent BIOS updates. The description of the BIOS provided here has to be a representative one, and the BIOS in your PC will inevitably be slightly different. The important features should be present in any BIOS, and it is only the more minor and obscure features that are likely to be different. The motherboard's instruction manual should at the least give some basic information on setting up and using any unusual features.

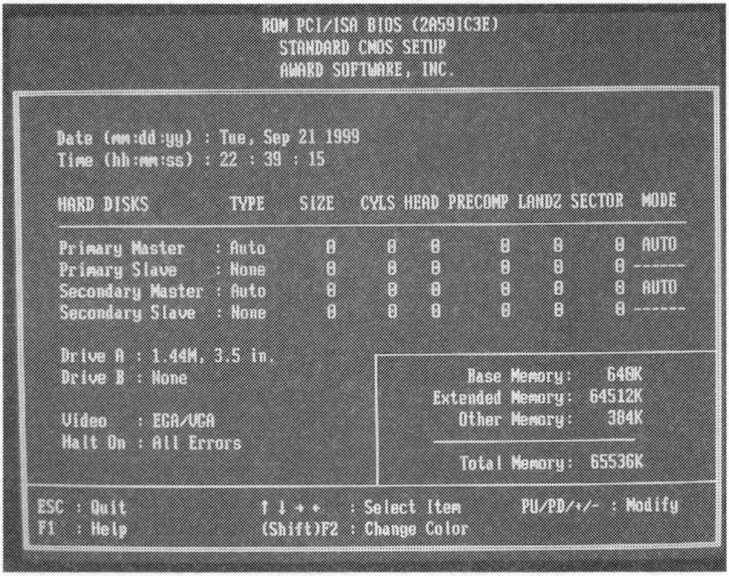

```
                    ROM PCI/ISA BIOS (2A59IC3E)
                        STANDARD CMOS SETUP
                       AWARD SOFTWARE, INC.


  Date (mm:dd:yy) : Tue, Sep 21 1999
  Time (hh:mm:ss) : 22 : 39 : 15

  HARD DISKS          TYPE    SIZE   CYLS HEAD PRECOMP LANDZ SECTOR  MODE

  Primary Master   : Auto      0      0    0      0      0      0   AUTO
  Primary Slave    : None      0      0    0      0      0      0   ------
  Secondary Master : Auto      0      0    0      0      0      0   AUTO
  Secondary Slave  : None      0      0    0      0      0      0   ------

  Drive A : 1.44M, 3.5 in.
  Drive B : None                          Base Memory:      640K
                                      Extended Memory:    64512K
  Video   : EGA/VGA                      Other Memory:      384K
  Halt On : All Errors
                                          Total Memory:    65536K

  ESC : Quit             ↑ ↓ → ←  : Select Item    PU/PD/+/- : Modify
  F1  : Help            (Shift)F2 : Change Color
```

*Fig.4.5 An example of a Standard CMOS Setup screen. Not every
BIOS now permits manual entry of drive parameters*

Standard CMOS

There are so many parameters that can be controlled via the BIOS Setup
program that they are normally divided into half a dozen or so groups.
The most important of these is the "Standard CMOS Setup" (Figure 4.5),
which is basically the same as the BIOS Setup in the original AT style
PCs. The first parameters in the list are the time and date. These can
usually be set via an operating system utility these days, but you may as
well set them from the Setup program while you are in that section of the
program. There are on-screen instructions that tell you how to alter and
select options. One slight oddity to watch out for is that you often have
to use the Page Up key to decrement values, and the Page Down key to
increment them.

With virtually any modern BIOS a help screen can be brought up by
pressing F1, and this will usually be context sensitive (Figure 4.6). In
other words, if the cursor is in the section that deals with the hard drives,
the help screen produced by pressing F1 will tell you about the hard
disc parameters. It would be unreasonable to expect long explanations

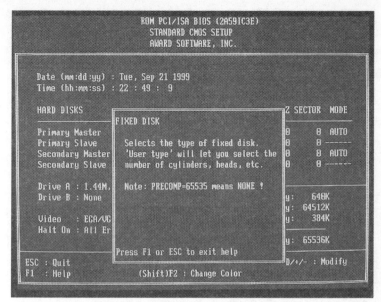

Fig.4.6 Pressing F1 will usually bring up a brief Help screen

from a simple on-line help system, and a couple of brief and to the point sentences are all that will normally be provided.

Drive settings

The next section is used to set the operating parameters for the devices on the IDE ports. For the sake of this example we will assume that the hard disc is the master device on the primary IDE channel (IDE1), and that the CD-ROM is the master device on the secondary IDE channel (IDE2). Note that CD-RW and DVD drives are straightforward CD-ROM drives as far as the BIOS is concerned. The additional features of these drives are provided by applications software such as Nero and Power DVD. Windows XP has some built-in support for CD-RW drives, but this is the operating system providing the extra features and not the BIOS.

If the manuals for the drives provide the correct figures to enter into the CMOS memory, and they certainly should do so in the case of hard disc drives, you can enter these figures against the appropriate device. In this case the hard disc drive is the "Primary Master". A modern AMI

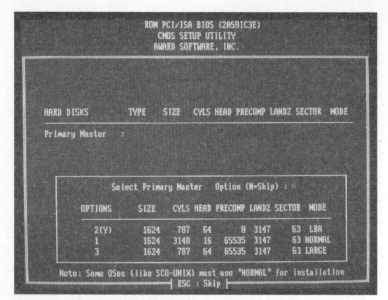

Fig.4.7 An IDE automatic detection screen in operation

BIOS should have a setting specifically for a CD-ROM drive, and this can be used for the "Secondary Master" device. Simply setting everything at zero usually works where no CD-ROM setting is available. There are no primary or secondary slave drives, so simply enter "None" for these.

If you do not know the appropriate figures for your drives it does not really matter, because there is always an "Auto" option. If this is selected, the BIOS examines the hardware during the start-up routine and enters the correct figures automatically. This usually works very well, but with some drives it can take a while, which extends the boot-up time.

There is an alternative method of automatic detection that avoids this delay. If you go back to the initial menu you will find a section called "IDE HDD Auto Detection" (Figure 4.7), and this offers a similar auto-detection facility. When this option is selected the Setup program examines the hardware on each IDE channel, and offers suggested settings for each of the four possible IDE devices. If you accept the suggested settings for the hard disc drive (or drives) they will be entered into the CMOS RAM. There may actually be several alternatives offered per IDE device, but the default suggestion is almost invariably the correct one. After using this auto-detection facility it is a good idea to return to the "Standard CMOS Setup" page to check that the settings have been transferred correctly. Also, make sure that "None" is entered for the drive type where appropriate.

The last parameter for each IDE drive is usually something like Auto, Normal, LBA (large block addressing), and Large. Normal is for drives under 528MB, while LBA and Large are alternative modes for drives having a capacity of more than 528MB. Modern drives have capacities of well in excess of 528MB, and mostly require the LBA mode. The manual for the hard drive should give some guidance here, or you can simply select Auto and let the BIOS sort things out for itself.

Some users get confused because they think a hard drive that will be partitioned should have separate entries in the BIOS for each partition. This is not the case, and as far as the BIOS is concerned each physical hard disc is a single drive, and has just one entry in the CMOS RAM table. The partitioning of hard discs is handled by the operating system, and so is the assignment of drive letters. The BIOS is only concerned with the physical characteristics of the drives, and not how data will be arranged and stored on the discs.

Non-standard IDE

If you are using IDE devices other than hard discs and an ordinary CD-ROM drive it is advisable to consult the instruction manual for these drives to find the best way of handling their BIOS settings. As pointed out previously, CD-RW and DVD drives are normally entered into the BIOS as normal CD-ROM drives. A modern operating system such as Windows ME should then recognise and install the drive, but only as a simple CD-ROM type. Some additional software, which is usually but not always supplied with the drive, will be needed in order to exploit the additional capabilities of these drives. It is a good idea to obtain a drive that comes complete with some bundled software since the extra cost is minimal, and buying the software separately can be quite expensive.

Other drives such as LS120 and Zip drives often have some specific support in the BIOS. It may even be possible to boot from these devices, although not necessarily with all operating systems. The instruction manuals for the drives should give detailed instructions on how to integrate them with any common BIOS.

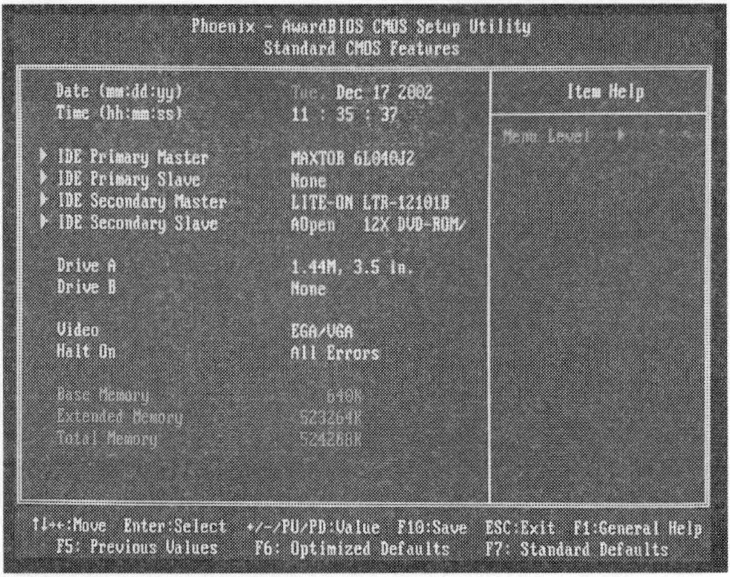

Fig.4.8 This Standard CMOS screen only permits automatic detection
of the IDE devices

Auto-only

There is a trend towards automatic detection with no manual override.
With the Phoenix-Award BIOS shown in Figure 4.8 the Page Up and
Page Down keys permit parameters such as the time and date to be
changed, but they have no effect on the IDE drive types. The BIOS
automatically detects the drives, displays its findings in the Standard
CMOS page, and sets the correct parameters. As most users opt for
automatic detection anyway, the lack of manual control is not likely to be
of any importance. On the other hand, if you should happen to use an
IDE device that the BIOS can not identify, it will probably be unusable
until a BIOS update becomes available.

Floppy drives

The next section in the "Standard CMOS Setup" is used to select the
floppy disc drive type or types. All the normal types of floppy drive are
supported, from the old 5.25-inch 360k drives to the rare 2.88M 3.5-inch
type. You simply select the appropriate type for drives A and B. Select

"None" for drive B if the computer has only one floppy drive. In days gone by you had to enter the amount of memory fitted, but with a modern BIOS the amount of memory is automatically detected and entered into the CMOS RAM. The "Standard CMOS Setup" screen will report the amount of memory fitted, and will display something like Figure 4.9.

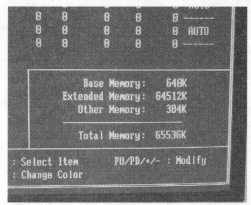

Fig.4.9 The BIOS reports the memory it finds. The user can not alter these settings

Note that there is no way of altering the memory settings if they are wrong. If the BIOS reports the wrong amount of RAM there is a fault in the memory circuits, and the correct amount will be reported if the fault is rectified. Sometimes what appears to be an error is just the way the amount of memory is reported by the BIOS. For those who are new to computing the way in which the amount of memory is reported can seem rather strange. It should look very familiar to those who can remember the early days of IBM compatible PCs. The original PCs had relatively simple processors that could only address one megabyte of RAM, but only the lower 640k of the address range were actually used for RAM. The upper 384k of the address range was used for the BIOS ROM, video ROM, and that sort of thing.

Modern PCs can address hundreds of megabytes of RAM, but the lowest one megabyte is still arranged in much the same way that it was in the original PCs. The BIOS therefore reports that there is 640k of normal (base) memory, so many kilobytes of RAM above the original one megabyte of RAM (extended memory), and 384k of other memory. This "other" memory is the RAM in the address space used by the BIOS, etc.

The final section of the standard Setup enables the type of video card to be specified, and the degree of error trapping to be selected. The BIOS will probably detect the video card and set the appropriate type, which for a modern PC will presumably be a EGA/VGA type. It might be possible to select the old CGA and mono adapters, but these are obsolete and

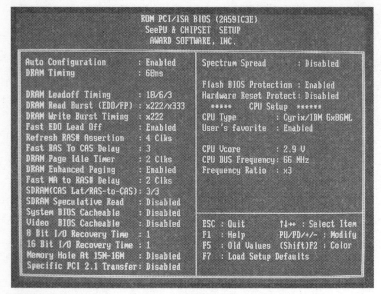

Fig.4.10 This screen provides control over the chipset features

not used in modern PCs. The error trapping controls the way in which the computer responds to errors that are found during the BIOS self-testing routing at switch-on. The default of halt on all errors is probably the best choice, particularly when you are testing a new PC. Once the PC has been fully tested and is running properly you may prefer to alter this setting, but I would not bother.

Chipset

Setting up the standard CMOS parameters is probably all you will need to do in order to get the computer running properly, but it is a good idea to look at the options available in the other sections of the Setup program. There will be a section called something like Chipset Setup or Advanced Chipset Setup (Figure 4.10), which controls things such as the port and memory timing. There are so many parameters controlled by a modern BIOS that a multi-level menu system is sometimes used. In the example of Figure 4.11 the DRAM timing option produces the submenu of Figure 4.12. You can "play" with these settings in an attempt to obtain improved performance, but higher speed may well produce lower reliability. Results

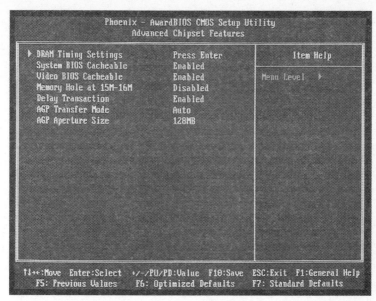

Fig.4.11 The Chipset Features menu might contain some submenus

should be quite good if you simply leave this section with the auto configuration enabled.

If you make a complete "dogs breakfast" of these settings it is possible that the PC could become unusable. This is not as drastic as it sounds because you can always go back into the BIOS and select the default settings from the initial screen. There will probably be an option to return to the "old" settings, which usually means the settings saved prior to the last time the BIOS Setup program was used. I suppose it is conceivable that changes made in the BIOS could render the computer unable to start up at all. I think that this is highly unlikely, but remember that the contents of the CMOS memory can always be wiped clean using the appropriate jumper on the motherboard. No matter how badly you scramble the BIOS settings it should always be possible to get back to the default settings and then "fine tune" things from there.

It is worth remembering that no changes are made to the settings unless you opt to save the changes when exiting the Setup program. If you know you have made a complete mess of things, simply exit the Setup program without saving the changes. The PC will then reboot, the Setup

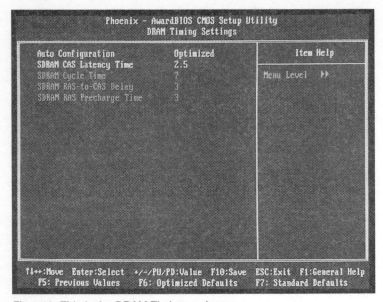

Fig.4.12 This is the DRAM Timings submenu

program can be entered again, and you can start from scratch with the changes.

If the PC is fitted with SDRAM, one of the timing settings will be the SDRAM CAS Latency. The default setting will probably be suitable provided the Standard Default settings are used. If the Optimised Default settings are used, or a low figure is set manually, make sure that the DIMMs used are up to the task. Trying to use memory modules beyond their ratings is not usually successful and can produce major problems when running applications programs.

The AGP Aperture Size controls the amount of system memory that is set aside for use with graphics adapter for such things as texture storage. The default value should be a sensible one for the amount of system memory installed in the PC and the amount of video memory fitted to the AGP card. There are various formulas for calculating the optimum setting, and you can try these if maximum video performance is important. In most cases any change in performance will be quite small.

The amount of memory allocated by default might seem to be large relative to the total amount of system memory. However, bear in mind that it is actually the maximum size that is being set. The actual amount of memory used depends on the video activity, and system memory is only used when it is essential to do so.

Cache

There are various BIOS address ranges listed or there may be just a list of BIOS names. There is the option of enabling or disabling shadowing of each one. By default the video BIOS will be shadowed, and possibly the video RAM as well, but the system BIOS and any others listed will probably not be cached. Shadowing of a BIOS is where it is copied into the computer's RAM and then run from there. The top 384k of the base memory is given over to the main BIOS, plus any other device that needs its own BIOS. In a modern PC this part of the memory map is occupied by RAM, but this RAM is normally disabled.

When shadowing is enabled, the relevant block of RAM is activated, and the contents of the BIOS at that address range are copied into it. The point of this is that the RAM is faster than the ROM used for the BIOS, and using shadowing should speed up operation of the video card. Usually the only peripheral that has its own BIOS is the video card, but shadowing of other parts of the top 384k of memory can be enabled if necessary. If you have a peripheral device that will benefit from this treatment its manual should say so, and specify the address range that must be shadowed.

Power Management

Most operating systems and all modern motherboards seem to support some form of power management facility. In other words, the computer goes into some form of standby mode if there is no mouse or keyboard activity for a certain period. Most motherboards can also be switched to and from a standby mode via a peripheral such as a modem, and this also comes under the general heading of power management. A modern BIOS usually has a section dealing solely with power management (Figure 4.13).

The Power Management Setup will probably be set to Disabled, and with some operating systems this is probably the best way to leave it. A lot of power management features can be controlled via the operating system these days, and you can sometimes get into a situation where the BIOS and the operating system are both trying to rule the power

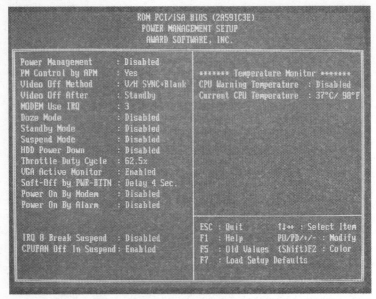

Fig.4.13 A typical Power Management Setup screen

management roost. Where possible I totally disable this feature and only enable it if there is good reason to do so.

These days it is not uncommon for the motherboard to support more than one standby mode. The idea seems to be that the computer progressively shuts down the longer it is left unused. It will typically go from normal operation into the "doze" mode, followed by the "standby" and "suspend" modes. Operating the mouse or keyboard should always result in the computer returning directly to the "normal" mode, but it may take a few seconds to become fully operational if the motor of the hard disc has been switched off. Due to the high rotation speed of a hard disc it takes several seconds for it to reach its normal operating speed.

The BIOS Setup program will probably permit adjustment of the delay times before each standby mode is entered, plus other details such as whether the processor fan is switched off when the "suspend" mode is entered. Of course, all this type of thing is only relevant if the power management feature is enabled. You may wish to "fine tune" the power management feature at a later time, but when initially setting up a PC it is probably best not to get deeply embroiled in this type of thing.

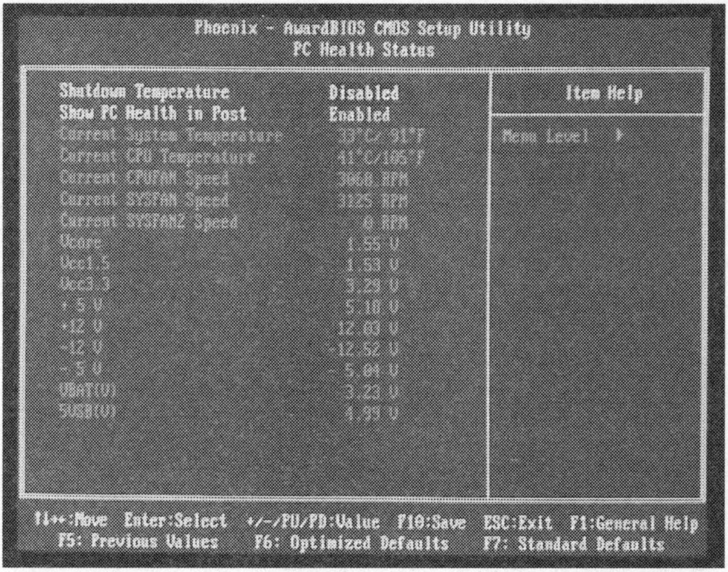

Fig.4.14 Voltages and temperatures can be monitored via the PC
Health Status screen

If the motherboard supports some form of external power management, and you wish to use this feature, it will have to be enabled in this section of the BIOS. Any feature of this type is always disabled by default. Any feature of this type will, of course, only operate if it is properly supported by the peripheral device or devices, and any extra cabling that it needed is properly installed.

Monitoring

Most motherboards now support at least a basic over-temperature detection circuit for the processor, and there are often various CPU threshold temperatures that can be selected. Figure 4.14 shows a typical BIOS screen that provides temperature and voltage monitoring. This screen usually shows the system temperate (the temperature inside the PC's case) in addition to the processor's temperature and various operating voltages. If the CPU goes above the selected temperature a warning can be produced, and the PC usually shuts down as well. It is probably best to activate this feature and simply leave the threshold temperature at its default setting.

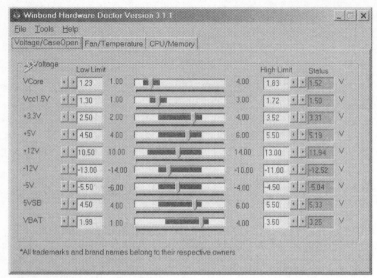

Fig.4.15 Many motherboards are supplied with a monitoring program that runs under Windows

The normal operating temperature varies considerably from one type of processor to another. In general, the processor should operate below about 50 degrees Celsius. However, some AMD chips seem to operate quite happily at around 60 degrees while many Intel chips settle down at around 40 degrees or even less. Unless you know what you are doing it is not a good idea to alter the default alarm temperatures.

Note that many motherboards are supplied complete with so-called health monitoring software that enables parameters such as the CPU temperature, fan speeds, operating voltages, etc., to be monitored while running Windows. It is well worthwhile installing any bundled software of this type. Figure 4.15 shows the main window of the Winbond Hardware Doctor program while it is monitoring a Pentium 4-based PC. A range of voltages are measured by this window, including the core voltage of the processor and the main 5-volt supply.

Whether monitoring via the BIOS or a Windows program, do not be surprised if the measured voltages are slightly different to the nominal voltages. There is a tolerance of plus and minus 5 percent or more on most voltages, and the measuring circuits will produce small errors that

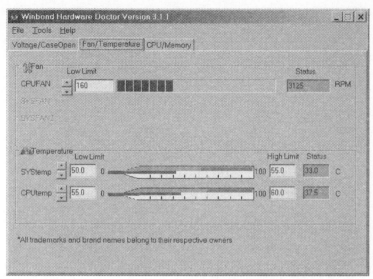

Fig.4.16 Further screens allow more parameters to be monitored

effectively widen the tolerance ratings. Another window of the Hardware Doctor program enables the processor's temperature, the system temperature, and the speed of the processor's fan to be monitored (Figure 4.16). Most of these monitoring programs can sound an alarm if (say) an excessive temperature is detected.

CPU settings

If the motherboard is one that uses software control to set the correct parameters for the PC there could be a separate page for this (Figure 4.17), but it is sometimes included in the chipset settings or in a miscellaneous section. The BIOS will automatically detect the processor type and should set the correct core voltage, bus frequency, and processor multiplier values. It is advisable to check that the BIOS has correctly identified the processor and set the correct values. It should be possible to set the correct figures manually if the BIOS makes a mistake, although it is very unlikely that it would do so. Otherwise, it should only be necessary to exercise manual control if overclocking is to be tried (see chapter 3).

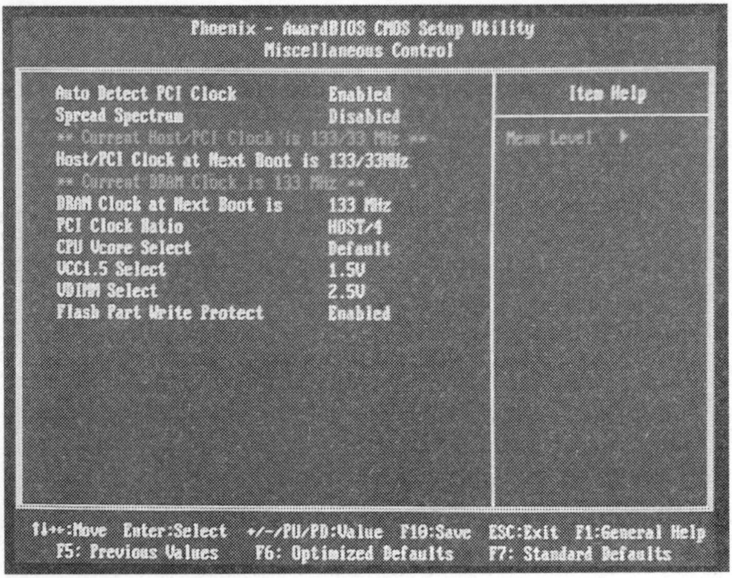

Fig.4.17 The CPU Settings menu of the Phoenix-Award BIOS

Note that any changes you make to the CPU settings may be ignored unless you activate an override setting. Also, with any modern Intel or AMD processor the motherboard will automatically set the correct multiplier value by reading information from the processor itself. It is not normally possible to set the multiplier manually even if the override setting is activated. The BIOS may seem to accept the new multiplier value, but when you exit the BIOS and reboot the computer it will operate with multiplier value set by the chip.

PNP/PCI

Unless you know what you are doing it is not a good idea to mess around with the PNP/PCI settings (Figure 4.18). The initial screen might be lacking in options (Figure 4.19), but things like the IRQ assignments will be tucked away in submenus like the one of Figure 4.20. The defaults should work perfectly well anyway. There will be the option of selecting "Yes" if a PNP (Plug N Play) operating system is installed or "No" if a non-PNP type is installed. Windows 95 and 98 are PNP operating systems, and the obvious setting is "Yes" if you will use either of these. In practice I

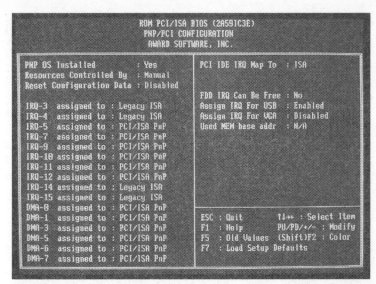

Fig.4.18 The PNP/PCI Configuration menu

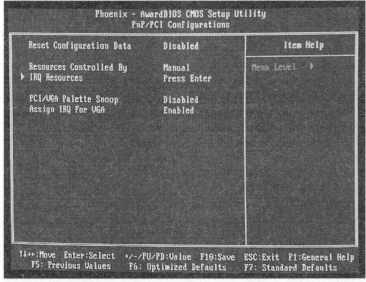

Fig.4.19 The PNP/PCI menu might rely on submenus

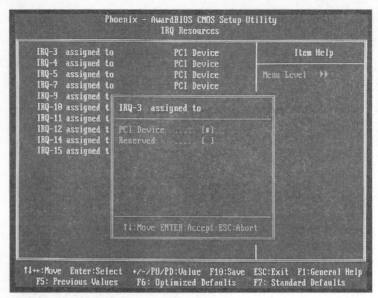

Fig.4.20 The IRQ Resources submenu

have sometimes encountered problems if "Yes" is selected when using Windows 95. Consequently, I usually leave the default setting of "No" when using this operating system.

It should only be necessary to alter the IRQ (interrupt request) settings if there are problems with hardware conflicts. While this problem was not exactly unknown in the past, the widespread use of PCI expansion cards and USB external peripherals has greatly eased the problem. It is definitely not a good idea to alter these settings unless you know exactly what you are doing. With this type of thing it is much easier to make matters worse than it is to cure a problem.

Integrated Peripherals

The Integrated Peripherals section (Figure 4.21) provides some control over the on-board interfaces. In particular, it allows each port to be switched on or off, and in the case of the serial and parallel ports it also enables the port addresses and interrupt (IRQ) numbers to be altered. This can be useful when trying to avoid conflicts with hardware fitted in

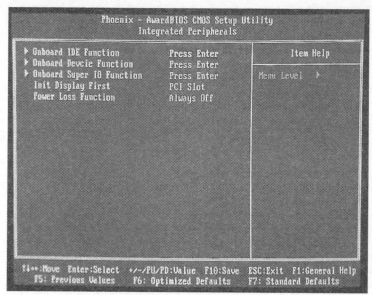

Fig.4.21 The Integrated Peripherals menu will probably use submenus

the expansion slots, but is unlikely to be necessary with a modern PC. The number of integrated peripherals on current motherboards is such that the options in this section of the BIOS will largely be handled by sub-menus.

With the example BIOS the serial and parallel ports are covered by the Super IO submenu (Figure 4.22). There will be various parallel port modes available, but with a modern BIOS it is unlikely that there will be a Standard (output only) mode. The choices will probably be SPP, EPP, and ECP, which are all bi-directional modes. For most purposes either SPP or EPP will suffice. Only set ECP operation if you use the port with a device that definitely needs this mode. There might be further options, such as a mode that can provide both EPP and ECP operation, and a choice of ECP versions. It is unlikely to matter which version is selected, but the relevant one should obviously be selected if the instruction manual states that a peripheral requires a certain ECP version.

If the motherboard supports infrared communications it may be possible to switch serial port two (COM2) between normal operation and infrared operation. When set to infrared operation it is possible for the PC to

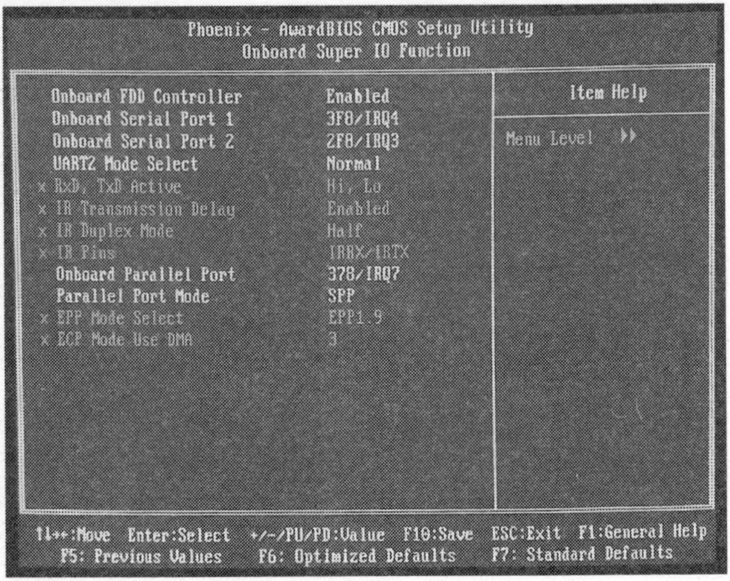

```
              Phoenix - AwardBIOS CMOS Setup Utility
                    Onboard Super IO Function

     Onboard FDD Controller         Enabled              Item Help
     Onboard Serial Port 1          3F8/IRQ4
     Onboard Serial Port 2          2F8/IRQ3         Menu Level   ▶▶
     UART2 Mode Select              Normal
   x RxD, TxD Active                Hi, Lo
   x IR Transmission Delay          Enabled
   x IR Duplex Mode                 Half
   x IR Pins                        IRRX/IRTX
     Onboard Parallel Port          378/IRQ7
     Parallel Port Mode             SPP
   x EPP Mode Select                EPP1.9
   x ECP Mode Use DMA               3




   ↑↓→←:Move  Enter:Select  +/-/PU/PD:Value  F10:Save  ESC:Exit  F1:General Help
       F5: Previous Values    F6: Optimized Defaults    F7: Standard Defaults
```

Fig.4.22 This is the Onboard SuperIO Function submenu

communicate with suitably equipped notebook computers and digital cameras that support infrared communications. However, the correct hardware add-on is needed on COM2 before this cordless communications will be possible.

This dual role for serial port two seems to be less common these days and most motherboards now have entirely separate hardware to implement the IrDA facility. It is likely that the BIOS Setup program will give some control over the settings for this port, but simply accept the default settings. Only change the settings if this port is used with a piece of equipment that requires changes to be made. If any changes should be required, the instruction manual for the device concerned should explain exactly what needs to be altered.

The Onboard IDE Function submenu (Figure 4.23) enables the IDE controllers to be switched on and off and permits the modes to be set manually. Auto operation will be selected by default, and manual control should only be contemplated if the automatic mode selection fails for some reason. This is very unlikely to happen.

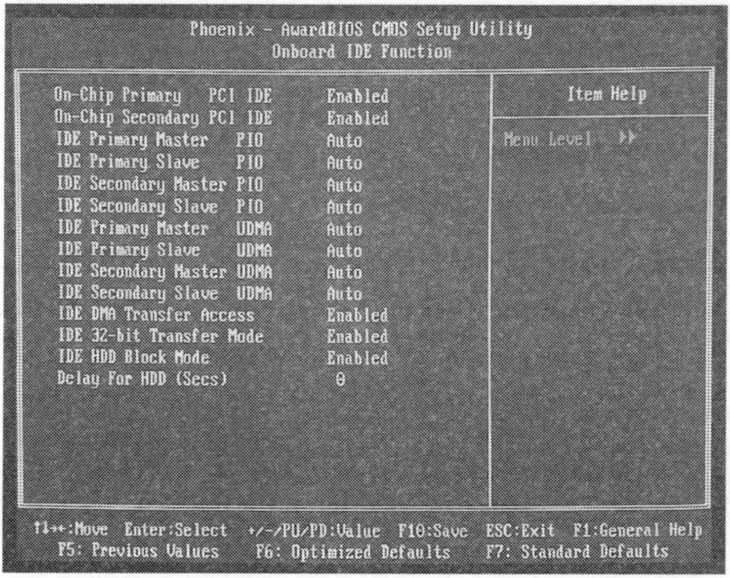

```
                    Phoenix - AwardBIOS CMOS Setup Utility
                           Onboard IDE Function

    On-Chip Primary   PCI IDE      Enabled              Item Help
    On-Chip Secondary PCI IDE      Enabled
    IDE Primary Master    PIO      Auto          Menu Level    ▶▶
    IDE Primary Slave     PIO      Auto
    IDE Secondary Master PIO       Auto
    IDE Secondary Slave  PIO       Auto
    IDE Primary Master    UDMA     Auto
    IDE Primary Slave     UDMA     Auto
    IDE Secondary Master UDMA      Auto
    IDE Secondary Slave  UDMA      Auto
    IDE DMA Transfer Access        Enabled
    IDE 32-bit Transfer Mode       Enabled
    IDE HDD Block Mode             Enabled
    Delay For HDD (Secs)           0



  ↑↓←→:Move  Enter:Select  +/-/PU/PD:Value  F10:Save  ESC:Exit  F1:General Help
   F5: Previous Values    F6: Optimized Defaults    F7: Standard Defaults
```

Fig.4.23 The Onboard IDE Function submenu. Automatic detection should set suitable operating modes

Onboard Device

The Onboard Device submenu (Figure 4.24) covers an assortment of onboard hardware. Many motherboards now have a built-in RAID interface with two additional IDE ports. This was once an expensive option, but it is a feature that is now found in quite low-cost motherboards. This means that your chosen motherboard may well come complete with a RAID interface that you do not actually need. It is unlikely that leaving the RAID hardware switched on will cause any major problems, but the boot process will be lengthened while the BIOS looks for absent drives on the RAID ports. It is therefore a good idea to switch off the RAID hardware if it is not needed.

If there is a built-in audio system there will probably be the option to disable it in this section of the BIOS. This should not be necessary unless a PCI soundcard will be used. In theory it should be possible to have both sound systems installed, but in practice there could be difficulties. Since having both audio systems installed is unlikely to bestow any advantages, it is advisable to disable the built-in sound circuits.

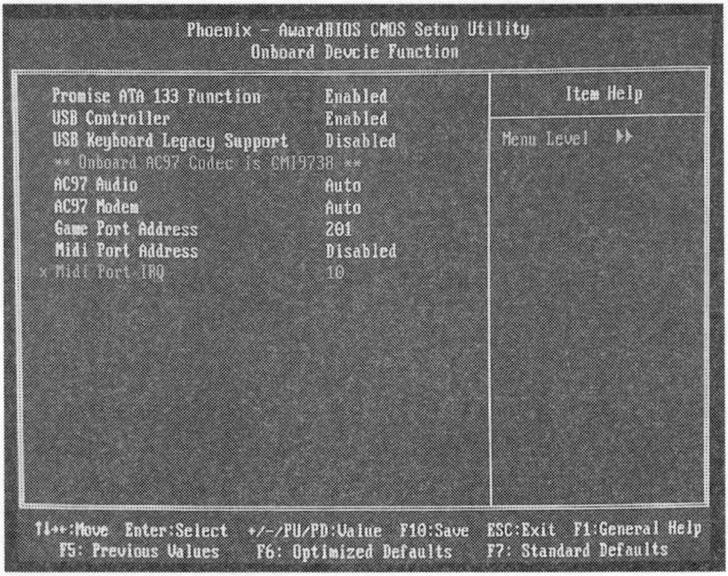

Fig.4.24 The Onboard Device Function menu. The Promise ATA 133
Function controls the built-in RAID controller

Similarly, it is probably best to disable the integral USB ports if a USB
expansion card is used for some reason.

It is only necessary to alter the game and MIDI port addresses and the
MIDI port IRQ setting in the event that hardware conflicts occur. This is
unlikely to be a problem with a modern PC. Note that the MIDI port is
often disabled by default. This is a common cause of problems, with
users finding that they can not output data to the MIDI port. Indeed, with
the port disabled it will not be listed by Windows as an output option. If
you are going to use the MIDI port or might use it in the future, it is a
good idea to enable it from the outset.

BIOS Features Setup

The BIOS Features Setup (Figure 4.25) controls some useful features,
but once again the default settings should suffice. Note that the larger
menus, which will probably include this one, can not show all the settings
simultaneously. A sort of scrollbar appears down the right-hand edge of
the section that contains the settings, and this indicates which section of

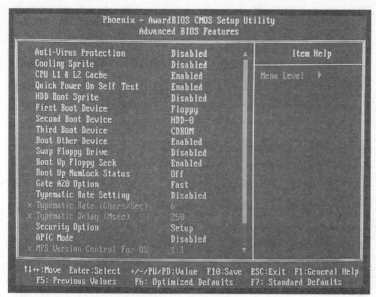

Fig.4.25 The Advanced BIOS Features menu

the page is being displayed. It is not possible to scroll the page using the scrollbar and the mouse. The up and down cursor keys are used to do this. Figure 4.26 shows the scrolled version of the BIOS Features Setup screen. Once into the menu system, the right-hand panel of the screen indicates the current menu level.

Returning to the BIOS features, the internal and external caches must be enabled if the computer is to operate at full speed. There are various boot sequence options, and eventually you might like to select C Only. In the meantime the boot sequence must include drive A if Windows 95, 98, or ME is to be installed on the PC. This is the drive that the computer must boot from until drive C is made bootable. It is advisable to have drive A as the first boot drive. There is otherwise a slight risk that the boot process will stall when the BIOS tries to boot from a blank hard disc drive.

Most other operating systems, including Linux and Windows XP, can be and normally are installed from a bootable CD-ROM. Any modern BIOS should have the option to use the CD-ROM drive as a boot drive, and this option must be selected if you intend to use this method of installation.

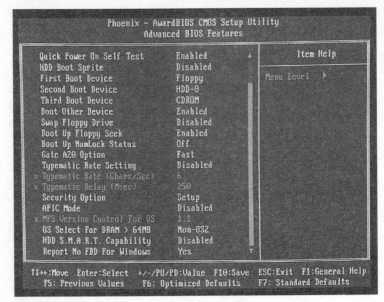

*Fig.4.26 Here the menu has been scrolled down to reveal
           further options*

The drives might be referred to as A, B, C, etc., in the BIOS Setup program, but these days different terminology is often used. In the example BIOS the hard drives are referred to as HDD-0, HDD-1, etc. Assuming drive C is the hard disc that will be used as a boot drive, it is HDD-0 (not HDD-1). To avoid possible confusion, this drive should be used as the master drive on the primary IDE interface.

Other drives are referred to by suitable names, such as CD-ROM, Floppy, and ZIP-100. If there are two of these drives of the same type, the BIOS will probably try to boot from the drive with the highest priority and ignore the other one. The primary IDE interface is searched first, followed by the secondary IDE interface. As one would expect, the master drive takes precedence over the slave device on the same interface.

If this option is present, make sure that the IDE HDD Block Mode is enabled, because the hard disc performance will be relatively poor if it is not. In a modern BIOS this function might be in the Onboard IDE Function submenu. After boot-up the NumLock key is normally on, but there is a useful option that enables it to be switched off after boot-up.

Floppyless

There are usually several options relating to the floppy disc drive or drives. One of these enables drives A and B to be swapped over. I am not sure why it would ever be necessary to have drive A operate as drive B and vice versa, but this facility is there if you should need it. Although at one time a floppy disc drive was an essential part of a PC, this is no longer the case. Other forms of removable disc are available, and with some operating systems it is now possible to install the system from a bootable CD-ROM. This removes the need to boot initially from a floppy disc.

The problem with leaving out the floppy disc drive is that the BIOS will produce an error message each time that the computer is booted. There should be an option called something like Floppy Seek or Boot Up Floppy Seek, and by disabling this option the BIOS will not check for a floppy drive, and the error message will be suppressed. In some cases there might be a setting called something like Report No FDD for Windows, and could be necessary to set this to No as well.

The Rest

Other sections of the BIOS Setup program allow you to select a user password that must be entered before the PC will boot-up, load standard or optimised default settings, save the new settings and exit, or exit without saving any changes to the settings. Being able to load the standard set of default settings is clearly useful if you experiment a little too much and end up with totally unsuitable settings. It is worth repeating that no settings are actually altered unless you select the Save and Exit option. If you accidentally change some settings and do not know how to restore the correct ones, simply exiting without saving the new settings will leave everything untouched. You can then enter the Setup program again and have another try.

Flash upgrade

If you look through the specifications for motherboards you will often encounter something like "Flash upgradeable BIOS" or just "Flash BIOS". In days gone by the only way of upgrading the BIOS was to buy a new chip, or pair of chips as it was in those days. Some of the ROMs used to store the BIOS were actually re-programmable, but only by removing them from the PC and putting them into a programmer unit. This was not a practical proposition for most users. New BIOS chips were very difficult to obtain and you were usually stuck with the BIOS supplied with the motherboard.

The rate at which modern computing changes makes it beneficial to upgrade the BIOS from time to time in order to keep PCs up to date, and not just to accommodate a major upgrade such as a change of processor. The BIOS sometimes has to be updated to cure compatibility problems with certain items of hardware. There could even be one or two minor bugs in the original BIOS.

With a modern BIOS there is no need to replace the BIOS ROM chip or to remove it from the motherboard for reprogramming. The ROM for a modern BIOS can be electronically erased and reprogrammed while it is still on the motherboard. This is why it is possible to download a new BIOS and a "blower" program and upgrade the BIOS. Of course, an upgrade of this type is dependent on the motherboard having the BIOS in Flash memory. However, there is little likelihood of a new motherboard lacking support for the Flash method of upgrading the BIOS. It is many years since I last used a motherboard that lacks this facility.

Write protection

If you get an error message such as "Flash type unrecognised" during the upgrade, this does not mean that the BIOS is a non-reprogrammable type. It usually just means that the Flash memory is write-protected, making it impossible for the upgrade program to alter its contents. Write protection is used as a means of preventing viruses and other malicious programs from corrupting the BIOS and rendering the PC unusable. It would be prudent to check for write-protection before trying to upgrade the BIOS.

The manual for your PC or its motherboard should give instructions for disabling this facility. In some cases the write protection is provided via a switch or jumper on the motherboard. These days it is more usual for this facility to be controlled via a setting in the BIOS itself (Figure 4.27), but you may have to do some searching to find the appropriate menu. There should be no difficulty in upgrading the BIOS once the write-protection has been switched off. Having completed the upgrade it is a good idea to enable this facility again, so that the BIOS is protected from attack.

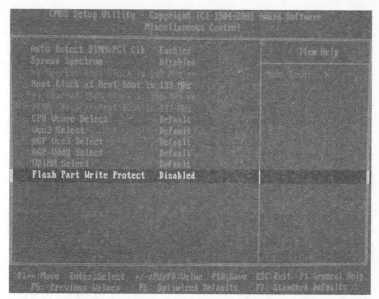

Fig.4.27 The BIOS can not be upgraded unless write protection
           is disabled

Risk factor

It is only fair to point out that a BIOS upgrade is a bit risky. For a start,
you need to be absolutely certain that the data file you are using is the
correct one for your motherboard. Using the wrong BIOS data file could
easily render the computer unusable, and if it will not boot-up correctly it
is impossible to restore the original BIOS.

Another slight worry is that a power failure during the upgrade could
leave the PC with a BI (half a BIOS)! With an incomplete or corrupted
BIOS it is unlikely that the PC could be rebooted to restore the original or
complete the upgrade. It only takes a few seconds to carry out the
upgrade, so you would be very unlucky indeed if a power failure
interrupted the process, but there is a slight risk. A serious error when
upgrading the BIOS could necessitate the fitting of a complete new
motherboard.

The upgrade program usually has to be run from MS-DOS, and is very
simple to operate (Figure 4.28). After you have supplied the name of the
data file for the new BIOS (including any extension to the filename) the

Fig.4.28 A typical Flash writer program in operation

program should give the option of saving the existing BIOS onto disc. It is as well to do this so that you can revert to the original BIOS if the new version proves to be troublesome. After you have confirmed that you wish to continue with the upgrade the new data will be written to the BIOS ROM chip. Do not touch the computer during the flash upgrade, just stand back and let the upgrade program get on with it. The computer is then ready for rebooting and checking to see if the new BIOS has the desired effect.

Boot disc

The boot disc used when upgrading has to be a very basic type that does not run some form of memory management software such as EMM386. Making a suitable boot disc from a system running Windows XP is very straightforward. Place a blank disc in the floppy drive, launch Windows Explorer, and then locate drive A in Windows Explorer. Right-click on the entry for drive A and select the Format option from the popup menu. This produces the window for the Format program, which looks like the one in Figure 4.29. Tick the Create an MS-DOS Startup Disc checkbox and then operate the Start button. A warning message will probably appear, pointing out that any data on the disc will be lost. Operate the Yes button to continue and create the boot disc.

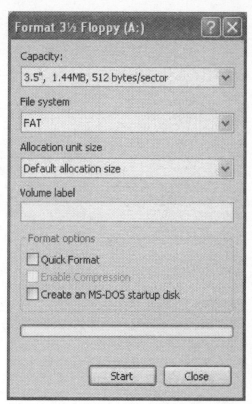

When the formatting has been completed, copy the BIOS data file and upgrade program to the floppy disc. Leave the disc in the floppy drive and restart the computer. With luck the floppy drive will be used as the boot drive and you will be ready to

Fig.4.29 Making a boot disc in Windows XP

proceed with the upgrade once the boot process has been completed. It is possible that the computer will simply boot into Windows. This occurs because the floppy drive is not set as the first boot disc in the BIOS. The BIOS therefore looks for the hard drive first, finds it, and then boots into Windows as normal. Restart the PC, go into the BIOS and set the floppy as the first boot disc, then save the changes and exit the BIOS Setup program. The computer should then boot into MS/DOS using the floppy disc in drive A.

Unfortunately, the Windows ME Format program does not provide a boot disc option. It is possible to make a Startup disc via the Control Panel and the Add/Remove Programs facility. However, this option results in various utilities being placed on the disc, and some of these could interfere with the upgrade process. Make sure that the Minimal Boot option is selected from the boot options menu during the initial boot process, and the memory management programs, etc., will not be run. It should then be safe to go ahead with the BIOS upgrade.

Switches

Most BIOS upgrade programs accept certain switches to be added after the command name. For example, it is possible to specify the file containing the data for the new version of the BIOS. Another common option is one that clears the CMOS memory of all the BIOS settings. It is generally considered advisable to use this switch, since some of the original settings might be inappropriate to the new BIOS. Using this switch means that the BIOS will have no setting when the PC is restarted, and you must enter the Setup program so that the Load Setup Defaults option can be selected. If necessary, the defaults can then be "fine tuned" to suit your requirements. The date and time will have to be reset, but this can be done from the Windows Control Panel.

If the BIOS has been updated correctly a new BIOS version number and date should be displayed on the initial screen at start-up. It is also likely that Windows will detect that there has been a change and respond with various messages to the effect that new hardware has been detected. Actually, it is just detecting the same old hardware and reinstalling the drivers for it. The change in BIOS presumably fools Windows into "thinking" that a different motherboard has been installed. Once this reinstallation has been completed the computer should perform much the same as it did before.

Some motherboards are supplied with a Windows program that permits the BIOS to be easily updated. A facility such as this should make it much simpler and easier to upgrade the BIOS, but as always with a BIOS upgrade, make sure that the manufacturer's instructions are followed "to the letter".

Points to remember

The BIOS helps the operating system to deal with the hardware, particularly the drives and memory. It stores masses of information about the hardware in CMOS RAM which retains its contents when the computer is switched off. These can be controlled via the Setup program built into the BIOS.

The normal way into the BIOS Setup program is by pressing the Del (Delete) key during the initial start up routine. A message will appear on the screen at the appropriate time. If the BIOS you are using has a different method of entering the Setup program the motherboard's instruction manual should explain what to do.

It is essential to go into the BIOS to ensure that it is set up correctly. If you simply try to bypass this part of PC building it is unlikely that the PC will work really well, and it may well be impossible to get it working properly at all. Vital information required by the operating system may be missing.

Do not be intimidated by the BIOS Setup program. With a modern BIOS there are numerous parameters that can be adjusted, but to a large extent you can leave the BIOS to sort things out for itself.

As a minimum, set the time and date and check that the various drives (including any floppy drives) are properly installed. It is advisable to check to see if there are any memory settings that might need adjustment. It might be necessary to alter the boot sequence in order to get the operating system installed.

The manual provided with hard disc drive should give the correct parameters to enter into the Setup program, but satisfactory results should be obtained if you simply opt for automatic detection. With a modern BIOS there might not be a manual option.

If the BIOS detects the processor and sets the core voltage, bus frequency, and multiplier value, check that they are correct. Do not experiment with overclocking unless you know what you are doing and are prepared to foot the bill for any damage caused.

Read the section of the motherboard's manual that deals with the BIOS. Each BIOS is slightly different, and the only way to find out if the one you are using has some special features you should know about is to read through the manual.

It is worthwhile adjusting things such as the Numlock setting to suit your own preferences, so check through the available parameters for any that you can usefully customise.

You may need to alter the parallel port's operating mode if you use any advanced parallel port devices that require high-speed data transfers.

Remember to save the new parameters before exiting the Setup program. Alternatively, if you have made a mess of things you can exit without saving the scrambled settings.

It is very unlikely that "playing" with the BIOS settings will cause any damage to the hardware, and if things get into a complete mess you can always return to the default settings. However, simply playing around with settings to see what happens is not really a good idea.

Do not experiment with the flash memory writing program. A careless error here could easily render the computer unusable, and the only solution might be a replacement motherboard. A BIOS upgrade is something you only undertake if you really need to, and it is then essential to proceed with great care.

Installing
Windows
95/98/ME

Operating system

With the BIOS set up correctly it is time to install the operating system. It has to be pointed out that it is not acceptable to simply "borrow" an operating system from one computer and install it on another. You should have a licence for each copy of an operating system that is installed on your PCs. If you are scrapping an old PC then it is perfectly legitimate to use all the software from the old PC on the new one, since it will still be running on a single computer. If you are not scrapping an old PC it is necessary to buy an operating system for your newly constructed computer.

In the past the full version of Windows 95/98 was only sold with new PCs or with major items of hardware. This meant that you had to buy the operating system when buying one of the main components of the PC such as the processor or motherboard. As far as I am aware, there is no restriction of this type currently in force with Windows 98 SE or Windows ME. They seem to be standard "off the shelf" items that can be purchased from practically any computer store.

There has never been any restriction of this type with other operating systems such as Windows XP, BEOS, and Linux. Of course, with a "free" operating system such as Linux you can install as many copies as you wish on as many PCs as you like. However, there may be some restrictions on the use of certain programs provided with the operating system, so it is as well to check the "fine print".

Formatting

The method used to install the operating system depends on which particular system you will be using, and there may be more than one way of handling things. With MS/DOS, Windows 3.1, Windows 95, Windows 98, and Windows ME the hard disc drive must be formatted before the operating system can be installed. Start by booting the computer from an MS-DOS boot disc or a Windows Startup disc in drive A. With the computer booted-up and running MS-DOS or the Windows 95/98/ME equivalent of MS-DOS, the hard drive will not be accessible. Modern hard disc drives are supplied with the low-level formatting already done, but they still require high-level formatted using the MS-DOS "FORMAT" program. However, you must first prepare the disc using the "FDISK " command.

The system disc used to boot the computer must contain copies of both FDISK and FORMAT, and it is also helpful if this disc contains a simple text editor program such as the MS-DOS EDIT program. With a Windows 98 setup disc both of these programs will be placed on the disc for you when it is created. To create the disc from the Windows 98 or ME desktop select Start, Settings, Control Panel, Add/Remove Programs, Startup Disc, and finally Create Disc (Figure 5.1). Note that you will be asked for the Windows 98 CD-ROM, because some of the files required are not normally stored on the hard disc.

With an MS/DOS boot disc you must copy the programs onto the disc yourself, from an MS/DOS installation on a hard disc drive. It is better to use a Windows 98/ME disc rather than the Windows 95 equivalent or a "real" MS/DOS disc. Windows 98 provides better support for large hard disc drives. Using earlier versions of MS/DOS you may find that the disc is used inefficiently, and that the disc has to be organised as if it were actually several relatively small discs. The drive may be supplied with software that helps to work around these problems, but it is better to use a modern operating system that can handle large hard disc drives properly.

Large drives

FDISK is used to create one or more DOS partitions. It is usually possible to have the whole of the disc as a single partition, but this depends on the size of the disc and the operating system that will be used. With a single partition the hard disc drive becomes drive C. By creating further

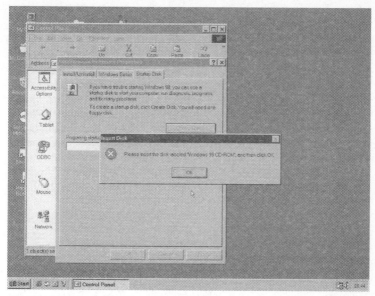

Fig.5.1 Creating a Windows Startup disc

partitions it can also operate as drive D, drive E, etc. The primary partition is the boot disc, and this is where the operating system must be installed.

The MS/DOS and Windows 95 file systems limits the maximum size of a partition at 2.1 gigabytes. There is also an 8.4-gigabyte limit on the physical size of the drive. With Windows 98 and any reasonably modern BIOS these limits do not apply, but you must use the FAT32 file system. With modern hard discs having capacities of 20 gigabytes or more it is definitely a good idea to upgrade to Windows 98 SE or Windows ME if you are still using Windows 95. Both of these operating systems can fully exploit the high capacities of modern hard discs.

In order to use the FAT32 file system simply answer yes when FDISK is first run, and you are asked if you require support for large hard disc drives. Even if you do not wish to have a large disc organised as one large partition, it is still best to opt for large hard disc support. FAT32 utilizes the available disc space more efficiently and reduces wastage. Note that if you only require a single partition you must still use the FDISK program to set up this single partition, and that the FORMAT program will not work on the hard drive until FDISK has created a DOS partition for it to format.

Some hard discs are supplied complete with partitioning software that will also format the disc and add the system files, which will be copied from the boot disc. Where a utility program of this type is available it is probably better to use it instead of the FDISK and FORMAT programs. These MS-DOS programs are fairly straightforward in use, but using the software supplied with the drive will almost certainly be even easier. Also, most of these programs do the job very quickly. If you use the FDISK and FORMAT programs, make sure that you are using modern versions of them. Versions of MS/DOS earlier than version 3.3 are not able to provide two partitions, and are not really suitable for use with a modern PC.

Using FDISK

Once you are in FDISK there is a menu offering these four choices (see also Figure 5.2):

1. Create DOS partition or logical DOS drive

2. Set the active partition

3. Delete partition or logical DOS drive

4. Display partition information

The first thing we need to do is create a DOS partition, so select option one, which will be the default. This takes you into a further menu offering these three options (Figure 5.3):

1. Create primary DOS partition

2. Create extended DOS partition

3. Create logical DOS drive(s) in the extended DOS partition

It is a primary DOS partition that is required, so select option one, which should again be the default. You will then be asked if you wish to use the maximum space for the partition and make it the active partition. If you answer yes, the whole disc, or as much of it as FDISK can handle, will be used for the partition. It will also be made active, which simply means that this is the partition that the computer will try to boot from. This is the partition to which the operating system should be installed.

If you answer no, you will then have to specify the size of the primary partition in megabytes. This creates the partition, but does not make it active. Having created the partition you then press the Escape key to return to the original menu. It is a good idea to select option four to check that the partition has been created successfully (Figure 5.4).

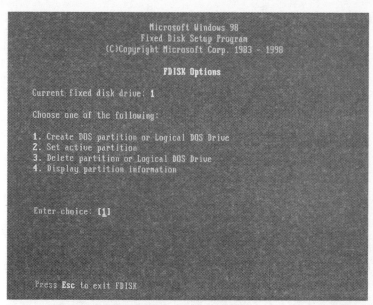

Fig.5.2 The main FDISK menu has four options

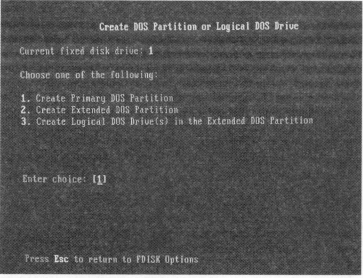

Fig.5.3 The FDISK partition creation menu

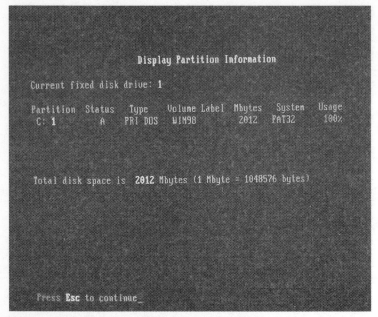

Fig.5.4 Using FDISK to check partition information

If you did not use the maximum space for the partition it will not have been made active. To do this select option two from the main menu and then enter the number of the partition you wish to make active. As there is only one partition this will obviously be partition number one. Press return to implement this command, and then press the Escape key to return to the main menu again. It is then a good idea to use option four once again to ensure that everything has gone smoothly. In the Status column there should be an "A" to indicate that partition one is active (as in Figure 5.4).

If a further partition is required select option one, and then option two, which is "Create extended DOS partition" (Figure 5.5). Enter the size of the partition you require and press the Return key to create the partition. Then press the Escape key, which will bring up a message saying "No logical drives defined" (Figure 5.6). In other words, you have created a partition, but as yet it does not have a drive letter. Assuming you require all the space in the partition to be one logical drive, simply press the Return key. This will make the partition drive D, and a screen giving this information will appear (Figure 5.7). Press the Escape key to return to

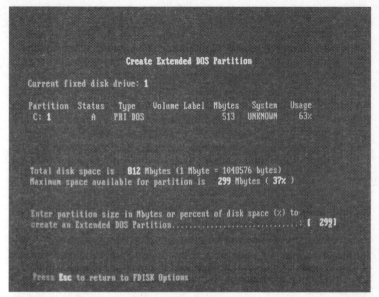

Fig.5.5 Creating an extended DOS partition

the main menu, and use option four to check that the partition has been created successfully.

Formatting

Having created the partitions you require, the "FORMAT" command can then be run. First you will have to press the Escape key twice to exit FDISK, and then the computer must be rebooted so that the new partition information takes effect. In the unlikely event that you wish to use MS-DOS and Windows 3.1 on the new PC, the system files must be placed onto the hard disc in order to make it bootable. This is not necessary if the PC will be used with any later version of Windows. To format drive C and place the system files onto it use this command:

format C: /s

To simply format the hard disc dive, use this command:

format C:

Either way, the command will bring up a warning to the effect that all data in drive C will be lost if you proceed with the format. As yet there is

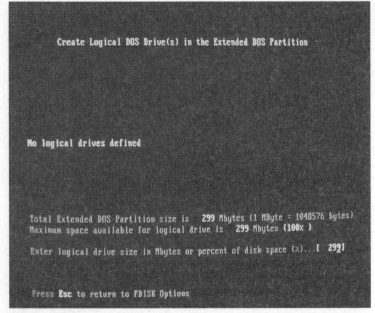

*Fig.5.6 Creating an extra partition does not automatically create a
logical drive*

no data to lose, so answer yes to proceed with the formatting. It might
take a several minutes to complete the task, since there are a large
number of tracks to be processed and checked. With a large disc it
could take around an hour.

If the hard disc has more than one partition and is operating as drive C,
drive D, etc., each partition must formatted using a separate "FORMAT"
command. Of course, the system should only be placed on disc C, so
for the other logical drives do not use the "/s" addition to the format
command. This would not actually prevent drive D from working, but it
would waste disc space on system files that would never be used. To
format drive D this command would be used:

format D:

Windows

If you are still using MS-DOS, the PC is more or less ready to use once
the hard drive is bootable. You will have to install all your applications

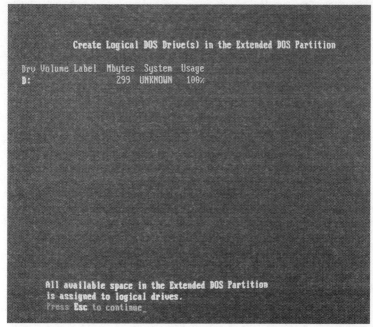

Fig.5.7 This screen confirms that logical drive D: has been created

software or course, and it is a good idea to copy the MS-DOS support files to a directory call "DOS", or something similar. The later versions of MS/DOS have an installation program that will do all this for you. Windows 3.1 can be installed onto the hard disc in much the same way as applications programs.

For most users, putting the MS-DOS operating system onto the hard disc is simply a stepping-stone to installing Windows 95, 98, or ME. In the unlikely event that you have the floppy disc version of Windows 95/98 there should be no difficulty in loading it onto the hard disc once the hard disc is bootable. You may find that you need to install the mouse in MS-DOS first, but otherwise it can be installed onto the bare drive.

The situation is similar with the CD-ROM version and with Windows ME, but it is necessary to install the mouse and the CD-ROM drive into MS-DOS before the Windows Setup program can be run. This is simply because MS-DOS will not automatically recognise the CD-ROM drive and designate it as drive D, or whatever. Just the opposite in fact, and

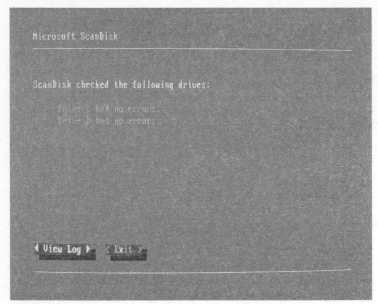

Fig.5.8 Scandisk will automaticall check for disc errors

MS-DOS will totally ignore the CD-ROM drive until the installation process has been completed and the computer has been rebooted.

The mouse and the CD-ROM drive should be supplied complete with installation software that largely does the installation for you. Some CD-ROM manufacturers supply the MS-DOS MSCDEX.EXE file, which is needed to integrate the CD-ROM drive with MS-DOS, but in most cases you will have to ensure that it is already on the hard disc. This file is supplied as part of MS-DOS 5 and 6, and should be placed on the hard disc if you install all the MS-DOS support files. It is installed into the C:\Windows\Command directory once Windows 95/98 is installed, but this is obviously of no use at this stage, as Windows is not yet installed on the PC. If necessary, "borrow" this file from another PC by copying it onto a floppy disc, and then copying it to the hard disc drive.

Alternatively, if you are using a Windows 98 or ME Startup disc, boot-up from this and choose CD-ROM support when asked to select the start-up mode. This should provide access to the CD-ROM drive so that the Windows installation disc can be run, and is a much easier way of handling things. Also, the mouse might work with the Windows Setup program without having to install its drivers.

Fig.5.9 The initial screen of the Windows ME Setup program

Windows Setup

Once the mouse and CD-ROM drive have been installed it should be possible to run the Setup program on the Windows 95/98 installation disc. It will probably not be necessary to direct the operating system to the drive that contains the Windows installation disc, so using this command at the MS-DOS prompt should run the Setup program:

setup

It will probably be necessary to specify the drive if the computer was booted from something other than a Windows Startup disc. For example, this command would be used if the installation disc is in drive D:

D:\ setup

First a welcome message will appear and then the Scandisk utility will check for errors on the hard disc drives and logical drives (Figure 5.8). Assuming all is well, press the "x" key to exit Scandisk and go into the first screen of the Windows Setup program (Figure 5.9). Installation is largely automatic, so from here onwards it is largely a matter of following the on-screen prompts.

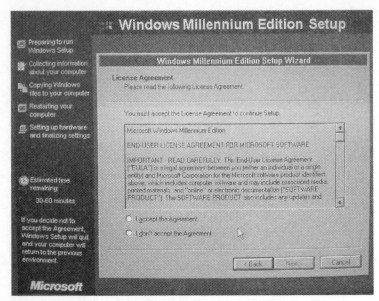

Fig.5.10 Windows can only be installed if you agree to the licence conditions

Note that you can install the upgrade version of Windows 95, 98 or ME onto a "clean" hard disc, and that it is not essential to load your old version of Windows first so that you have a Windows installation to upgrade. However, during the installation process you will probably be asked to prove that you have a qualifying upgrade product by putting the Setup disc into the floppy drive or CD-ROM drive, as appropriate. Do not throw away or recycle your old Windows discs, as this could leave you unable to reinstall the Windows upgrade.

The basic installation process is much the same for Windows 95, 98, and ME. Although the description provided here is for an installation of Windows ME, the basic procedure is therefore much the same for Windows 95 and 98. Also, the process is much the same whether the operating system is installed from scratch or on top of an existing Windows installation. If Windows is already on the hard disc it will be detected by the Setup program, which will then reinstall it on top of the existing Windows installation, by default. Any Windows applications programs on the disc should remain properly installed with the new Windows installation.

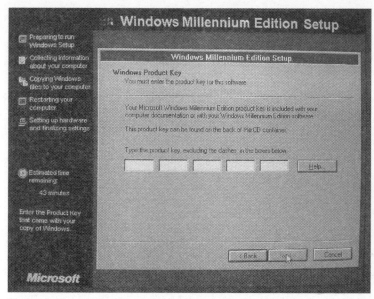

Fig.5.11 The product key must be entered at this screen

Therefore, if the Windows installation becomes damaged in the future, the process described can be used to reinstall it and, hopefully, repair the damage. Of course, the partitioning and formatting processes are not used when a Windows installation is being repaired. Formatting can be used to completely wipe the hard disc if you wish to reinstall Windows from scratch, which can sometimes be necessary with an installation that has become badly damaged.

Installation

First you have to agree to the licensing conditions (Figure 5.10), and it is not possible to install Windows unless you do. At the next screen the Windows Product Key has to be entered (Figure 5.11). This code number will be found on the Windows certificate of authenticity and (or) on the back of the CD's jewel case. Next you are asked to select the directory into which Windows will be installed (Figure 5.12), but unless there is good reason to do otherwise, simply accept the default (C:\Windows).

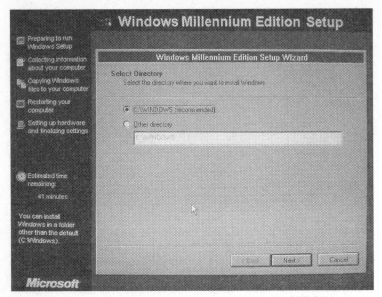

Fig.5.12 It is normally best to install Windows in the default folder

After some checking of the hard disc you are offered several installation options (Figure 5.13), but for most users the default option of a Typical installation will suffice. Remember that you can add and delete Windows components once the operating system is installed, so you are not tied to the typical installation forever.

The Custom option enables the user to select precisely the required components, but this can be time consuming and you need to know what you are doing. The Compact option is useful if hard disc space is limited, but with a new PC the hard disc will presumably be large enough to make this option superfluous. The Portable option is optimised for portable PCs, and is the obvious choice when installing the system on a computer of this type.

At the next screen you type your name and company name into the dialogue boxes (Figure 5.14). If an individual owns the PC the box for the company name can be left blank. The purpose of the next screen (Figure 5.15) is to give you a chance to check the information entered so far, and to provide an opportunity to change your mind before moving on to the actual installation process. Operating the Next button may

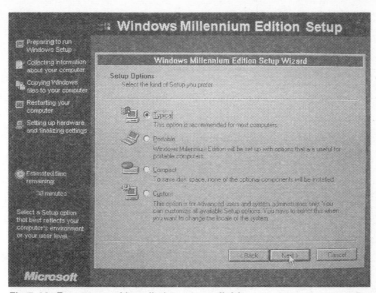

Fig.5.13 Four types of installation are available

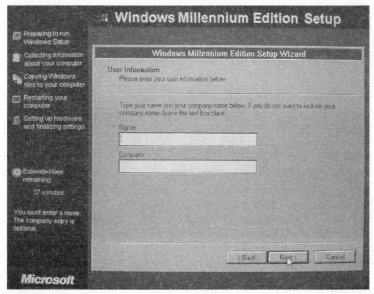

Fig.5.14 You must enter your name, but the company name is optional

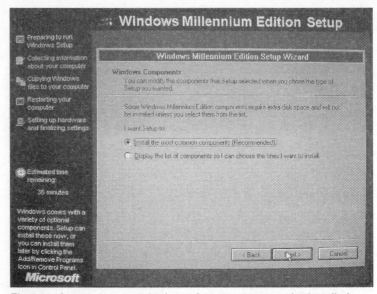

Fig.5.15 A custom or standard set of components can be installed

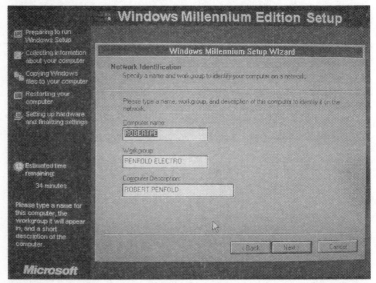

Fig.5.16 The network selection screen is not relevant to most users

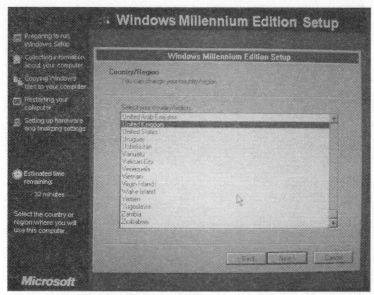

Fig.5.17 The country selection screen

bring up a network identification screen (Figure 5.16). Where appropriate, make sure that this contains the correct information. In most cases the PC will not be used on a network, and the default settings can be used.

Time zone

Next the appropriate country has to be selected from a list (Figure 5.17), and then the required time zone is selected (Figure 5.18). This screen also provides the option of automatically implementing daylight saving changes. The next screen (Figure 5.19) enables a Windows Startup disc to be produced. If you already have one of these you may prefer to skip this section by operating the Cancel button and then the OK button. Unfortunately, floppy discs are not the most reliable of storage mediums. If you only have one Startup disc already, I would suggest that you go ahead and make another one so that you have a standby copy.

If you are using an upgrade version of Windows there will be an additional section in the setting up procedure where you have to prove that you have a qualifying product to upgrade from. The screen of Figure 5.20 will appear, so that you can point the Setup program towards the disc

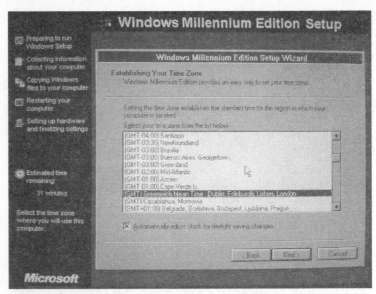

Fig.5.18 This screen is used to select the correct time zone

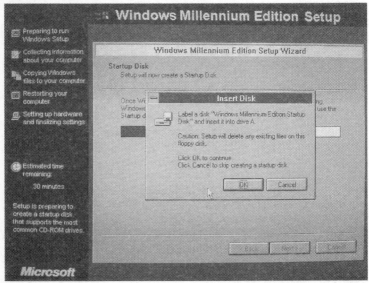

Fig.5.19 There is the option of making a Windows Startup disc

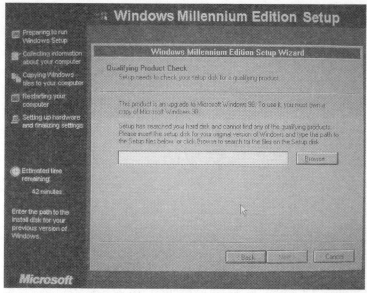

Fig.5.20 An upgrade product requires evidence of a previous version

that contains the earlier version of Windows. To do this you will have to remove the upgrade disc from the CD-ROM drive and replace it with the disc for the previous version of Windows. Then either type the path to the CD-ROM drive in the text box (e.g. E:\) or operate the Browse button and point to the appropriate drive in standard Windows fashion. The checking process is something less than instant, and the usual progress bar will appear to show how things are going (Figure 5.21).

Note that this stage will be passed over if

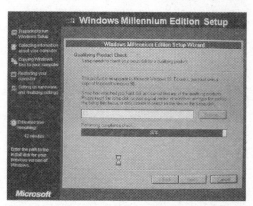

Fig.5.21 A progress bar is displayed during the checking process

Fig.5.22 The main installation screen

at some later time you reinstall an upgrade version on top of an existing Windows installation. Windows will find the existing installation and will deduce from this that you are a bona fide user. This assumes that the existing installation is not so badly damaged that the Setup program fails to recognise it.

Main installation

Having completed all this you will have finally progressed to the main installation screen (Figure 5.22), and from thereon installation is largely automatic. A screen showing how the installation is progressing will appear (Figure 5.23). The computer will reboot itself two or three times during the installation process, so if you opted to produce a Windows Startup disc during the initial setup procedure remember to remove this from the floppy drive. Otherwise the computer might reboot from the floppy rather than the hard disc, which would interfere with the installation process.

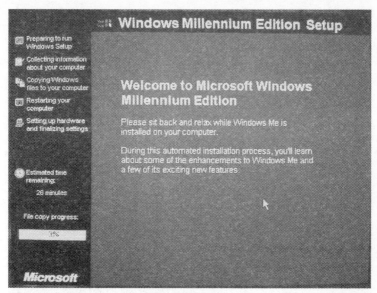

Fig.5.23 Eventually the installation begins

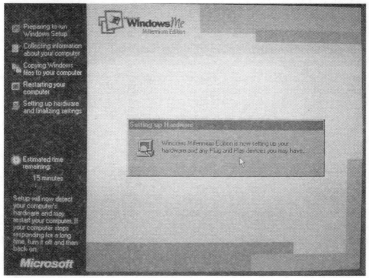

Fig.5.24 The Setup program keeps you informed of what it is doing

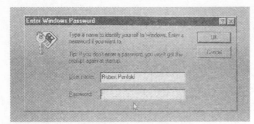

Fig.5.25 The password is optional

In the later stages of the installation there will be further screens telling you what the computer is doing, and giving an indication of how far things have progressed (Figure 5.24). No input is required from the user during all this, so you can let the computer get on with the installation. The one exception is that near the end of the installation process you will be asked to supply a user name and password (Figure 5.25). Simply leave the password text box blank if you do not require password protection. Eventually you should end up with a basic Windows installation, and the familiar initial screen (Figure 5.26).

Sometimes the Windows Setup program comes to a halt. Either the computer shows no signs of any disc activity for some time, or there may be repeated disc activity with the installation failing to make any progress.

Fig.5.26 The familiar Windows screen appears once installation is complete

progress. The usual cure is to switch off the computer, wait a few seconds, and then switch on again. The Setup program will usually detect that there was a problem, and will avoid making the same mistake again. If the computer is switched on and off on several occasions, but the installation still fails to complete, it will be necessary to reboot using the Startup disc, wipe the hard disc clean, and try again. If Windows repeatedly refuses to install it is likely that the PC has a hardware fault.

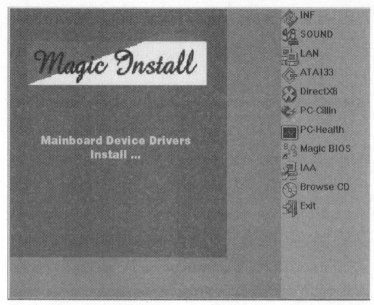

Fig.5.27 Most motherboards are supplied with an installation program for the device drivers, etc.

Hardware drivers

There will probably still be a certain amount of work to be done in order to get all the hardware fully installed, the required screen resolution set, and so on. Windows 95/98/ME might have built-in support for all the hardware in your PC such as the sound and video cards, but this is unlikely. In order to get everything installed correctly you will probably require the installation discs provided with the various items of hardware used in the PC. These discs may be required during the installation of Windows 95/98/ME, or they may have to be used after the basic installation has been completed.

The instruction manuals provided with the hardware should explain the options available and provide precise installation instructions. These days even the motherboards seem to come complete with driver software for things such as special chipset features and the hard disc interface. It is once again a matter of reading the instruction manual to determine which drivers have to be installed, and how to go about it. Get all the hardware properly installed before you install the applications software.

The order in which the hardware is installed in Windows can be important. In general, it is advisable to install any drivers for hardware on the motherboard first. Other items of hardware might be reliant on the motherboard's hardware being properly installed into Windows. For example, the AGP and PCI slots might require additional driver software to be installed once the basic Windows installation has been completed.

Most motherboards are supplied with an installation program that gives a list of the software that can be installed (Figure 5.27), making the installation process very straightforward. There might be other optional pieces of software such as an anti-virus program and monitoring software. With the software for the motherboard installed, the drivers for the video card should be installed next. The video card will work with Windows once the basic installation has been completed, but it will only function as a simple VGA type. The full range of facilities will be available once the video drivers have been installed. Any remaining drivers can then be installed, and the order in which these are installed is unlikely to be of any consequence.

Device Manager

Once everything is supposedly installed correctly it is a good idea to go into the Control Panel program and double-click the System icon. Then select the Device Manager tab to bring up a window of the type shown in Figure 5.28. Look down the various entries to check for any problems. These are indicated by yellow exclamation marks, or possibly by yellow question marks.

Certain items of hardware will not be picked up properly by Windows, and some types of modem fall into this category. The question mark in Figure 5.28 is caused by Windows modem that the system is unable to sort out on its own. A Windows modem uses a relatively simple hardware plus software in the computer to provide the encoding and decoding. Unlike a conventional modem, a Windows modem does not interface to the computer via a true serial port. It is interfaced via a sort of pseudo serial port, and it is this factor that makes it difficult to correctly identify the hardware.

If a problem is indicated, or an item of hardware is missing from the list, it will be necessary to load the drivers for the hardware concerned in order to get things working properly. This would be a good time to search the relevant web sites for updated driver software for the hardware in your PC. You may well find some newer and better drivers for the

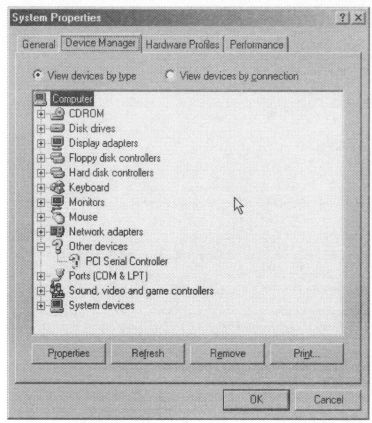

Fig.5.28 Device Manager is used to look for installation problems with the hardware

hardware in your PC. The hardware can be integrated into Windows using the Add New Hardware facility in the Control Panel. However, many items of PC hardware do not take the standard Windows route and have special installation programs instead. Read the installation manuals carefully and use the exact methods described therein.

Awkward hardware

Any awkward hardware will have to be added via the Add New Hardware facility without utilizing Windows hardware detection facility. First

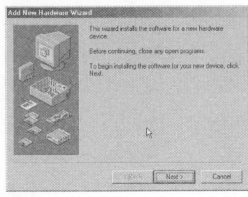

Fig.5.29 The initial Add New Hardware screen

Windows tries to detect Plug and Play devices, and then it can try to find non-Plug and Play hardware. Failing that, the new hardware has to be installed manually using the drivers disc or discs provided with the item of hardware. The process is slightly different depending on the version of Windows you are using, but the basic process is the same with all three versions. Here we will consider the Windows ME version.

The opening screen of Figure 5.29 appears when the Add New Hardware program is run. Heed the warning and close any programs that are

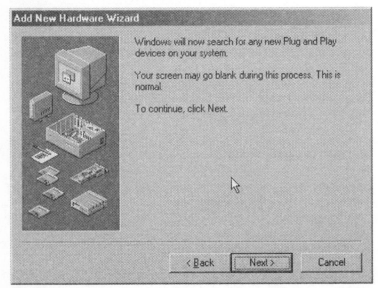

Fig.5.30 A search for Plug and Play devices is made first

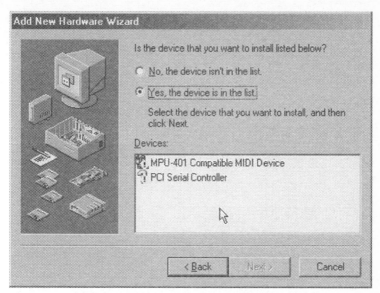

Fig.5.31 Any Plug and Play devices that are found are listed

running before proceeding further. To continue left-click on the Next button, which will bring up a screen like the one in Figure 5.30. This informs you that the program will look for Plug and Play devices connected to the system, and not to panic if the screen goes blank for a time. Press the Next button to proceed with the search. Eventually you will get a screen something like the one in Figure 5.31, complete with a list of any Plug and Play devices that have been found. If the device you wish to install is in the list, leave the Yes radio button checked, left-click on the device you wish to install, and then operate the Next button to proceed with the installation.

Any non-Plug and Play devices will not be in the list, and it is then a matter of checking the No radio button and operating the Next button. This brings up the window of Figure 5.32, which provides the option of having the program search for the hardware you wish to install. There is no harm in letting the program search for the hardware, although this can be quite time consuming. It is likely that a standard item of hardware such as an additional serial or parallel port will be detected, but it is by no means certain that anything exotic will be located.

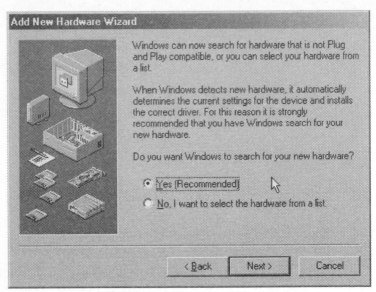

Fig.5.32 A search can be made for non-Plug and Play devices

If you decide not to opt for automatic detection, check the No radio button and operate the Next button. This produces the window of Figure 5.33 where you can select the appropriate category for the hardware you are installing. A wide variety of devices are covered, with more available under the "Other" category. In this example the modem category was selected, and operating the Next button moved things on to the window of Figure 5.34. Here you are once again offered the option of automatic detection, but this does not work

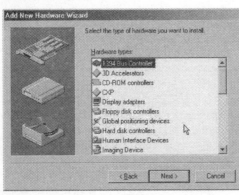

Fig.5.33 This screen enables the type of device to be selected manually

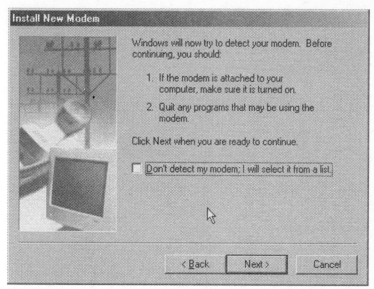

Fig.5.34 Even at this stage, automatic detection is still possible

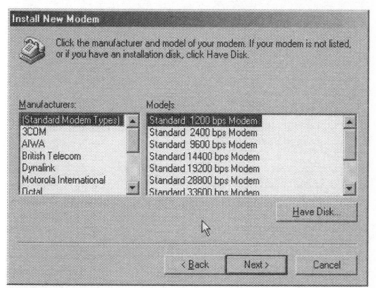

Fig.5.35 The Have Disk option is used if you have a drivers disc

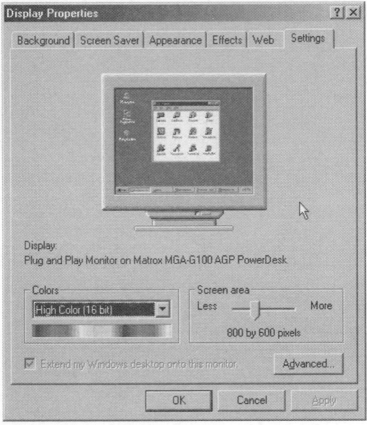

Fig.5.36 The Display Properties screen is used to set the screen resolution, colour depth, etc.

properly with most "soft" modems, so the No button was checked and the Next button was operated.

If you opt for manual selection you will eventually be shown a window containing a list of devices, as in Figure 5.35. The right device might appear in the list, but with recent hardware or generic devices you will probably be out of luck. It is then a matter of selecting the Have Disk option, which brings up a file browser so that you can direct the program to the correct disc drive, and where appropriate, the correct folder of the disc in that drive. With the drivers installed the computer will probably have to be rebooted before the hardware will operate properly.

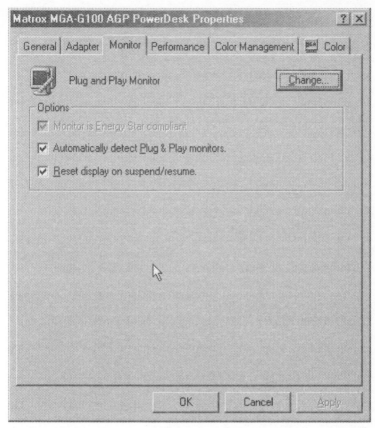

Fig.5.37 If there is screen instability check that the correct monitor is installed

Screen settings

Once the video card has been installed properly the required screen parameters can be set. To alter the screen resolution and colour depth, go to the Windows Control Panel and double-click on the Display icon. Then left-click on the Settings tab to bring up a screen of the type shown in Figure 5.36. It is then just a matter of using the onscreen controls to set the required screen resolution and colour depth. To use the new settings left-click the Apply button. It may be necessary to let the computer reboot in order to use the new settings, but in most cases they can be applied without doing this. Instead Windows will apply the new settings for a few seconds so that you can see that all is well. Simply left-click on the Yes button to start using the new screen settings.

If there is a problem with the picture stability do nothing, and things should return to the original settings after a few seconds. This should not really happen if the monitor is installed correctly, because Windows will not try to use scan rates that are beyond the capabilities of the installed monitor. If a problem of this type should occur, check that the monitor is installed properly. In the Display window of Control Panel select Settings, Advanced, and then Monitor. This will bring up a screen like Figure 5.37, which shows the type of monitor that is installed.

If the installed monitor is not the correct one, or is just one of the generic monitor types, left-click the Change button and select the correct one. If the picture is stable with the new settings but the size and position are completely wrong, there is probably no problem. It should be possible to position and size the picture correctly using the monitor's controls. Many graphics cards are supplied with utility software that helps to get the best possible display from the system, and it is worth trying any software of this type to see if it gives better results.

Disc-free ME

It has been assumed in this chapter that you have a Windows installation CD-ROM. Some computers are supplied with Windows ME pre-installed, and they do not come complete with a normal Windows installation CD-ROM. Instead, the hard disc has two partitions with drive C acting as the main disc and a much smaller drive D containing the Windows files. There is usually a CD-ROM that can be used to recover the situation in the event of a hard disc failure, but this is not an ordinary Windows installation disc.

On the face of it, there is no problem if you wish to take this type of Windows ME from a defunct PC and use it on your newly constructed PC. Unfortunately, in practice it is unlikely that this will be possible. Apart from any problems caused by differences in the hardware of the two PCs, this type of Windows is tied to a particular make and model of PC. The serial number of the BIOS is checked as part of the installation process, and the new motherboard will not have an appropriate number. Consequently, the installation program will refuse to go ahead with the installation.

This might seem slightly unreasonable, but the computer manufacturers buy this form of Windows at relatively low prices. This is reflected in a lower price when you buy the PC, but when the PC reaches the end of its operating life the copy of Windows supplied with it also expires. Therefore, it is not possible to take this type of Windows installation on to another PC, and a new copy of the retail version has to be purchased.

Points to remember

In order to place MS-DOS, MS-DOS and Windows 3.1, or Windows 95/98 onto the hard disc it must first be partitioned with the MS-DOS FDISK program. It must then be formatted with the MS-DOS FORMAT command. Choose support for large hard discs when it is offered (you are using an old version of FDISK if this option is not offered).

You must produce at least one partition on the disc, even if it will be used as a single drive. You produce one partition that utilizes all the disc's capacity. An extended partition can be created and used as one or more logical drives if required.

When Installing Windows 95/98/ME it is advisable to boot from a Windows Startup disc, opting for CD-ROM support when the menu appears. It should then be possible to run the Windows Setup program from CD-ROM, and most mice will work with this program without having to install any further drivers.

The basic installation process is largely automatic. The user provides some basic information and then the Setup program installs the Windows files and sets up the essential hardware. Some further installation is then required to get all the hardware properly installed, the screen resolution and colour depth set correctly, etc.

The order in which drivers are installed is often important. It is best to start with any drivers supplied with the motherboard, and then install the video card's driver software. The drivers for modems and other hardware on expansion cards are then added.

Not all hardware can be installed with the aid of the automatic detection facilities. Manual installation of hardware drivers is not difficult, but where appropriate, make sure that items of hardware are supplied complete with a disc or discs containing the driver software. Some hardware has its own installation routines and does not go through the normal Windows routes. Always install hardware in accordance with the manufacturer's instructions.

Use Device Manager to check that all the hardware is installed correctly. Where any problems are highlighted, try reinstalling the relevant device drivers. If that fails to cure the problem, see if more up-to-date drivers are available from the manufacturers web site.

PCs that are supplied with Windows ME preinstalled are not necessarily supplied with a normal Windows installation disc. It is only possible to use Windows that was supplied with a defunct PC if it was supplied in the form of a standard Windows installation CD-ROM.

Installing Windows XP

Boot from CD-ROM

Windows XP is easier to install than Windows 95/98/ME, since there is no need to format the hard disc drive when installing Windows XP. This can be done during the installation process. In fact the partitioning of the disc can also be handled by the installation program, so FDISK is not needed either. Windows XP is designed to operate totally independently from MS-DOS, and this it achieves. The Windows XP installation CD-ROM is a bootable type, so it is possible to boot from the CD-ROM straight into the Setup program. No floppy boot disc of any kind is required.

The first step is to boot from the installation CD-ROM, and this might require changes to the BIOS settings. These days the normal default boot sequence is the floppy disc, the first hard disc (drive C), and then the first CD-ROM drive. However, it is good idea to go into the BIOS Setup program to check that the CD-ROM is one of the boot devices, as there is no guarantee that this drive will be in the boot sequence.

Ideally the BIOS should be set to boot from the CD-ROM drive before it tries to boot from the hard disc. In theory the BIOS will look for a bootable floppy disc first, and then a boot sector on drive C, and then finally try to boot from the CD-ROM drive if the first two attempts fail. In practice the process can hang up when the BIOS tries to boot from the hard drive, especially if it is not partitioned and formatted.

It is therefore a good idea to temporarily set the CD-ROM drive as the first boot device, the hard drive as the second option, and the floppy disc as the third boot drive. The hard disc and the CD-ROM can be made the first and second boot devices respectively once installation is complete. Booting from a floppy disc is not usually necessary with Windows XP, even in an emergency, so the floppy can be left as the third boot device.

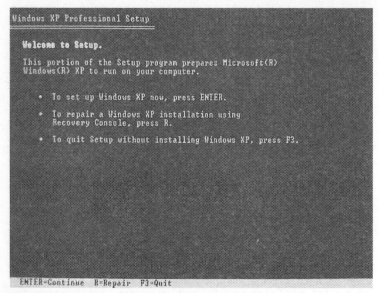

Fig.6.1 The opening screen of the Windows XP Setup program

With a suitable boot sequence set, place the Windows XP installation disc in the first CD-ROM drive and try to boot from it. If all is well, a message will appear on the screen indicating that any key must be operated in order to boot from the CD-ROM drive. This message appears quite briefly, so be ready to press one of the keys. The computer will try to boot from the hard disc if you "miss the boat". It will then be necessary to restart the computer and try again.

After various files have been loaded from the CD-ROM, things should come to a halt with the screen of Figure 6.1. The Setup program is needed to install Windows XP, so press the Enter (Return) key. The Next screen (Figure 6.2) is the usual licence agreement, and the F8 key is pressed in order to agree with the licensing terms. Note that Windows XP can not be installed unless you do agree to the licensing conditions.

Things should now move on to a screen like the one of Figure 6.3 where there is sometimes the option of repairing any existing installation or installing Windows XP from scratch. In this case there is no existing installation, so you are presented with various options for the "raw" hard disc space.

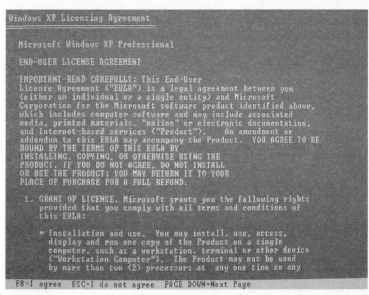

Fig.6.2 You must agree to the conditions in order to proceed

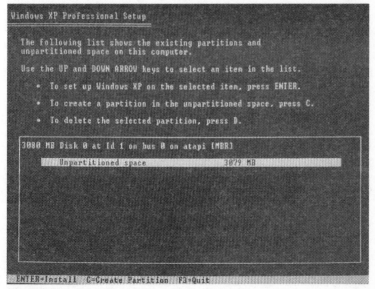

Fig.6.3 There are a few options for the "raw" disc space

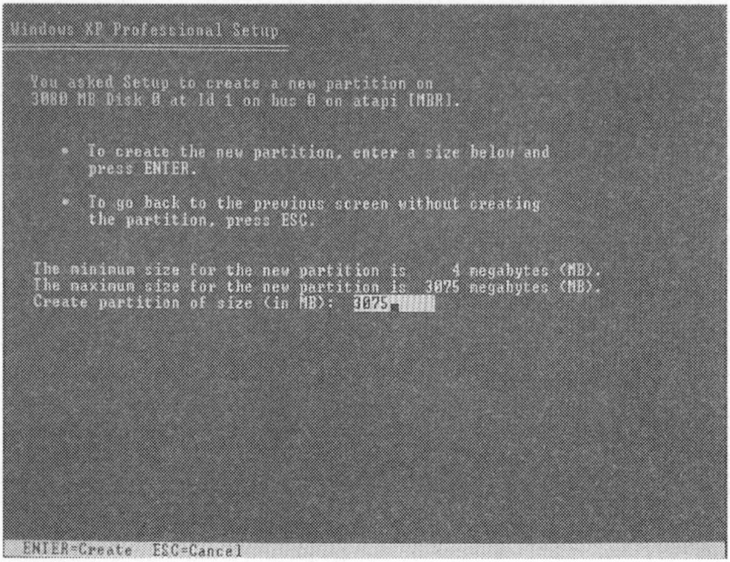

Fig.6.4 The first task is to produce a new partition

XP repair

Obviously the repair option should be selected when reinstalling Windows XP in an attempt to make a damaged installation usable again. Note that the Setup program will not offer the repair option if the installation is badly damaged. It is then a matter of backing up any important data that can be recovered from the hard disc and then installing Windows XP from scratch. This will delete any data on the hard disc, so it is essential to rescue any important data if at all possible.

The first task with a fresh installation is to produce a new partition by operating the C key, which produces the screen of Figure 6.4. By default the Setup program will use the whole disc as a single partition, but you can enter a smaller size if desired. The remaining space can then be partitioned using the same method used to produce the first partition. Here we will keep things simple and settle for a single partition equal to the full capacity of the disc. This is achieved by pressing the Return (Enter) key, which brings up the screen of Figure 6.5. Operate the Return key again, which will produce the new partition and start the preparations for installing Windows XP onto it.

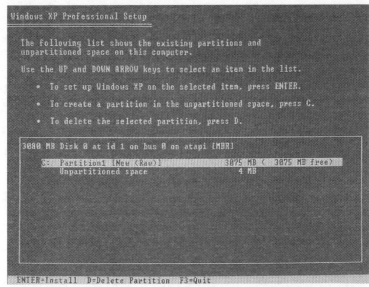

Fig.6.5 *Press Return to create the partition and install Windows on it*

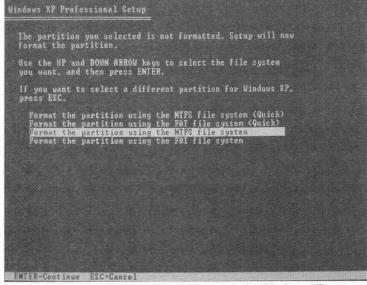

Fig.6.6 *NTFS is the file system normally used with Windows XP*

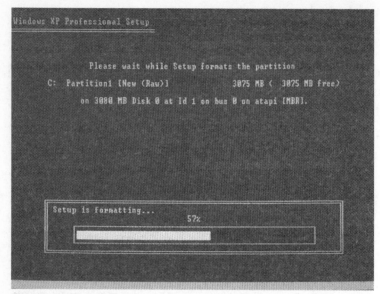

Fig.6.7 The bargraph shows how the formatting is progressing

Things now move on to the screen of Figure 6.6 where the desired file system is selected. Unless there is a good reason to use the FAT or FAT32 file systems, such as compatibility with another file system, choose the NTFS option. This file system makes the best use of Windows XP's capabilities. Having selected the required file system, press the Return key to go ahead and format the partition. This brings up the screen of Figure 6.7, complete with the usual bargraph to show how far the formatting has progressed.

Once the partition has been created and formatted, the Setup program will start copying files to the hard disc (Figure 6.8). Once this stage has been completed you are prompted to restart the computer (Figure 6.9), but this will happen in a few seconds if you do not respond. Having rebooted, the computer will go into the initial screen of the Setup program (Figure 6.10), and installation then carries on in more or less normal Windows fashion, but the exact procedure depends on whether the installation is completely new or repairing an existing one that has become damaged. Extra information has to be entered if Windows XP is being installed from scratch.

Windows XP Professional Setup
Please wait while Setup copies files
to the Windows installation folders.
This might take several minutes to complete.
Setup is copying files...
2%

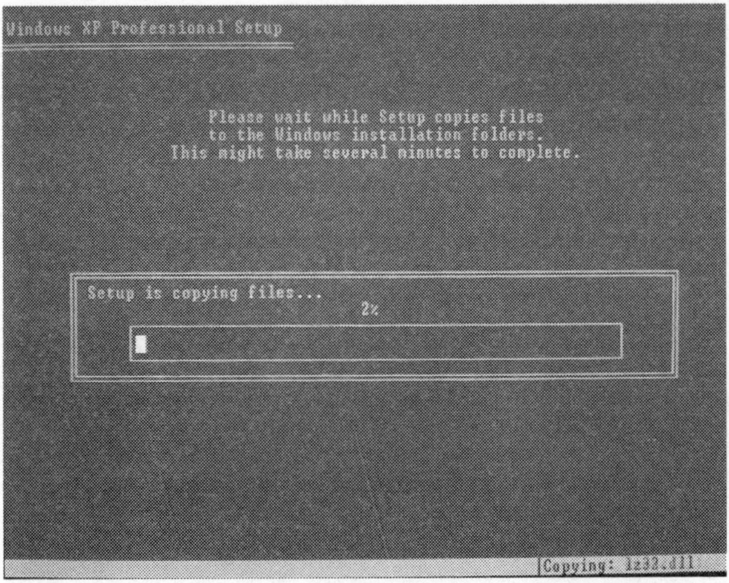

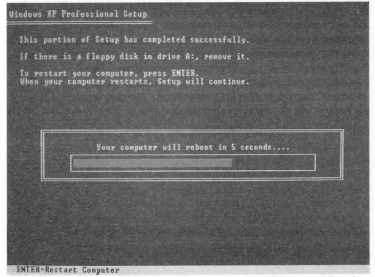

Fig.6.8 With the formatting completed, files are copied to the disc

Windows XP Professional Setup
This portion of Setup has completed successfully.
If there is a floppy disk in drive A:, remove it.
To restart your computer, press ENTER.
When your computer restarts, Setup will continue.
Your computer will reboot in 5 seconds....
ENTER=Restart Computer

Fig.6.9 Restart the computer once the copying has been completed

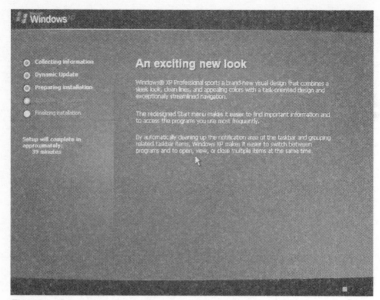

Fig.6.10 Once restarted, Windows XP is installed on the disc

XP compatible?

First, the stages that always occur during installation will be considered. The Setup screen keeps you informed about the progress of the installation. A warning message like the one in Figure 6.11 might appear during the reinstallation. This points out that one of the device drivers in use on the computer is not one that has officially passed the Windows XP compatibility test. This does not necessarily mean that it will cause problems with Windows XP if you go ahead and install it, but it is obviously a possibility that has to be given serious consideration.

In this case the audio driver in question was loaded and was in use for some weeks without any problems arising. Although everything seemed to be all right, a change in the computer's hardware did eventually cause problems with the system crashing, and odd audio happenings. The audio driver proved to be the source of the problem. By that time a new driver had been produced, and this proved to be entirely satisfactory. If in doubt, the safe option is to operate the No button so that the driver is not loaded, but this will render the relevant item of hardware inoperative.

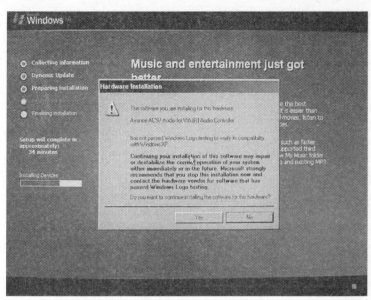

Fig.6.11 A warning message appears if a non-approved driver is found

The more practical approach is to load the driver but use an approved one as soon as it becomes available from the manufacturer's web site. If a device driver proves to be troublesome it can be uninstalled using the Windows XP version of Device Manager. Locate the device in the list of installed hardware and then right-click the mouse on its entry. This produces a small popup menu like the one in Figure 6.12, where the Uninstall option is selected. Answer yes when asked if you really wish to remove the driver and Windows will go ahead and uninstall it.

Language settings

Eventually the installation process will reach a point where further input is required from the user, and a screen like the one in Figure 6.13 will appear. This permits the language settings to be customised, and it is advisable to operate the Customise button and check that the settings are suitable. This brings up an initial window like the one on Figure 6.14, but further windows and menus can be brought up by operating the Customise buttons and the tabs. Figures 6.15 and 6.16 show a couple of examples.

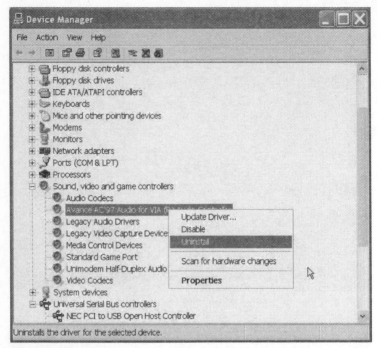

Fig.6.12 If necessary, a faulty driver can be uninstalled later

Look through the various windows and menus, changing any settings that are incorrect. Mistakes here will not have dire consequences, but there could be a problem such as the keyboard producing some incorrect characters. It should be possible to correct any mistake of this type once Windows XP has been installed, but it can save a lot of hassle later if you get it right first time.

Even when Windows is being installed over an existing installation, it is still necessary to enter the product key when the screen of Figure 6.17 appears. The Windows XP installation disc is supplied in a cardboard folder rather than the usual jewel case. The 25-digit product key is on the rear of this folder. Keep the folder safe because it is not possible to reinstall Windows XP without the product key. It is a good idea to keep a copy of the product key in case the folder becomes lost or damaged. With the correct product key typed into the textboxes, operating the Next button will produce a screen like the one in Figure 6.18, and the installation

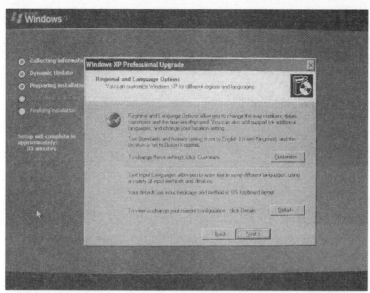

Fig.6.13 This window enables the language settings to be altered

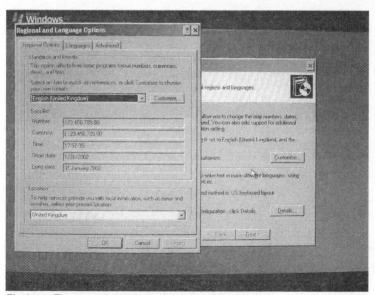

Fig.6.14 These settings control the time format, etc.

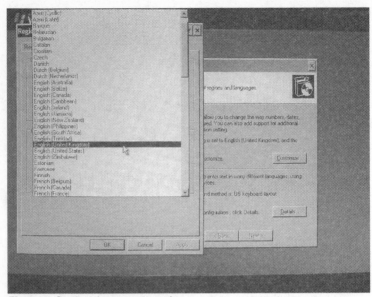

Fig.6.15 Setting the correct region

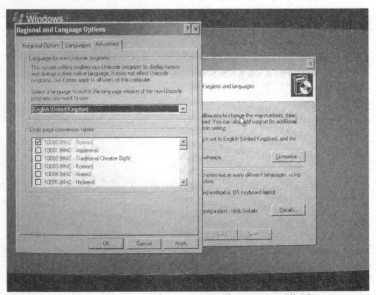

Fig.6.16 Various regions and language settings are available

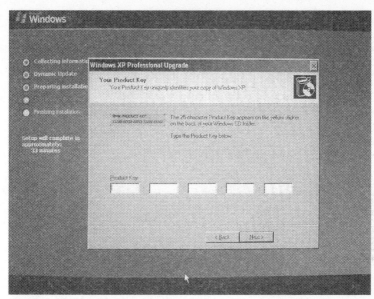

Fig.6.17 The product key is entered here

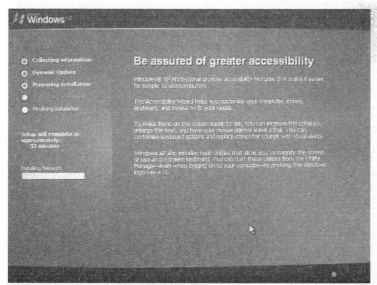

Fig.6.18 The installation process resumes

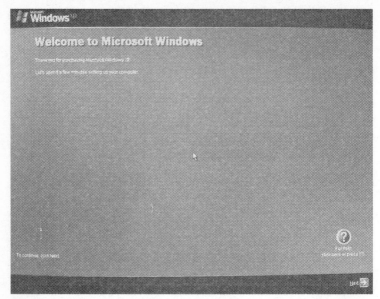

Fig.6.19 With installation complete, the Welcome screen is displayed

process will continue. The computer may then reboot, and the Welcome screen of Figure 6.19 will eventually appear.

Operate the Next button to move on to the screen of Figure 6.20. Using the two radio buttons you can opt to activate the new Windows XP installation or leave this until later. As the computer is proving troublesome, it is probably best to defer the activation process. Activating Windows was described in a previous chapter and it will not be considered further here. At the next screen (Figure 6.21) you can sign on to MSN or continue with reinstallation. It will be assumed here that the second option is taken. The Windows reinstallation is then finished, and the screen of Figure 6.22 will appear to confirm that the process has been completed.

To try out the new installation, operate the Finish button. The computer should then boot into the usual login screen (Figure 6.23). Login using your normal password, and the computer should go into the Windows XP desktop (Figure 6.24). After reinstalling Windows 9x it is necessary to adjust some of the settings in order to provide normal operation. In particular, the reinstalled version of Windows uses very basic video

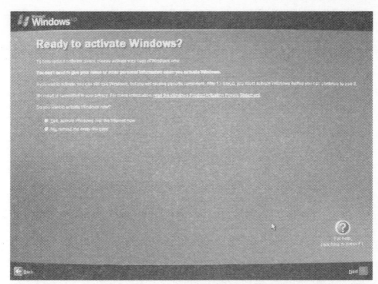

Fig.6.20 It is not essential to activate Windows XP at this stage

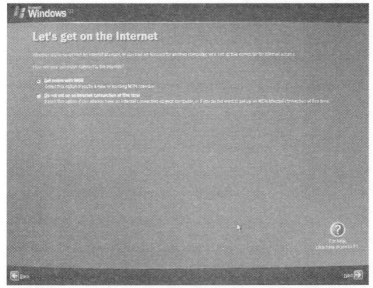

Fig.6.21 You are given the opportunity to get online with MSN

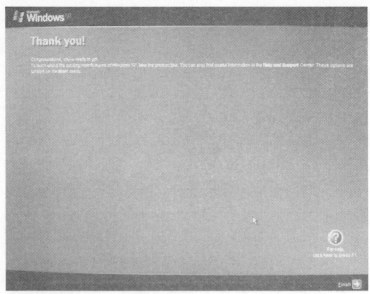

Fig.6.22 This screen confirms that the installation is complete

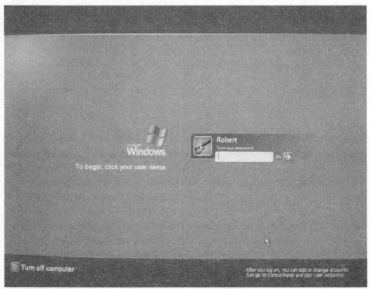

Fig.6.23 The next screen is the usual login type

*Fig.6.24 With reinstallation, the Windows desktop should look as it
did before*

settings, which have to be adjusted to your normal settings. As can be
seen from Figure 6.24, Windows XP uses the previous video settings for
reinstallation, and the new installation should be usable without any
adjustments. With luck the applications programs should remain installed
and fully usable. This depends on exactly what went wrong with the
original installation.

From scratch

The Setup program operates in much the same way when installing
Windows XP from scratch, but there are one or two differences though.
There is no existing installation, so it is not possible for the new installation
to read any information from one. Some additional information therefore
has to be provided during the installation process. You must enter your
details when the screen of Figure 6.25 appears. The same is true of the
passwords, and a new administrator password must be used when the
screen of Figure 6.26 appears. Some general information has to be
entered at the screens of Figure 6.27 and 6.28.

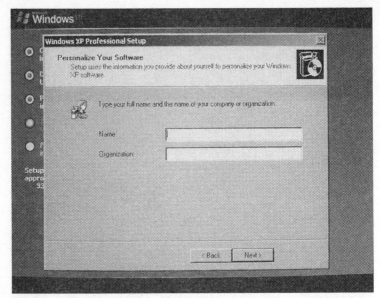

Fig.6.25 Add your name and (optionally) organisation in the textboxes

Near the end of the installation process there may be a small window that asks if Windows can automatically adjust the screen settings. Normally it is best to operate the OK button if this appears. Windows will then start in something better than the basic 640 by 480 pixel resolution. It will probably opt for only 800 by 600 pixel resolution, but this is still much more usable that the basic 640 by 480 pixel mode. After negotiating the usual login screen the computer should go into Windows XP (Figure 6.29). A window asking if you wish to activate Windows XP might appear, but it is probably best to leave activation until you are sure that everything is installed and working perfectly.

Hardware drivers

At this stage you have Windows XP installed or reinstalled, but it is likely that some items of hardware will be either partially operational, or will be simply ignored by Windows. It is possible that Windows will detect all the hardware on the motherboard and install the necessary drivers. If the motherboard hardware is more recent than the version of Windows XP that you are using, then Windows is unlikely to have the correct drivers in its standard repertoire.

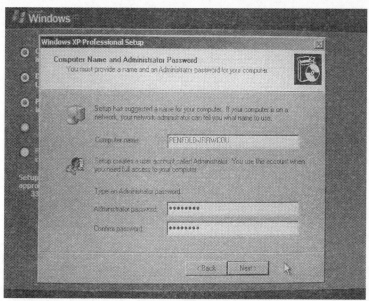

Fig.6.26 *Type the administrator password into the textboxes*

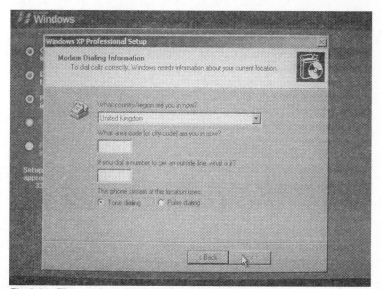

Fig.6.27 *The modem dialling information is added here*

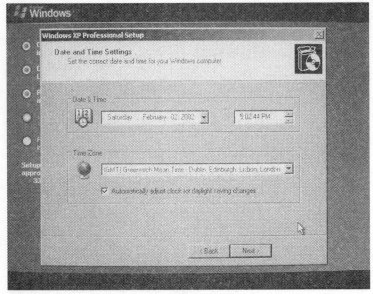

Fig.6.28 Use this window to set the time zone, etc.

It is virtually certain that proper video drivers will be needed. Even if the graphics card can be set to use high resolutions and colour depths, it is almost certainly using a generic driver rather than one designed specifically for the video card in use. Although high resolutions and colour depths can be used, the video system will probably be very slow in operation. There are likely to be other items of hardware that Windows has missed completely or has been unable to identify, especially when it has been installed from scratch.

The installation CD-ROM for the video card will usually auto-run, as in this example, and Figure 6.30 shows the initial window. This provides two options, and in this case is clearly the default "Install the drivers" option that is required. The next window (Figure 6.31) has the usual copyright notice, and operating the Next button moves things on to the licence agreement. Left-clicking the Yes brings up a further window (Figure 6.32), and this one gives the option of loading the on-disc instruction manual onto the hard disc. Since the manual is unlikely to require much disc space it is a good idea to install the documentation onto the hard disc when this option is available.

Fig.6.29 Finally, you are into the newly installed Windows XP

The next window simply shows the options that have been selected, and assuming everything is in order it is just a matter of left clicking the Next button to start installation. Once the files have been copied to the hard disc the window of Figure 6.34 appears. It is definitely advisable to restart the computer immediately rather than waiting until later. This finalises the installation of the drivers and gives you an opportunity to check that the video system is functioning correctly. Installing several sets of device drivers and then restarting the computer might seem to be a more

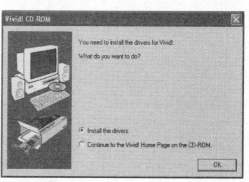

Fig.6.30 The initial window of the installation program

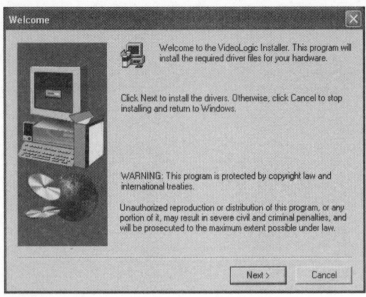

Fig.6.31 The Welcome window includes the usual copyright notice

efficient way of doing things, because the computer only has to be restarted once. In practice it is not a good idea and is simply inviting problems.

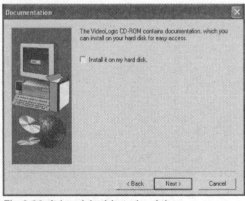

Fig.6.32 It is advisable to load the on-disc manual

Video settings

Windows will almost certainly detect that a new video card has been installed, and it will then produce the message window of Figure 6.35 when the reboot has been completed. Operate the OK button and then adjust the video

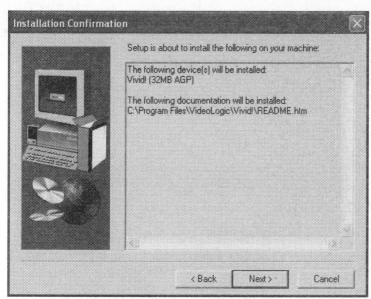

Fig.6.33 This window gives you an opportunity to review the options that have been selected

settings using the Display Properties Window (Figure 6.36), which will be launched automatically. If the newly installed video card is not detected by Windows, the display settings window must be run manually. Launch the Control Panel, double-click the Display icon, and then operate the Settings tab in the window that appears.

Having set the required screen resolution and colour depth, operate the Apply button. It is likely that Windows is overestimating the

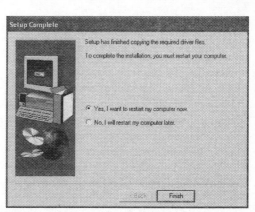

Fig.6.34 Restart the computer to complete the installation

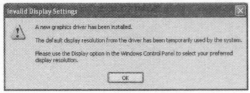

Fig.6.35 Windows will probably detect the newly installed video card

abilities of the monitor if the screen goes blank or produces an unstable image. The screen should return to normal in a few seconds though. One way of tackling

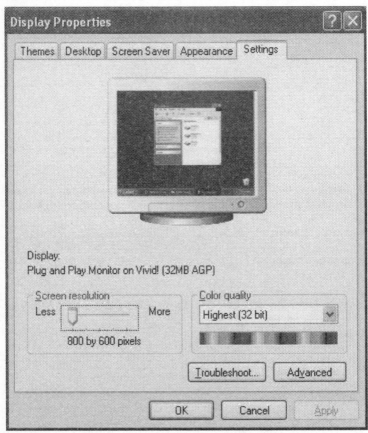

Fig.6.36 Set the required screen resolution and colour depth

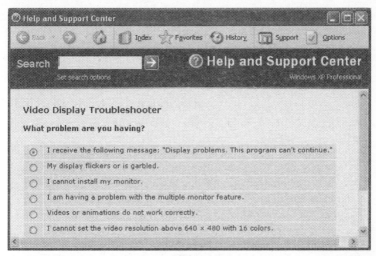

Fig.6.37 The Video Display Troubleshooter

the problem is to operate the Troubleshoot button, which launches the Video Display Troubleshooter, as shown in Figure 6.37. By going through the questions and suggested cures it is likely that the problem would soon be solved. However, the most likely cause of the problem is Windows setting a scan rate that is too high for the monitor, and this is easily corrected.

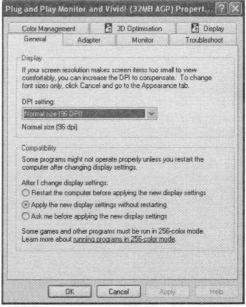

Fig.6.38 The Advanced Settings window

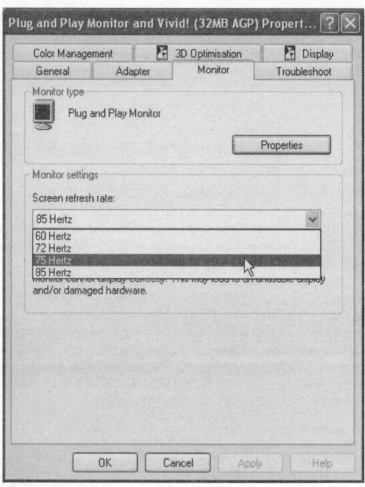

Fig.6.39 A lower scan rate might be needed at high resolutions

Scan rate

First set the required screen resolution again, and then left-click the Advanced button to bring up a window like the one in Figure 6.38. Next, operate the Monitor tab to switch the window to one like Figure 6.39. Activate the Screen refresh rate menu, and choose a lower rate than the

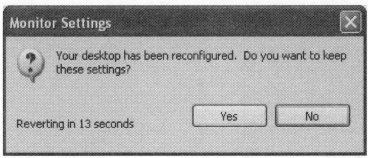

Fig.6.40 The settings return to normal unless the Yes button is operated

one currently in use. In this example the rate was reduced from 85 hertz to 75 hertz. Left-click the Apply button and observe the screen. With luck, this time a small window like the one shown in Figure 6.40 will be visible on the screen. If so, operate the Yes button to keep the new scan rate. If not, wait for a proper display to return and then repeat this process using an even lower scan rate.

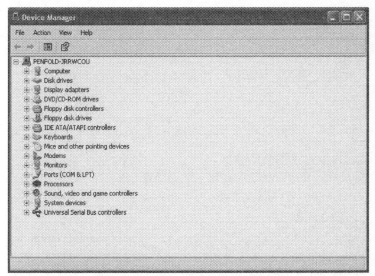

Fig.6.41 Device Manager shows that there are no hardware problems

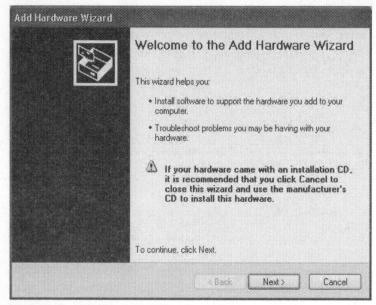

Fig.6.42 The Add Hardware Wizard

Note that the maximum scan rate for a monitor generally reduces as the screen resolution is increased. Consequently, the higher the screen resolution used, the lower the scan rate that will have to be set. Unfortunately, with some monitors there can be noticeable screen-flicker when they are used at the highest resolutions. In general, it is better to use a lower screen resolution in order to obtain a higher scan rate and a flicker-free screen. This is particularly so if you will work at the PC for long periods.

Obviously the installation of the video card will vary slightly from one card to another, but most cards are installed using the general method outlined here. With the video card installed and set up correctly, any further drivers that are needed can be installed. In this example it was only necessary to install some additional device drivers for the audio system. Device Manager then showed no problems with any of the hardware (Figure 6.41), indicating that all the hardware was installed successfully. With the hardware installed properly, it is then a matter of installing all the applications software, undertaking any customisation of

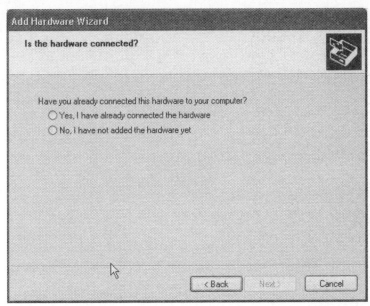

*Fig.6.43 The first check determines whether the hardware
     is connected*

the software, and then installing your data files. The PC is then ready for
use again.

Correct channels

The installation CD-ROMs supplied with most hardware includes a Setup
program. However, in some cases the disc contains device drivers but it
does not include a program to install the drivers. Device drivers
downloaded from the Internet are often in the form of the driver files with
no installation program included. If the instruction manual gives
installation instructions, then follow them. Unfortunately, with some low-
cost hardware you are simply left to your own devices. The same is true
of many device drivers obtained via the Internet, but check for a Readme
file or installation advice on the source web site.

It is not strictly necessary to have an installation program, and Windows
has a built-in system for tackling the installation of hardware that lacks
this facility. The first step with this type of hardware is to launch the Add

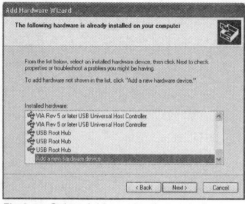

Fig.6.44 Select Add new hardware device

Hardware Wizard. Go to the Control Panel, double-click the System icon, and then operate the Hardware tab in the System Properties window. In the upper section of this window there is an Add Hardware Wizard button, and operating this launches the wizard (Figure 6.42).

Heed the warning notice about using the manufacturer's installation program wherever possible. Double-check the installation CD-ROM or web site to ensure

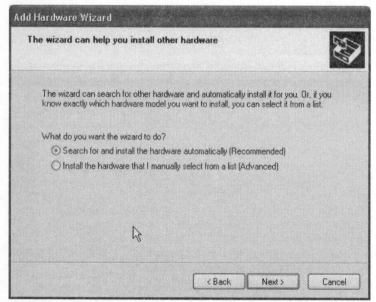

Fig.6.45 Manual installation is probably the best option here

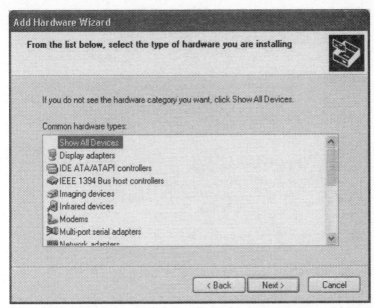

Fig.6.46 Select the correct category for the new hardware

that it does not contain an Install or Setup program. If you are sure that it does not, operate the Next button to move the wizard on to the next stage (Figure 6.43). The Add Hardware Wizard uses the normal technique of suggestions and questions to (hopefully) find the right answers. The first screen simply determines whether the hardware is already connected to the PC. Unless the manufacturer specifically advises otherwise, the hardware must be physically installed before the device drivers are loaded.

Assuming that the hardware is already connected, the next window provides a list of the detected hardware. Obviously the entry for the hardware should be selected if it is found in the list. If it has not been detected and listed by Windows, select the Add a new device option (Figure 6.44). The next window (Figure 6.45) gives the option of installing the device manually or having Windows try to detect it. There is no harm in trying the detection method, but it is likely Windows is incapable of detecting the hardware if it has not done so already. Taking the manual route produces a window like the one of Figure 6.46. This gives a list of hardware types, and you must select the correct category for the device you are trying to install.

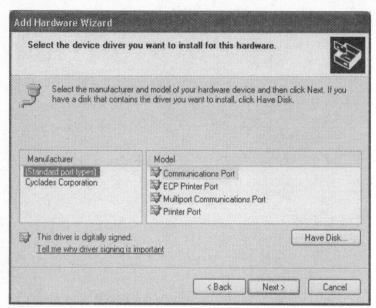

Fig.6.47 It is normally the Have Disk option that is needed here

Moving on to the next window (Figure 6.47) gives a list of manufacturers in the left-hand section, and devices for the selected manufacturer in the right-hand section. Obviously you should select the appropriate entry for your device if it is listed, but this is unlikely. It is normally necessary to operate the Have Disk button, which brings up a window like the one

Fig.6.48 Give the location of the driver files

of Figure 6.48. Either type the path to the disc and folder containing the device drivers, or use the Browse option to locate the drivers. Having pointed Windows to the drivers, the installation process then follows along normal lines.

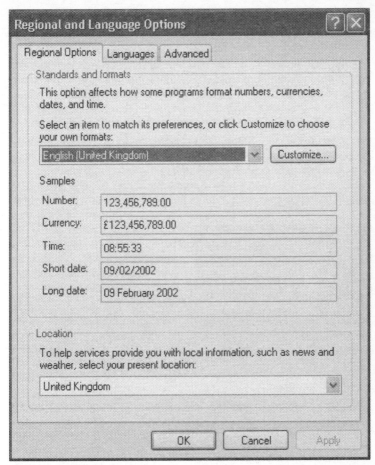

Fig.6.49 Check that the Regional and Language settings are correct

Language problems

Back in the days of MS-DOS it was often quite tricky to persuade the operating system that you were using a keyboard having the English (UK) version of the English layout, rather than one having the US English characters and layout. The differences are quite minor, but they result in the double quotes and @ symbol being transposed. Also, the pound sign (£) tends to disappear or be replaced with the hash (#) symbol. Some of the little-used symbols also disappear or become assigned to the wrong keys.

Windows XP can suffer from a similar problem after it has been reinstalled from scratch, even if you did make the appropriate changes to the Regional settings during installation. If you are not careful the result is that both English and US English keyboards are installed, with the US version set as the default. Fortunately, this problem is easily cured.

The obvious first step is to go to the Control Panel and double-click the keyboard icon. This is the first thing to try if the keyboard is not working at all, but with a language problem it is unlikely to be of any help. It is better to start by going to the Control Panel and double-clicking the Regional and Language icon. This produces a properties window like

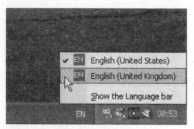

the one in Figure 6.49, which is essentially the same as the one that appears during the installation process. Check the various sections to make sure that the correct language is set.

If everything is correct, look at the bottom right-hand corner of the Windows desktop. Here there will be a button that indicates the language in use. This will usually be marked EN for English, but as

Fig.6.50 Choose the correct language version

pointed out previously, more than one version of the language will probably be available. Left-click the button to produce a small popup menu (Figure 6.50), and then select the English (United Kingdom) option. The keyboard should then function properly, producing the pound sign, etc. However, the wrong version of English will be set as the default.

To correct this, activate the menu again and select the Show the language bar option. This removes the button and produces a small floating bar instead (Figure 6.51). Operate the tiny

Fig.6.51 Choose the Settings option from the popup menu

button in the bottom right-hand corner of the bar and select Settings from the popup menu. This launches the Text Services and Input Languages window (Figure 6.52). Use the pop-down menu near the top of the window to select the correct default language. Next operate the Apply and OK buttons, and then restart the computer to check that the default has switched to the right language.

Fig.6.52 Set the correct default language

User accounts

By default, only one account with administrator privileges is normally produced when Windows XP is installed from scratch. Any other accounts you require have to be set up manually. The Administrator account is usually reserved for making changes to the system or troubleshooting, since it gives full control over the system. There is no real need to add an extra account if the computer will only be used by one person. The situation is different when the computer will have two or more users, and it is preferable to have a separate account for each user in addition to the Administrator account.

The first step in adding a new account is to go to the Control Panel and double-click the User Accounts icon. This launches a window like the one in Figure 6.53. Left-click the link for Create a new account, which switches the window to the one shown in Figure 6.54. Type a name for the account into the textbox and then operate the Next button.

The type of account is selected at the next window (Figure 6.55). An administrator account provides freedom to make changes to the system,

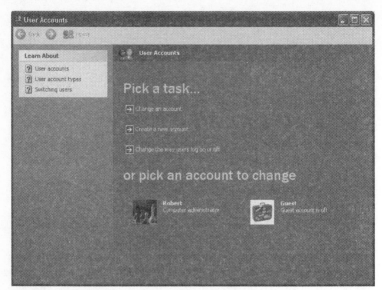

Fig.6.53 The initial version of the User Accounts window

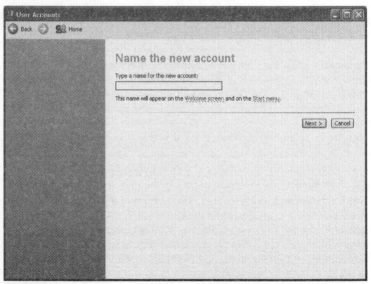

Fig.6.54 Type a name for the account into the textbox

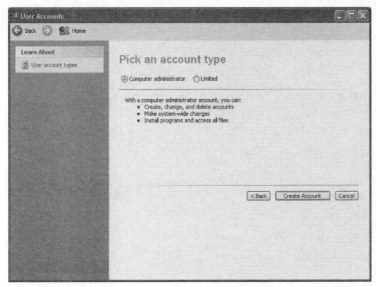

Fig.6.55 Use this window to select the most suitable type of account

but these abilities are not needed for day to day use of the computer. A limited account is generally considered to be the better choice for normal use, since the restrictions reduce the risk of the system being accidentally damaged. Note that you might not be able to install programs when using a limited account. Also, some programs produced prior to Windows 2000 and XP might not be usable with a limited account. Consequently, there is no alternative to an administrator account if maximum flexibility is required.

Having selected the type of account using the radio buttons, operate the Create Account button. The original User Accounts window then returns, but it should now contain the newly created account (Figure 6.56). There are other facilities in the User Accounts window that enable the login and logoff settings to be altered. By default, the Welcome screen is shown at start up, and you simply have to left-click the entry for the new account in order to use it. Note that the new account will start with a largely blank desktop. Each account has its own desktop and other settings, so each account can be customised with the best settings for its particular user.

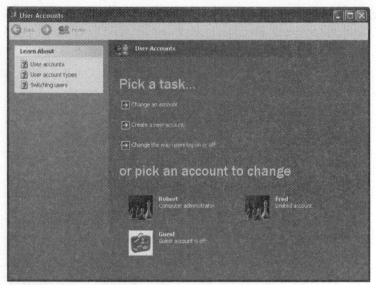

Fig.6.56 An icon has been added for the newly created account

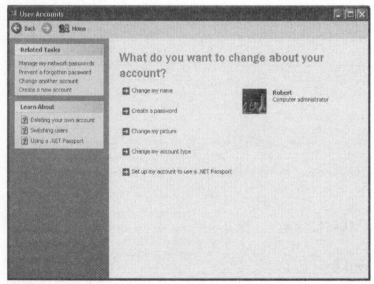

Fig.6.57 Operate the Create Password link

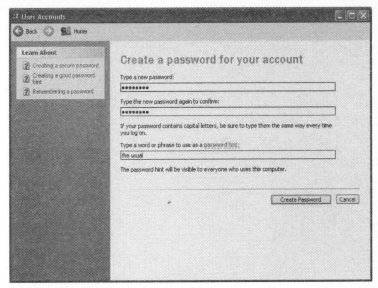

Fig.6.58 Type the password into the top two textboxes

Accounts are not password protected by default. To add a password, go to the User Accounts window and left-click the entry for the account that you wish to password protect. This switches the window to look like Figure 6.57, and here the Create password link is activated. At the next window (Figure 6.58) the password is typed into the top two textboxes, and a hint is entered into the other textbox. The hint is something that will jog your memory if you should happen to forget the password.

Next operate the Create Password button, which moves things on to the window of Figure 6.59. This window explains that password protection does not prevent other users from reading your files. Operate the Yes Make Private button if you would like to prevent other users from accessing your files. This completes the process, and the password will be needed the next time you login to that account.

Registering

It is important for Windows XP users to realise that, unlike previous versions of Windows, registering the program is not optional. Strictly speaking, it is not necessary to register Windows XP in order to go on

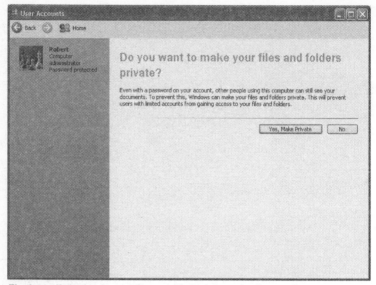

Fig.6.59 If desired, your files and folders can be kept private

using it indefinitely. It is the Windows Product Activation (WPA) that is essential, but this is normally done as part of the registration process. In effect, the Windows XP CD-ROM contains a fully working 30-day demonstration version of the operating system. If you ignore the onscreen warning messages and do not go through the WPA/registration process, the operating system will refuse to boot properly.

All is not lost if you reach this stage, because it is still possible to go through the WPA/registration process and get the operating system working again. When you try to boot into Windows a message like the

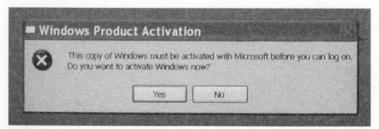

Fig.6.60 Operate the Yes button to go ahead with activation

one shown in Figure 6.60 appears. In order to go on using the operating system it is necessary to operate the Yes button and proceed with the WPA process. Note that you can not log on to Windows by selecting the No option. You can only log off and shut down the computer if this button is operated.

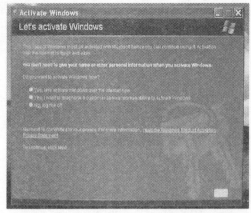

Fig.6.61 Activation can be via telephone or the Internet

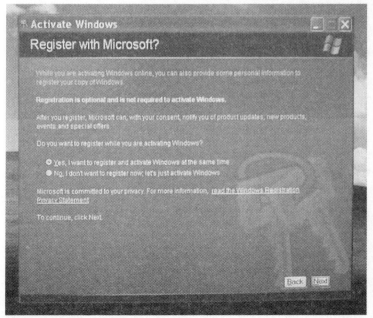

Fig.6.62 You can register at the same time as activating Windows XP

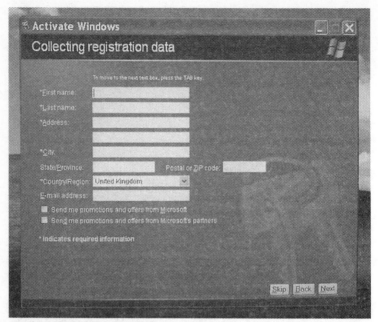

Fig.6.63 This form appears if you opt for online registration

Having opted to go ahead with the activation procedure, the window of Figure 6.61 appears. This gives the option of registering by telephone, over the Internet, or halting the activation process and logging off. It is definitely a good idea to use the Internet option if the PC is suitably equipped, since this is much quicker and easier than verbally exchanging multi-digit product keys and activation numbers over the telephone. It virtually guarantees that the process will be free of errors and will work first time. The Internet method is the only one that we will consider here, but the program provides full instructions if you have to use the telephone route to activation.

After selecting the required option, operate the Next button to move the process on to the next window (Figure 6.62). This gives the choice of activating the program, or activating and registering it at the same time. The obvious choice is to activate the program and also register it while you are at it. If this option is selected, at the next screen the usual registration details are entered (Figure 6.63). Moving on to the next screen

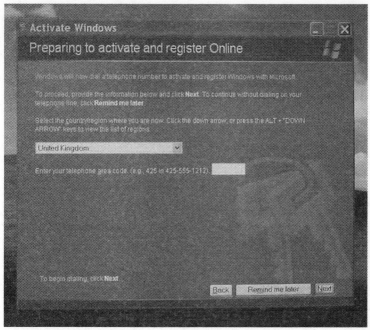

Fig.6.64 Select your country from the pop-down menu

(Figure 6.64), your country is selected from the pop-down menu and you telephone area code is entered in the textbox.

Operating the Next button brings up the window of Figure 6.65, and the program dials the server. The activation and registration processes are fully automated, and after a minute or two the screen of Figure 6.66 should appear, indicating that both processes have been completed successfully. After operating the OK button to close this window, the PC is ready for you to log on to Windows.

Anti-piracy

Windows Product Activation is a new feature of Windows XP, and to say the least, this feature is bit controversial. The idea is to prevent casual piracy of the XP operating system. However, like most anti-piracy systems, it does not make life any easier for legitimate users of the

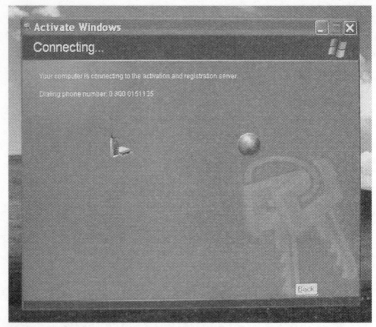

Fig.6.65 The registration/WPA process is then automatic

product. It can make life very much more difficult for legitimate users, although it will not necessarily do so.

As pointed out previously, the program on the disc when you buy Windows XP is effectively just a 30-day demonstration version. Entering the product identification number during installation was sufficient to get earlier versions of Windows fully working, but with Windows XP it is only the first step in the activation process. You are locked out of the system if you do not activate Windows within 30 days of installing it, so you have to activate Windows or keep installing it from scratch!

Where possible, it is definitely advisable to opt for automatic activation via the Internet. The telephone alternative requires you to read a 50-digit code to a Microsoft representative. This code appears onscreen during the activation process. This is bad enough, but you then have to enter a 42-digit code supplied by the representative. This is clearly an awkward and time-consuming way of doing things, and there is plenty of scope

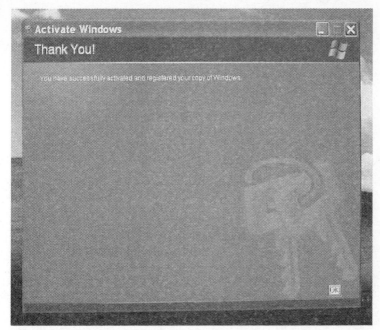

Fig.6.66 This screen will appear if the process is successful

for errors to occur. By contrast, activation over the Internet is quick and there is virtually no chance of errors occurring.

WPA problems

Having to go through the WPA process should be no more than a minor inconvenience, and it is not the necessity for activation that is the main "bone of contention". The activation key is derived from your Windows product identification number and the hardware installed in the PC. To be more precise, it is these items of hardware that are used to produce the number:

Microprocessor type

Microprocessor serial number

Display adapter

SCSI adapter (if fitted)

IDE adapter

Network adapter (if fitted)

RAM amount

Hard drive

Hard drive volume serial number

CD drives

When Windows XP is booted, as part of the boot-up process the installed hardware is checked. The boot process is only completed if the installed hardware matches the full product key that is stored on the hard disc drive during the activation process. On the face of it, two computers having identical hardware could use the same activation key. In practice, this is not possible because the network adapter and processor serial numbers are unique. Two seemingly identical PCs would actually need different activation keys due to the processors and (where appropriate) the network card having different serial numbers.

There is a potential problem, in that any changes to the hardware will cause a mismatch during the checking process at boot-up. This problem is not as great as it might seem, because you are allowed a certain amount of leeway. Up to four of the items of hardware listed previously can be altered without the need to reactivate the operating system. If more than four items are changed, the activation mechanism will probably assume that the system has been copied to another computer, and it will halt the boot process.

This does not mean that you will have to buy Windows XP again. It will be necessary to call the WPA clearing house though, in order to obtain a new activation key. Frequent changes to the computer's hardware and calls to the WPA centre would presumably result in Microsoft refusing to provide further activation codes. You are permitted four changes to the hardware in 120 days or less. This suggests that you can make as many changes to the hardware as you like provided they are made slowly so that there are no more than four changes in each 120-day period. I have not tested this in practice though.

There is little likelihood of problems unless you undertake a massive hardware upgrade. A call to the WPA centre should then get things working again. However, it is best not to be too eager to activate a newly installed copy of Windows XP. This is especially important when upgrading from an earlier version of Windows or installing Windows XP on a new PC. In both cases there will be a few doubts about the compatibility of some pieces of hardware.

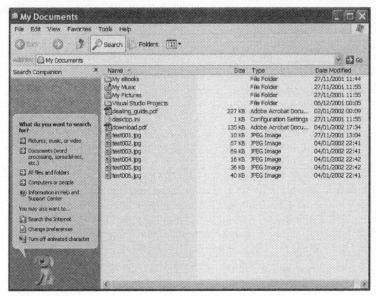

Fig.6.67 The Windows XP version of Windows Explorer

You are given the opportunity to go through the activation process once installation has been completed, but it is probably best not to do so at that stage. First, load any hardware drivers that are required, and try out the new system. If necessary, obtain new versions of device drivers, and only go through the activation process when everything is working properly. You have 30 days to get everything working properly, which should be more than ample. It is not necessary to wait for the 30 days to expire before activating Windows XP. The activation process can be started at any time by going to the Start menu, selecting All Programs, followed by Accessories, System Tools, and Activate Windows.

WPA file

Computer hardware is not infallible, and it is possible that it will be necessary to reinstall Windows XP at some point during the computer's operating life. Some PC users reinstall Windows from time to time as a means of clearing out the defunct files that tend to accumulate on the hard disc, and to keep the system working efficiently. There is no limit to

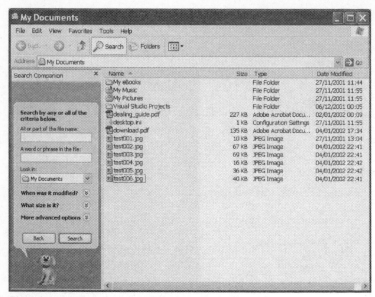

Fig.6.68 Using the Windows Explorer Search facility

the number of times that Windows XP can be reinstalled on the same PC, but reactivation is necessary each time Windows is reinstalled.

There is an alternative to reactivation, and the first step is to make a backup copy of a certain file before deleting the old installation. After Windows XP has been reinstalled, the backup copy of the file is copied to the hard disc. The file in question is called wpa.dbl, and it will normally be placed in the C:\Windows\System32 folder. If it proves to be elusive, track it down using the Search facility of Windows Explorer. Run Windows Explorer and then operate the Search button in the upper part of the window. The screen should then look something like Figure 6.67.

In the left-hand section of the window there is an animated character called Rover, and this is Windows XP's answer to the infamous animated paperclip of Word For Windows. Left-click on the All Files and Folders button to bring up the form that enables the search criteria to be defined (Figure 6.68). Type the name of the file (wpa.dbl) into the textbox at the top of the form, and select drive C: using the menu near the middle of the form. Operate the Search button, and after scanning the hard disc the program should produce an entry for the file in the right-hand section

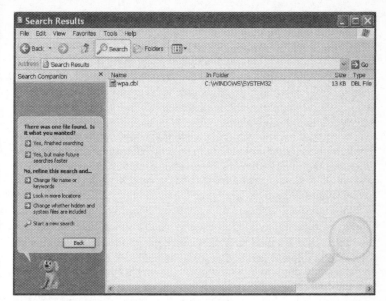

Fig.6.69 The required file has been located

of the window (Figure 6.69). The size of the file is only about 10 to 15 kilobytes, so it can be copied to a floppy disc using the Copy and Paste facilities. It can be restored using the same method once Windows XP has been reinstalled.

There is no guarantee that this will always work, but it is merely necessary to go through the activation process if it fails. In the event that the restored wpa.dbl file is not accepted by the system, next time you log on there will be the choice of going through the activation process or logging off again. If you elect to log off it will be possible to log on to the system at the next attempt, but you will then have the usual 30 days before the system times out and locks you out of the system.

Disc cloning

On the face of it, there is an easy way of setting up the hard disc of a new PC if you have an old PC that has the operating system, programs, etc., already installed. Using a program such as Power Quest's Drive Copy or Drive Image it is possible to make a clone of the old hard disc using the new one. The old hard disc is temporarily installed in the new PC so that the old installation can be copied across to the new disc. The advantage of this method is that it sets up the new disc with the operating system, applications programs, and your data files installed and ready for use. Any customisation should also be intact on the cloned system.

Unfortunately, there is a problem with this system when used in this fashion. There should be no major difficulties when it is used to upgrade to a larger hard disc on a system that is otherwise the same as before. One or two passwords stored in hidden files might not be copied to the cloned version, and they will have to be entered again when the relevant programs are used for the first time. Apart from this the system should work as before, since the hardware and the device drivers are the same for the cloned version.

The situation is different when a system is copied from one PC to another. The hardware in the new PC will presumably be substantially different to the hardware in the old PC. This tends to get Windows confused when the cloned system is first booted, and the hardware does not match up with the hardware drivers on the disc. Due to the Plug and Play facility, Windows will detect the problem and should not go ahead with the installation of unsuitable device drivers. Instead, it will start installing the new hardware.

In theory, after a lot of rebooting and supplying driver discs at the appropriate times, the computer should boot into Windows and operate properly. In practice the changes can be too drastic, causing the reinstallation process to fail at some point. Windows 95 is not good at adjusting to large changes in the system, but later versions of Windows tend to be more accommodating. Even if Windows does manage to make the necessary adjustments, there is no guarantee the system will operate reliably and efficiently. Some aspects of operation could be very slow and (or) there could be frequent crashes. Of course, there is no harm in trying this approach. The operating system, etc., can be installed from scratch if the cloning method fails to give a fully working installation.

XP second drive

As pointed out previously, Windows XP has been designed as an MS-DOS-free zone, and it is not necessary to use the MS-DOS FDISK and FORMAT programs when a second hard disc is added to a Windows XP system. I suppose that these programs could be used, but it would

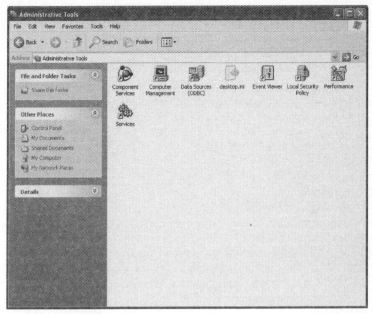

Fig.6.70 The Administrative Tools window

definitely be doing things the hard way. There is a built-in program that greatly simplifies the partitioning and formatting of hard drives.

This program can be run by going to the Windows Control Panel and double-clicking the Administrative Tools icon, which produces a window like the one of Figure 6.70. Double-clicking the Computer Management icon produces the new window of Figure 6.71. Several utilities are available from the Computer Management window, but the one required in this case is Disk Management. Left-clicking this entry in the left-hand panel changes the window to look something like Figure 6.72.

Details of the boot drive are given at the top of the right-hand panel. The bottom section gives details of both drives, and the new drive is Disk 1. This is described as "Unallocated", which means that it is not partitioned or formatted at this stage. The black line to the right of the Disk 1 label and icon also indicates that it is not partitioned.

To partition the disc, right-click on the black line and then select the New Partition option from the popup menu. This launches the New Partition Wizard (Figure 6.73). Windows XP can use two types of disc, which are

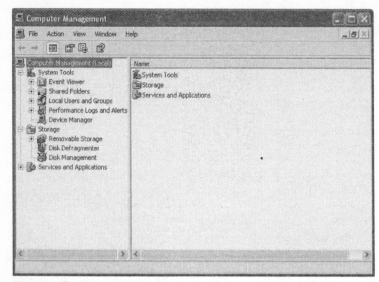

Fig.6.71 *The Computer Management window provides access to several utilities*

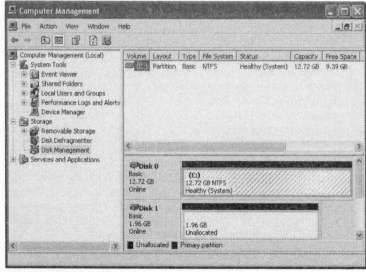

Fig.6.72 *The window with the Disk Management utility selected*

the basic and dynamic varieties. The New Partition Wizard only handles basic discs, and these use conventional partitions that are essentially the same as those used by MS-DOS and earlier versions of Windows. For most purposes a basic disc is perfectly adequate.

Fig.6.73 The opening screen of the Partition Wizard

Operate the Next button to move on with the partitioning, and a window like the one in Figure 6.74 should appear. Either an extended or a primary partition can be selected using

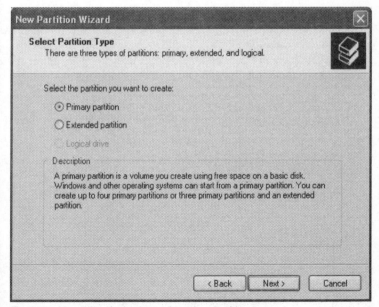

Fig.6.74 Use this window to select the partition type

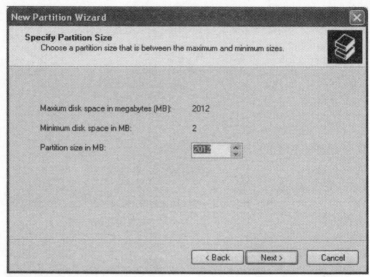

Fig.6.75 This window is used to set the partition size (in megabytes)

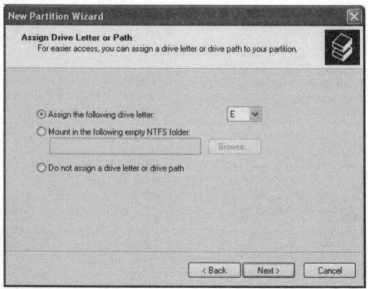

Fig.6.76 Here a drive letter is assigned to the new partition

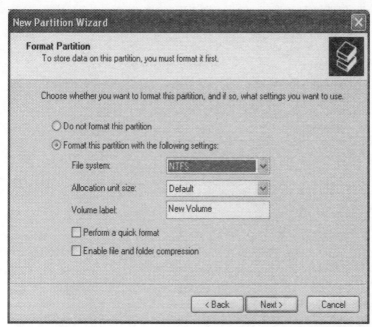

Fig.6.77 The partition can be formatted as a NTFS, FAT, or FAT32 type

the radio buttons, and in this case it is a primary partition that is needed.
The size of the partition is selected at the next window (Figure 6.75), and
the maximum and minimum usable sizes are indicated. All the available
disc space will be used by default, but a different size can be used by
typing a value (in megabytes) into the textbox. Operating the Next button
brings up the window of Figure 6.76 where a drive letter is assigned to
the new partition. Unless there is a good reason to do otherwise, simply
accept the default drive letter.

Formatting

At the next window (Figure 6.77) you have the choice of formatting the
new partition or leaving it unformatted. Since the partition will not be
usable until it is formatted, accept the formatting option. One of the
menus offers a choice of FAT, FAT32, or NTFS formatting. Settle for the
default option of NTFS formatting unless you need compatibility with
another Windows operating system. Also settle for the default allocation

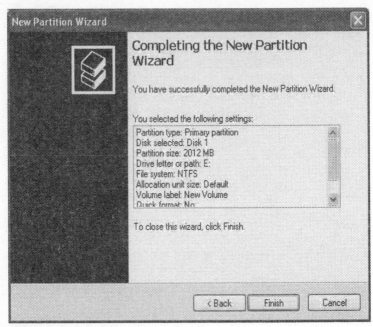

Fig.6.78 This window lists the parameters that have been selected

unit size, which will be one that is appropriate for the partition size. A different name for the drive, such as "Backup", can be entered into the textbox if desired. Tick the appropriate checkbox if you wish to enable file and folder compression.

Left-click the Next button when you are satisfied with the settings. The next window (Figure 6.78) lists all the parameters that have been selected, and provides an opportunity to change your mind or correct mistakes. If necessary, use the Back button to return to earlier windows and change some of the settings. Operate the Finish button if all the settings are correct. The partition will then be created, and it will appear as a blue line in the Disk Management window.

It will then be formatted, and this may take half an hour or more for a large partition. The area below the blue line indicates how far the formatting process has progressed. Eventually the formatting will be completed, and the Disk Management window will show the new disc as

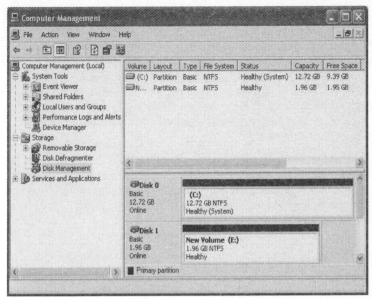

Fig.6.79 The Disk Management window shows the new partition

containing a primary partition using the appropriate file system (Figure 6.79). Once the formatting has been completed, files on the main drive can be copied to the new partition using the Cut and Paste facilities of Windows Explorer.

If space has been left for a further partition on the disc, right-click on the black section of the line that represents the vacant disc space. Then select the New Partition option from the popup menu, and go through the whole partitioning and formatting process again. A maximum of four primary partitions can be used on each physical disc.

Points to remember

PCs that are supplied with Windows XP preinstalled are not necessarily supplied with a normal Windows installation disc. There should be no problem in using Windows from a defunct PC provided the PC was supplied with a standard installation CD-ROM. Versions of Windows that only have some form of quick recovery disc are usually restricted to use with the original PC.

When installing or reinstalling Windows XP from scratch it is not necessary to reformat the hard disc prior to installation. Any necessary partitioning, formatting, and reformatting can be carried out using the Windows XP Setup program.

The installation process for Windows XP is largely automatic. The user provides some basic information and then the Setup program installs the Windows files and sets up the essential hardware.

Once Windows XP has been installed, some further work is required to get all the hardware properly installed, the screen resolution and colour depth set correctly, etc. Some hardware has its own installation routines and does not go through the normal Windows routes. In fact, most hardware is now installed in this way. Always install hardware in accordance with the manufacturer's instructions.

Install the device drivers for system hardware on the motherboard first, followed by the video drivers, and then any other drivers that are needed. Do not install applications software until all the hardware is fully installed and working properly.

The Text Services and Input Languages window can be used to correct things if the computer defaults to using the US English keyboard layout.

It is a good idea to have an Administrator account plus an account for each user if a PC will have more than one user. The Administrator account is normally produced during the installation process. Other accounts can be generated by going to the User Accounts window, which is accessed via the Control Panel.

Unlike previous versions of Windows, it is necessary to go through the activation process after installing Windows XP. You have 30 days after installation before the system will refuse to boot, so there is time to get the system working properly before going through the activation process.

An existing installation can be cloned onto the hard disc of the new PC. This is a quick way of getting the operating system, etc., installed, but there is no guarantee that it will produce an efficient and reliable set up.

Troubleshooting

Prevention

Provided you proceed carefully, checking and double-checking everything as you go, and observing the basic anti-static handling precautions, you will be very unlucky indeed if the finished computer fails to start up correctly. However meticulous you are though, there is still an outside chance that things will not go perfectly, and if you take an "it will be all right on the night" approach to things it is likely that things will be far from all right when the new PC is switched on.

This is definitely something where the old adage that "prevention is better than cure" applies. Most computer components are reasonably idiot-proof, and if an error should be made it is unlikely that any damage will occur. This possibility can not be totally ruled out though, and there is a small but real risk of mistakes proving to be quite costly. Check everything as you go along, and then carefully recheck the finished PC before switching it on.

If possible, get someone to check everything for you. Having fooled yourself into making a mistake it is easy to make the same mistake when you check the finished unit. The mistake will probably be glaringly obvious to a fresh pair of eyes.

Blank expression

A faulty PC may start to go through the initial start-up routine and then fail at some stage, usually after the initial BIOS checks as the computer goes into the boot-up phase. Alternatively it may simply refuse to do anything, or sit there on the desk producing "beeping" noises with a blank screen. We will start by considering likely causes if the computer does very little, or even nothing at all.

If switching on the PC results in nothing happening at all, with no sign of cooling fans operating or front panel lights switching on, the obvious first step is to check that power is getting to the computer. Is the power lead plugged in properly at both the computer and the mains outlet, and is the mains supply switched on at the outlet? It is a silly mistake to forget to plug the computer into the mains supply or to switch on the supply, but it is easily done in your haste to try out the new PC. Also check that the fuse in the mains plug is present and correct.

A PC power supply is a fairly sophisticated piece of electronics that contains numerous protection circuits. The fact that it fails to operate even though it is receiving power does not necessarily mean that it is faulty. It could simply be that a protection circuit is detecting a problem somewhere and is shutting down the supply circuit. An overload on one of the supply lines could cause this, but is not a likely cause of the problem with a new PC. However, you can not totally rule out the possibility that the cause of the problem is a fault in one of the components that the supply is powering.

Leads

A more likely cause is that the leads carrying the output of the supply are not connected properly. In the unlikely event that the supply is an AT type, it is possible to get the two supply connectors swapped at the motherboard. Fortunately, the supply should detect this problem and fail to switch on, ensuring that costly damage is avoided. With the power supply connected correctly the black leads should be grouped together in the middle (refer back to Figure 3.58 in chapter 3). If the black leads are at the ends of the row of leads the two connectors have been swapped over.

A normal ATX power supply only has one lead and connector that goes to the motherboard and this can only be connected the right way round. In theory this makes it impossible to get things wrong, but in practice this type of power connector can be difficult to get properly into place. In fact this applies to most types of power connector, and I suppose it is a byproduct of making the connectors fit very firmly together so that good connections are produced.

It is worth removing and refitting the power connector to the motherboard to make quite sure that it is fully pressed down and into place. An ATX power supply is switched on and off via a simple pushbutton switch on the front of the case, and not by way of a conventional on/off switch in the mains supply. Check that the on/off switch is connected to the motherboard correctly. If the PC uses a Pentium 4 motherboard that requires the two supplementary power leads, make sure that these are both connected to the motherboard correctly.

AMD approved

Occasionally there is a problem with a PC that seems to power-up correctly, but does not go into the POST routine. In fact the PC will usually start correctly on some occasions, but not on others, with the fault occurring randomly. This seems to occur more with PCs based on AMD processors than those having Intel chips. It seems to stem from a problem with the power supply, which is probably failing to establish the main supplies with suitable rapidity, or perhaps there is some initial noise on the supply lines that is causing problems.

Anyway, whatever the cause, you either have to learn to live with the problem or try fitting a new supply. When building a PC based on an AMD processor it is advisable to obtain a power supply that is AMD approved. This should avoid these start-up problems. Also, if the supply should fail to work properly with a motherboard fitted with an AMD processor, you then have good grounds for complaint.

If the mains supply seems to be getting through to the power supply unit all right, and the on/off switch and motherboard are connected to the power supply correctly, it is time to look further afield for the problem. It is unlikely that a faulty drive is causing an overload, but it is as well to check this by disconnecting the drive power leads.

It is worth making the point that you should not disconnect and reconnect any leads with the computer switched on. Doing so with power or data leads could result in costly damage, with you creating more faults than you fix! If any changes to the cabling are required, switch off the computer, make the changes, and then switch on again. Ideally the drive data cables should also be disconnected when making this test. With no power supplied to the drives they could provide abnormal loading on the data cables and could conceivable cause damage to the motherboard, although the chances of this occurring are admittedly quite remote.

It is possible that the problem is simply that the power supply is overloaded. This is very unlikely to happen provided you use a supply having a rating of at least 350 watts. Bargain PC cases having supplies rated at 300 watts or less are fine for rejuvenating an ageing PC, but are not well suited for use as the basis of a new computer. A rating of 350 watts is usually adequate, but a supply rated at 400 watts or more is better if the PC has a lot of drives or expansion cards.

An overloaded power supply may not simply result in the PC refusing to start. In my experience it is more likely that the PC will start up all right but it will tend to sporadically reset or switch off for no apparent reason. The power drain varies from one instant to another depending on what the PC is actually doing. Presumably one of the supply rails drops to an inadequate level during peaks of power consumption, causing the PC's monitoring circuits to reset or switch off the computer.

On the cards

If removing power from the drives does not effect a cure it is time to restore power to the drives and move on to the expansion cards. Switch off the computer, remove all the expansion cards, and then switch on again. In my experience the expansion cards are often the cause of problems, and removing them will often result in an otherwise "dead" PC bursting into life. If the cause of the problem is a faulty card, reinserting the cards one by one will soon reveal which card is at fault. When the computer ceases to start up again, the last card restored is the faulty one. Of course, the computer must be switched off before each card is installed. Adding or removing a card with the computer switched on does not guarantee that something will be damaged, but it nearly does.

Do not be surprised if having restored all the cards in the computer it still starts up properly. This will not be due to the faulty card having been miraculously cured, but is simply due to the fact that it was not originally installed correctly. If a card is not slotted into the motherboard correctly it can cause short circuits that will prevent the power supply from operating. The expansion card system used in PCs is a decided asset, which makes it easy to produce custom PCs that exactly suit given requirements. It also makes it easy to change the configuration of a PC to suit changing circumstances.

The drawback of this system is that there are numerous contacts on the expansion card connectors, and the card and motherboard connectors must be accurately aligned if everything is to work properly. Some PCs fit together better than others, but it can sometimes be difficult to get the cards into place, and nothing seems to fit correctly. When this happens the usual cause is the motherboard being slightly out of position on the base panel of the case.

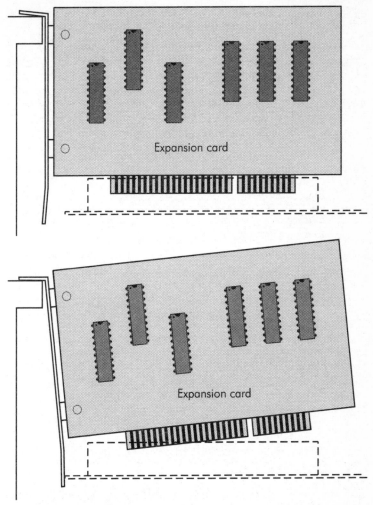

Fig.7.1 A mounting bracket can cause problems if it does not have the correct right-angled bend

On the level

Do not simple wrestle with the expansion cards until they are eventually forced into place. Apart from the very real risk of damaging the cards and the motherboard, boards forced into place in this fashion are unlikely

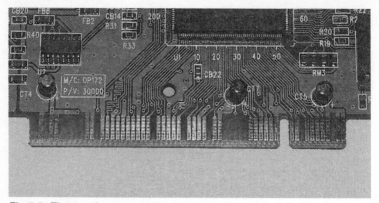

Fig.7.2 The gap between adjacent contacts on an expansion card is very small, making accurate alignment of the card and slot absolutely essential

to stay in place very long. If expansion cards are proving troublesome it is usually possible to sort things out by slightly loosening the screws that hold the motherboard in place. Fit the expansion cards and then tighten the motherboard's mounting bolts again.

You may occasionally find that an expansion card plugs into place perfectly well, but when its retaining bolt is tightened it tends to lift up out of its expansion slot. In most cases it is only the front end of the card that shifts out of position. The usual cause of this is the metal mounting bracket on the card not having a proper 90-degree bend at the top where it bolts to the rear of the case. This results in the card tending to lift out of the expansion slot at one end when the fixing bolt it tightened. This is shown in somewhat exaggerated form in Figure 7.1. The cure is to carefully bend the bracket to the correct angle with the aid of a small vice or some sturdy pliers.

Note that it only needs the card to lift slightly at one end or the other to totally "gum up" the computer. There are only minute gaps between the metal contacts on the connector of an expansion card (Figure 7.2). If the connector fits into the expansion slot at a slight angle this produces short-circuits along the rows of terminals. This in turn produces short-circuits on the supply lines, causing the power supply to shut down. With luck this should prevent any damage from occurring, but it is much better if you can spot a badly fitting card before you switch on the PC.

Another occasional cause of problems is a mounting bracket that is too high or too low on the expansion card. If it is mounted too low down on the card it will prevent the card from going down into the slot correctly. When this occurs it is usually possible to loosen the screws that fix the bracket to the card, pull the bracket into the correct position, and then retighten the screws.

Another problem with the expansion card system is that it only needs one bad connection to prevent the entire computer from working properly. This is something that tends to be more of a problem after a computer has been in use for some time and the connectors start to corrode slightly. Nevertheless, even with new equipment it is possible that the metal terminals on one or other of the connectors could be slightly dirty or corroded, and that bad connections could cause problems. There are special cleaning fluids, etc., for use with connectors, but simply inserting and removing an expansion card a few times should do the trick.

The problem could be due to a faulty memory module short-circuiting the supply, and removing the module or modules from the motherboard might bring results. It could also be that the processor is faulty and is overloading the supply, but this is not very likely. It is not a good idea to power up the motherboard without a processor installed, so unless you have another processor that can be tried on the motherboard it is difficult to test for this.

Substitution

If none of this gets the power supply operating it is likely that either the motherboard or the power supply itself is faulty. Do not be tempted to open up the power supply unit and prod around inside to see if you can see what is wrong. A modern PC power supply is a complex piece of equipment that uses a lot of specialised components and quite advanced techniques. Many electronics engineers are not qualified to sort out this type of equipment and it is certainly well beyond the scope of an electronics handyman. Also, it is potentially lethal to dabble with any equipment that connects direct to the mains supply, and it is certainly not something that should be undertaken by anyone who is not properly qualified.

So how can you determine whether it is the supply or the motherboard that is at fault? Sorting out problematic PCs is much easier if you have some old parts that can be used as an aid to fault finding. This is one reason for me not recommending do-it-yourself PC building to people who have little or no previous experience with PCs. Most long-standing

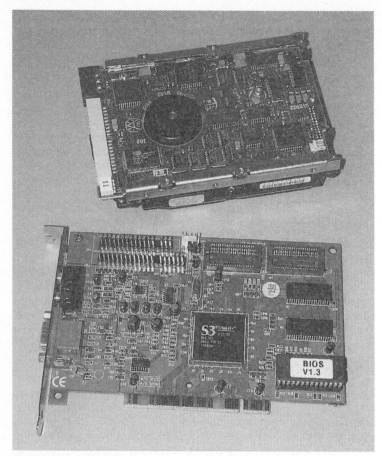

Fig.7.3 Keep old hard disc drives, video cards, etc. They can be invaluable when things go wrong

PC users have a collection of old components that have been replaced by more up-to-date components. These days they often have one or two complete but ageing PCs.

I would certainly recommend that you hold on to any PCs or PC components that are working and not totally obsolete, as these can often be useful when sorting out a troublesome PC. Items such as old PCI audio cards, AGP or PCI video cards, and low-capacity IDE hard disc drives (Figure 7.3) can be invaluable when trying to sort out a faulty PC. Old but working floppy or CD-ROM drives are also valuable for fault finding and are well worth keeping for this purpose.

In this case an old motherboard could be temporarily installed in the case to see if the power supply can be persuaded to burst into action. Alternatively, the new motherboard could be installed in an old case to see if it functions correctly. In either example there could be problems if the new case and motherboard are of the ATX variety, and the old equipment has AT connectors. For some years now it has been standard practice for AT motherboards to be ATX compatible, so unless the "spare" motherboard is really old it should be compatible with a new case. The old power supply might have a low power rating by current standards, but it should be sufficient to power a basic PC having a minimal set of drives and expansion cards.

If the new motherboard works in an old case, then clearly the new motherboard is not faulty. Presumably it is the new power supply that has the problem. If the old motherboard works properly in the new case, then the new power supply is functioning correctly and it is almost certainly the new motherboard that is faulty. This method of substituting a component that is known to work for one that is thought to be faulty is the basis for much PC faultfinding. Without specialised and expensive pieces of test equipment to check individual components it is the only practical method of determining which parts of a faulty PC work properly, and which do not.

Incidentally, if you return a component that is suspected of being faulty, it is unlikely to be tested on a special test bed or using some advanced piece of test equipment. It is much more likely that it will be installed in a working PC to see what happens. In other words, professional testers make great use of the substitution method, which is the quickest, easiest, and most reliable method of testing practically any computer component.

Partial failure

It is unusual for a faulty PC to simply "play dead" at switch-on, and the more usual problem is the computer starting up but reporting an error and failing to boot-up. Sometimes it fails to boot because the error brings things to a halt before the boot-up phase is reached. In other cases the error message will include a phrase like "boot failure", which means that the BIOS has tried to boot the PC but has failed to find a valid operating system. We will consider pre-boot failures first.

If the computer seems to be starting up normally, but there is no video signal, the obvious first check is to see whether or not the video card is installed correctly. In the past it was the video card that was most likely to give problems if there is a problem with physical alignment of the cards. These days the video card will presumably be an AGP type, complete with a locking mechanism to prevent any lifting at the front of the card. It is still worth checking that the card is properly in place, and that the locking lever has properly hooked into the card's cut-out and locked into place.

Also check that the signal lead for the monitor is connected properly to the video card and at the monitor if it is detachable at this end as well. If none of the monitor's indicator lights switch on it is likely that the problem is a complete lack of power to the monitor rather than an absence of video output from the computer. There is normally an indicator light switched on even if a modern monitor is receiving no video signal. Either another light switches on or the light changes colour when a video signal is received. If the monitor is completely "dead", it is not receiving power and the power lead and plug must be checked. If the monitor is powered via the power supply unit, try powering it directly from the mains supply. This will require a different power lead, but monitors can normally use a standard mains lead of the type used with most modern electrical and electronic gadgets.

If necessary, borrow the computer's power lead and try using the monitor on its own. Obviously you will not get any response from the screen, but an indicator light should switch on if power is getting through to the monitor. If this results in it working, either the original power lead is faulty or the power supply unit is faulty and is not providing any power on the mains output socket.

If the monitor itself appears to be faulty, do not be tempted to open the case and start delving around inside. There are very high voltages present inside a conventional (CRT) monitor, and these voltages can remain for some time after the unit is switched off. The interior of a monitor is potentially lethal and only trained engineers should attempt repairs to this type of equipment.

Lead checking

When faultfinding on PCs you will soon need to check leads for broken wires. There are inexpensive test meters available that have a continuity tester setting that is ideal for this sort of thing. In addition to any visual

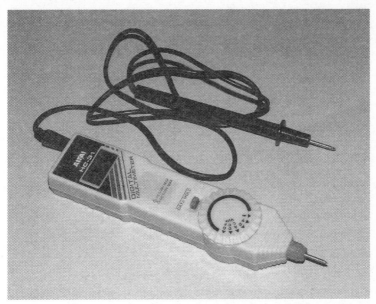

Fig.7.4 A digital test meter having a continuity tester function

indication, the unit normally produces a "beep" if a short-circuit is detected across the test prods. A miniature digital instrument (Figure 7.4) is well suited to this type of testing, but is somewhat over-specified. A basic analogue multimeter (Figure 7.5) is likely to be much cheaper and will do the job well.

In fact something much more basic is adequate for testing leads, and even an old torch bulb and battery style continuity checker (Figure 7.6) will do the job perfectly well. The test prods and leads can be the "real thing", but they need consist of nothing more than two pieces of single-strand insulated wire with a few millimetres of the insulation stripped away to produce the prods. This is admittedly a bit crude, but when testing computer leads it is often necessary to get the prods into tiny holes in the connectors. With the improvised prods there is no difficulty in doing so because they are so narrow, but with proper prods they are often too thick to fit into the connectors.

Testing cables is often rather awkward because you need four hands! You require one hand per test prod and another hand per connector.

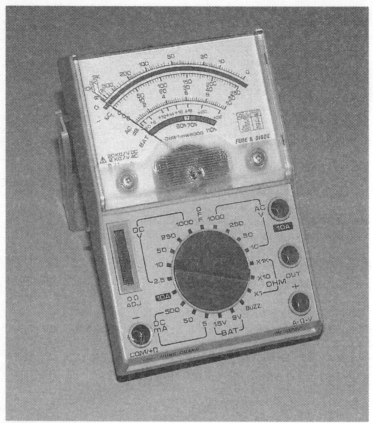

Fig.7.5 A cheap analogue multimeter is useful for checking leads

The easy way to tackle the problem is to fix both connectors to the workbench using clamps, or something like Bostik Blu-Tack or plasticine will often do the job quite well (Figure 7.7).

With heavier cables such as printer types it is better to clamp the connectors in place, because Blu-Tack and the like may not have sufficient sticking power to keep everything in place. With the connectors fixed to the bench and the metal terminals facing towards you it is easy to check for continuity because you then have both hands free to hold the test prods. Provided the workbench is well lit you can also see exactly what you are doing, which should help to avoid errors.

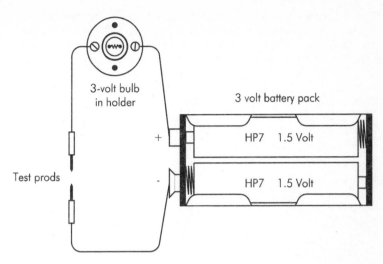

Fig.7.6 A simple continuity checker for testing leads

*Fig.7.7 Fixing both connectors to the work table makes it much easier
to test leads*

Incidentally, if you use a test meter for cable testing, on the face of it the meter is also suitable for checking the supply levels on the motherboard and other simple voltage checks. I would definitely advise against prodding around on the motherboard or an expansion card using a test meter. With the intricacy of modern boards it is quite tricky to do this, and there is a high risk of the test prods causing accidental short circuits. These could in turn ruin expensive items of hardware. The meter can be used to check for the correct voltages on a disc drive power cable and for simple continuity tests on cables that have been totally removed from the PC, but it is advisable to go no further with it than that.

Error messages

Returning to the subject of problems during the initial testing by the BIOS, it is possible for things to simply grind to a halt, but a more likely cause of the problem is that the BIOS has detected a problem and brought things to a halt. The screen may display a message along the lines "Press F1 to continue", but there is probably no point in trying to continue with the boot process if there is a major fault present in the system.

The error message may be rather cryptic, giving nothing more than a number for the error. The computer may also do a certain number of "beeps" from the internal loudspeaker over and over again, which is another way of indicating the nature of the fault. Unfortunately, motherboard instruction manuals do not usually give any information about the exact meaning of the error messages, but this information might be available at the web site of the BIOS manufacturer. It is worthwhile looking in the manual to see if it gives any guidance. Some instruction manuals are much more comprehensive than others.

These days the error message usually gives some indication of what is causing the problem, with an error message along the lines "keyboard error or no keyboard present". With the BIOS telling you the cause of the problem you can obviously go straight to the component that has failed to work properly. It is then a matter of checking that the keyboard is connected correctly, the memory modules are seated correctly in their holders, or whatever.

Once again, the substitution method can be used to nail down the exact nature of the fault. It the BIOS reports something like a memory or keyboard problem and everything seems to be plugged in correctly, there is a tendency to jump to the conclusion that the keyboard or a memory module is faulty. This could well be the case, but it is also possible that the problem is due to a fault in the motherboard.

If the keyboard is not functioning, try swapping over the keyboard with that of another PC. If the new PC fails to work with the replacement keyboard, but the other PC works perfectly well with the keyboard from the newly constructed PC, it is clearly the motherboard that is faulty. On the other hand, if the new PC works with the replacement keyboard and the other PC fails to work with the keyboard from the new PC, it is clearly the keyboard that is faulty.

Anomalies

Things in the computing world are not always as clear-cut as they should be, and if you are very unlucky you may be faced with an anomaly. For example, in our keyboard substitution example you might find that on swapping the keyboards both computers work fine, but on swapping them back again the new PC fails to work again. I can not say that I have ever experienced this problem with keyboards, but I have certainly encountered one or two memory modules and expansion cards that are rather selective about the computers they will work in. I have also heard of others having similar problems with mice and CD-ROM drives.

It is difficult to explain this sort of thing, and there is probably more than one cause. In days gone by there were certainly problems with expansion slots and cards that were not engineered with adequate accuracy. Some combinations of motherboard and expansion card would just about fit together well enough to work while others would not. Obviously there should never have been any problems of this type, but a lot of PC components were in the "cheap and cheerful" category, and were simply not up to the task.

This sort of thing seems to be extremely rare these days, and the more likely cause of problems is some slight electrical incompatibility, or two components in the system refusing to peacefully coexist for some obscure reason. Some makes of hard disc drive do not get on well together for example, particularly when trying to use an old drive alongside a new one. Some CD-ROM drives and hard drives seem to suffer from a lack of compatibility, although it is not advisable to use this combination on the same IDE interface for performance reasons.

If you are unlucky enough to find yourself saddled with one of these incompatibility problems you may be entitled to return the item that is causing the trouble. The difficulty is in determining which component is the cause of the problem, and it is understandable if suppliers are reluctant to take back items that work fine when they try them in their test PCs. If you persist with your complaint most suppliers will reluctantly do so, but you may prefer to be pragmatic about this sort of thing and rearrange the PCs slightly so that they all work, and the incompatibilities are avoided.

It is probably not worthwhile spending large amounts of time trying to get incompatible components to function together. Bitter experience suggests that in most instances they will never do so. Fortunately, this type of thing is relatively rare these days, so you would be very unlucky to encounter a serious problem of this type. Problems with device drivers rather than with genuinely incompatible hardware are another matter. If you have a PC that almost works but there are a few obscure problems it is odds on that the trouble is due to a faulty device driver. As pointed out previously, a visit to the relevant manufacturer's web site will usually produce a fully working device driver that cures the problem. Failing that, the manufacturer's product support team might have a solution or a way of working around the problem.

Memory

In some cases the BIOS will detect and report a memory problem, but if there is a total failure of the memory circuits or a problem with the processor the BIOS start-up routine may grind to a halt or never get started properly in the first place. Often the PC will slowly beep away without entering the POST, rather than doing the usual one or two beeps and then starting the POST routine. There are other problems that can cause this, but in my experience it usually indicates a memory problem.

When a memory fault is suspected, carefully check again the section of the motherboard's manual that deals with memory matters. Make sure that you are using an acceptable memory arrangement, and that the motherboard is not fitted with an unacceptable mixture of memory types. Unlike SIMMs, DIMMs can usually be used in multiples of one. Also, it does not usually matter which DIMM holders are used and which are left empty.

However, check the motherboard's instruction manual to make sure that there are no restrictions on the way that the memory modules are used. It might be necessary to fit the modules in the correct bank of sockets for the memory to work correctly. When using RIMMs, make sure that everything is in accordance with the fitting instructions in the motherboard's manual. Where appropriate, make sure that dummy modules are included in the appropriate sockets.

Fig.7.8 A close-up showing the locking arm of a holder within the notch of a DIMM

DIMM capacities

When the memory is in the form of DIMMs, the motherboard will probably not accept DIMMs of all capacities. Are you using memory modules that are supported by the motherboard? Where the motherboard has provision for both standard DIMMs and the DDR variety it will probably not be possible to use all the memory sockets. In most cases a mixture of normal DIMMs and the DDR type is not allowed at all, and you can therefore only use one of the other.

Modern motherboards are generally more accommodating than those of a few years ago, but when choosing the memory for a modern PC it is still essential to read the "small print" in the relevant section of the motherboard's manual. Also be very careful to avoid expensive mistakes and obtain the right type of memory first time.

A problem with the memory is most likely to be caused by one of the memory modules not fitting into its holder correctly. The quality of holders for memory modules is often quite poor even on some of the more upmarket motherboards. This tends to make it quite difficult to fit the modules into the holders, and in some cases they can be difficult to remove as well. When in place correctly the modules should lock into position, so try giving the modules a gentle tug to see if they pull free from the holders. If a module pulls away from its holder, even at just one end, it is not fitted in the holder correctly, and is unlikely to work reliably.

Although polarised, it was often possible to fit SIMMs the wrong way round. DIMMs are less problematic than SIMMs, and I have not experienced a similar problem with them. Nevertheless, perform a visual check to ascertain that the DIMMs are fitted the right way round, fully pushed down into their sockets, and fully locked in place. If a DIMM is fully pushed down into its holder the locking arms on the holder should fit into the cutouts at the ends of the module. One end of a properly locked DIMM is shown in the close-up shot of Figure 7.8.

With two polarising keys, one of which is well off-centre, there is no excuse for trying to fit a DIMM the wrong way around, and in theory anyway, it should not even start to fit into the holder. Whenever problems with the memory are suspected it is a good idea to remove the memory modules and refit them. This often seems to cure the problem.

Processor

The chance of a problem occurring with the microprocessor are very low, because the processor will only fit onto the motherboard the right way round, and very high quality ZIF sockets are used on even the cheapest of motherboards. If the processor fails to function properly the most likely cause is the motherboard being configured incorrectly. If the motherboard has some form of automatic processor detection facility, check that the right processor is specified on the initial start-up screen. If the wrong processor is identified it will be necessary to go into the appropriate section of the BIOS Setup program and set the processor parameters manually.

Note that if you are using a processor that has a clock frequency that is actually lower than its "equivalent" speed rating, it may well be the true clock frequency that the BIOS will use on the initial start-up screen. This depends on whether or not the BIOS specifically supports the processor you are using, and in most cases it will. Usually the name of the processor and its actual clock frequency will be displayed by the POST routine. Obviously there is a problem if the reported speed does not match up with the nominal or actual clock frequency of the processor.

If the motherboard is configured via jumpers or DIP switches, check the motherboard's instruction manual carefully again to ensure that you are using precisely the required settings. Sometimes there is a problem with the reported speed of the processor being about 25 percent slower than the correct figure. This usually means that the motherboard's bus frequency is too low, and that it is running at 100MHz instead of 133MHz for example.

Setting the correct bus frequency via the BIOS or a jumper on the motherboard, as appropriate, will take the processor's clock frequency to the correct figure and take the PC up to full speed. An error in the opposite direction is rarer, since the BIOS will usually default to the lower setting. Similarly, where the bus frequency is set via a jumper, the default setting will usually be the lower operating frequency. Erroneously setting the bus frequency to the higher frequency would probably result in the PC grinding to a halt soon after switch-on, so it is worth checking the relevant jumper if the PC exhibits this problem.

It might also be worthwhile clearing the CMOS memory in case this has become scrambled and is causing start-up problems. This is achieved by removing the relevant jumper from the motherboard, waiting about half a minute or so, and then replacing it. Most manufacturers recommend that the power supply should be disconnected from the motherboard while the CMOS memory is cleared. Presumably there is otherwise a slight risk of a residual charge in the power supply keeping the memory operational.

Discs

Discs and the BIOS were covered in chapter 4, and this topic will not be covered in detail again here. With the automatic detection systems of the average BIOS, the discs may all function perfectly well without the user altering any settings. Even so, it is advisable to carefully check the relevant BIOS settings if any drive problems are experienced. It is definitely a good idea to go into the BIOS Setup program to check the main settings when a new PC is first switched on.

As pointed out previously, there can be rare problems with incompatibility between certain IDE devices. This mainly occurs when using an old hard disc drive and a new one, and it can also occur when using some hard drive and CD-ROM combinations. This seems to be an innate problem with the drives, but it can often be resolved by shifting one of the drives from one IDE interface to another. In most cases this means having the problem devices on separate IDE interfaces, but apparently in some cases it can be necessary to move them from separate interfaces to the same IDE channel.

Note that if you are using a UDMA33 or later disc drive, special drivers will be needed in order to get maximum performance from these. These days any new hard disc drive will be UDMA100 or later, and some CD-ROMs, etc., have UDMA33 interfaces. The motherboard and (or) drive should be supplied with any necessary Windows drivers and full installation instructions. Remember also, that UDMA66 and later hard disc drives require a cable specifically for this type of drive and not an ordinary IDE cable. In the interest of performance, try to avoid having fast and slow devices on the same IDE interface.

Floppy problems

The most common mistake with floppy disc drives is to get one of the connectors on the data cable fitted the wrong way round. If you try to boot from the floppy drive it is inevitably unsuccessful, but it can also result in the data on the disc being corrupted. Having cleared the fault you try to boot from the disc, but this again proves to be unsuccessful. This gives the impression that the floppy disc drive is faulty or still installed incorrectly, but it is actually the corrupted disc that is causing the problem. It is advisable to have one or two spare boot discs handy so that you can try an alternative disc if the computer refuses to boot from the floppy disc for no apparent reason.

If there is a problem with a floppy connector fitted the wrong way round, or with the wrong ends of the cable connected to the drive and the motherboard, this should be immediately obvious. During the initial BIOS checks and the boot-up sequence the drive light of the floppy disc drive will usually switch on and off a few times, but with the cable connected wrongly the light usually stays on continuously. If the drive light comes on at switch-on and stays on, switch off and check the data cable.

The 5.25-inch power connectors are reasonably foolproof, but they are often a very tight fit. If a drive that uses one of these power connectors fails to do anything at all, make sure that the connector is fully pushed into the drive. The smaller power connectors used on 3.5-inch floppy discs are a different matter. Some drives have properly polarised connectors that only permit the power lead to be fitted correctly. Unfortunately, most 3.5-inch drives seem to have very "cheap and cheerful" power connectors that do permit errors to occur. Mistakes

Fig.7.9 The power connector is erroneously fitted one set of terminals to the right

here can result in damage to the drive and (or) the power supply unit, so it is definitely a good idea to get it right first time.

The most common mistake is for the power connector to be shifted one terminal out of alignment. In Figure 7.9 the connector is fitted one terminal too far to the right, and it is not difficult to see that there is something wrong. Apart from the fact that the connector is too far to the right, it is also at a slight angle to the drive's connector. It is easy to spot the mistake with the drive outside the case, but it can be more difficult to see this problem in a real-world situation with the drive installed in the case. Often you will be able to feel that the connector has not fitted into place properly, because it will not fully push into place. The mistake should be obvious if you take the time to look carefully at the connector.

Late problems

Problems do not always come to light when a PC is going through its initial testing or booting into Windows. Everything might seem to be all right until the operating system has been installed, after which some of the hardware may fail to work properly. Having installed Windows on a new PC it is always a good idea to go into the Windows Device Manager to check for any problems.

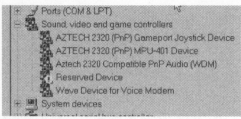

Fig.7.10 The exclamation mark indicates a problem with one of the soundcard's device drivers

To do this with Windows 95/98/ME, operate the Start button and then select Settings, Control Panel, System, and operate the Device Manager tab. You can then look down the list of devices in search of the dreaded yellow exclamation marks that indicate a problem (Figure 7.10). With Windows XP it is a matter of first selecting Control Panel from the Start menu and then double-clicking the System icon. Then operate the Hardware tab and finally operate the Device Manager button.

Initially there will usually be a few problems reported by the Device Manager, and this is simply because some of the drivers for the motherboard's built-in hardware have not been installed. These days motherboards are invariably supplied with a disc and (or) CD-ROM with various driver programs that have to be installed before everything will operate to perfection. The motherboard's instruction manual should give full details of the drivers provided, and how to install them. With the particular configuration you are using you may not need all the drivers supplied, so read the manual carefully to determine which software must be installed.

The ports can often be switched on and off via the BIOS Setup program, so if there is a problem with a port it is as well to go into the BIOS and check that any absent port is actually turned on. If a port is active, but is not detected by the operating system or an error is reported, it is likely that the port hardware is faulty. Unfortunately, since the standard ports are integrated with the motherboard these days, this means that the motherboard is faulty and must be replaced. One possible exception is if you are having problems with the USB ports under Windows 95. Most versions of Windows 95 do not have proper USB support, and it is advisable to upgrade to Windows 98 or ME if you intend to use the USB ports.

Most soundcards have a game port that can also act as a MIDI port. Integrated audio systems almost invariably have the same facility. These days it seems to be the convention to have the MIDI port switched off by default, so it is usually necessary to enable this port before it can be used. Where appropriate, the manual for the soundcard or motherboard should explain how the port is switched on and off. In the case of an integrated audio system, the MIDI port is usually controlled via the BIOS Setup program. Note that the MIDI port is not a standard type and that it can not be used with standard MIDI data cables. Special PC MIDI cables are required, and these include a small amount of interface electronics.

I have very occasionally had Device Manager show a problem with a piece of hardware that actually performs flawlessly. This was not exactly a rarity with Windows 95, but it seems to be much less common with later versions of Windows. I am far from certain about the cause of this problem, but there is presumably a minor flaw in the device drivers that "fools" Windows into thinking that there is a problem. In this situation it is best to take a pragmatic approach and not waste time trying to cure a nonexistent problem.

The opposite problem can also occur, with Device Manager reporting that everything is all right when there is clearly a problem. This is rare, but it can happen from time to time. One possibility is that the device drivers for the hardware are faulty or that the wrong ones have been installed. Try going into Device Manager, uninstalling the drivers, and then reinstalling them again. If that fails to cure the problem, visit the hardware manufacturer's web site and look for updated device drivers. It is likely that there is a hardware fault if loading the correct drivers fails to cure the problem. Windows will detect some hardware faults, but by no means all of them. The "all clear" in Device Manager is not a reliable indicator that the hardware is functioning perfectly.

Right leads

When you have been building PCs for some time you inevitably end up with a lot of leads and other odds and ends. When building a PC based on an AT motherboard it is tempting to simply grab the first serial or parallel port lead and blanking plate that comes to hand. This is not really a good idea though, since leads that look much the same may actually be wired up very differently. The serial and parallel port leads supplied with motherboards are not all the same, and you could certainly end up with a non-operating port by using the lead from one motherboard with a different motherboard.

When dealing with apparently faulty serial and parallel ports on AT motherboards it can be helpful to use a continuity check to determine

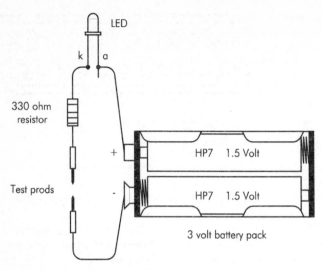

Fig.7.11 A low-current continuity tester using a LED

whether or not the port is connected properly to the motherboard. However, a torch bulb continuity tester of the type described earlier is not suitable for this type of testing. The test current used is too high, and could damage the port hardware. Only use a proper test meter that is designed for this sort of testing.

Alternatively, use a modernised version of the continuity tester that uses a LED rather than a torch bulb. Figure 7.11 shows a suitable arrangement. All the parts should be available from a shop or mail order company selling electronic components and equipment. Note that the LED will only work if it is connected the right way round. The cathode ("k") terminal is normally indicated by that lead being shorter than the anode ("a") lead and the cathode side of the body is usually (but not always) flattened slightly. Do not omit the resistor. Without this component a high current will flow, resulting in almost instant destruction of the LED.

Down to earth

The quick and easy way of checking that the leads are connected properly is to check for continuity between the chassis of the computer and whichever terminal or terminals of the port connector should be earthed.

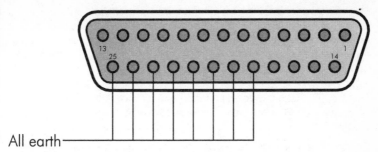

All earth—

Fig.7.12 The earthed pins on a parallel port connector

For a parallel port it is pins 18 to 25 that should be earthed (Figure 7.12). For 25 and nine pin serial ports it is respectively pins seven and five that should be earthed (Figure 7.13). If the right pins are not earthed and some of the other pins are, either the cable is connected incorrectly at the motherboard or you are using an unsuitable cable.

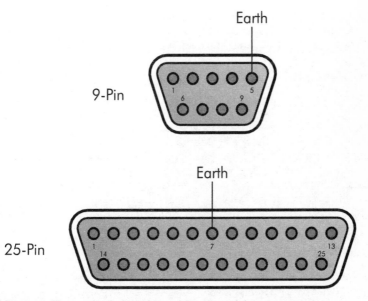

Fig.7.13 The earthed pins of 9 and 25-pin serial port connectors

The serial and parallel port connectors on motherboards are often simplified versions of IDE connectors, making it possible to connect the lead either way round. With a motherboard of this type you must refer to the manual to find pin one on each of the connectors, and then make sure that the red lead of the cable connects to this pin. It is also possible to fit many of these connectors one row of pins out of alignment. Fortunately, these cut-down connectors are now relatively rare, but due care needs to be taken if you should encounter a motherboard that uses them.

Of course, these days the vast majority of motherboards are of the ATX variety, with the main ports fitted direct on the motherboard. This largely avoids problems with leads to off-board port connectors. However, there are sometimes leads that connect to additional USB ports, front-panel mounted audio connectors, and this sort of thing. These are often optional extras and not supplied as standard with the motherboard. Be careful to obtain the correct items for the make of motherboard and to fit them correctly.

Minor problems

Most problems with a newly constructed PC are actually quite minor. Probably the most common of these is one of the front panel lights failing to operate. As pointed out in chapter three, these lights are light emitting

Fig.7.14 The power LED connector is out of position

diodes (LEDs) and not miniature light bulbs. Consequently they will only operate properly if they are fed with a supply of the correct polarity. If a light fails to operate, try reversing the connector to see if that cures the problem.

If the integral loudspeaker or any of the LEDs and switches that connect to the motherboard fail to work, carefully check the connections to the connector block on the motherboard. Getting these items plugged into

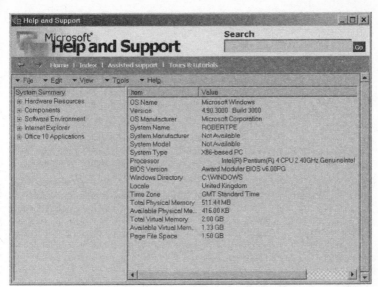

Fig.7.15 Some basic information about the finished PC can be obtained from the built-in facilities of Windows

the motherboard tends to be a bit fiddly, and it is often difficult to see what you are doing. Unless you have small fingers it will probably be easier using a pair of long-nose pliers or tweezers to manoeuvre the connectors into position. Incidentally, these tools are also useful for setting jumpers on the motherboard.

It can be helpful to shine a torch on the connector block so that you can see exactly what connects to where. Better still, get a helper to hold the torch so that you are free to concentrate on the connections. It is easy to get a plug shifted along the block by one set of pins so that one pin is unconnected, or it connects to the wrong pins. In the example of Figure 7.14 the power LED connector is shifted one row of pins to the left. A close visual inspection should soon reveal any problem of this type.

Be meticulous

Obscure problems can occur with a new PC, but they are relatively rare with modern PCs. In the vast majority of cases the computer will boot-up properly and work well if you are careful to get everything connected properly. When a newly assembled PC fails to work properly it is hardly

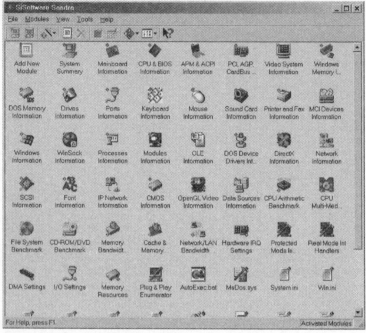

*Fig.7.16 The opening screen of Sisoft Sanda 2003. Double-clicking an
icon runs the appropriate utility program*

ever due to a faulty component, and is usually due to something very
fundamental like a connector that has come adrift or is fitted the wrong
way around.

When something goes wrong we would all rather blame someone else,
but if you check through a troublesome PC and fix any mistakes it will
almost certainly work flawlessly when you try it out again. Always resist
the temptation to rush at things. Trying to put a PC together in the shortest
possible time more or less guarantees that mistakes will be made.
Concentrate on getting everything right and give each part of construction
as much time as it requires. The newly completed PC should then work
first time.

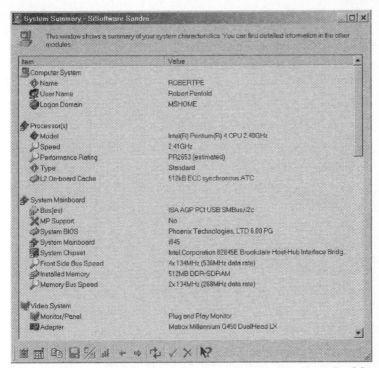

Fig.7.17 This screen provides some general information about the PC

Check-up

Having completed the PC and installed the operating system, many users like to check that the computer is running reliably and that the amount of memory, processor speed, etc., is all correct. Windows can provide some basic information about the processor and the amount of memory installed. With Windows ME and XP, go to the Start menu and then select Accessories, System Tools, and System Information. The System Information will take a few seconds to probe the system and then a Window like the one in Figure 7.15 will appear. This indicates the type of processor, its clock speed, and the amount of memory fitted (Total Physical Memory).

There are numerous diagnostic and testing programs that can provide further information and test the reliability of various parts of the PC. The

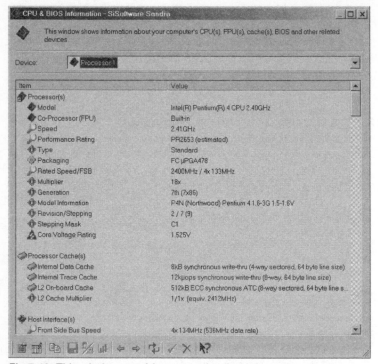

Fig.7.18 This window provides some detailed information about the processor

basic version of Sisoftware's Sandra is a very useful program that can be downloaded free of charge. A more advanced version is available as a commercial product. This is the web address to visit:

www.sisoftware.co.uk/sandra

The opening screen (Figure 7.16) has numerous icons that are used to access the various test and information screens. The two screens of Figures 7.17 and 7.18 respectively show some general information about the PC and some detailed information about the processor. Figure 7.19 shows the result of testing the maths co-processor of a 2.4GHz Pentium

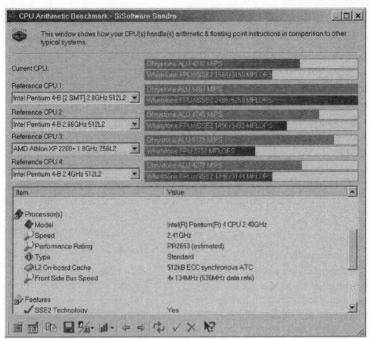

*Fig.7.19 This test of the maths co-processor shows that it is operating
at an appropriate speed*

4 PC. Typical test results for a range of processors are provided in addition
to the results from the PC being checked. This makes it easy to assess
the results, and in this case the test figures seem to be in line with the
typical results for a 2.4GHz Pentium 4 PC.

Memory testing

Detailed memory information is available (Figure 7.20) and the speed of
the memory can also be tested (Figure 7.21). In this example the memory
seems to be fractionally slow compared to the reference memory figures,
but the memory in the test PC is slower than the memory types supplied
for comparison purposes. The memory of the test PC is actually
performing quite well for its type.

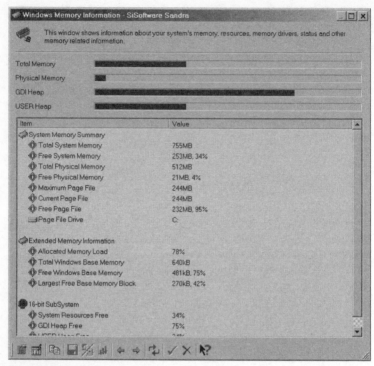

Fig.7.20 *Information about the memory and its use is provided here. In diagnostics and testing programs the RAM is usually referred to as "physical memory"*

Various other tests and information are available from the other modules, and most programs of this type can be set to repeat tests a large number of times so that the computer's reliability can be checked. It is certainly a good idea to give a new PC the "once over" with some test and diagnostics software. Some of these programs can also be used as an aid to diagnosing faults.

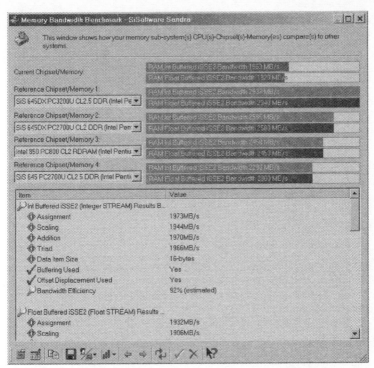

Fig.7.21 The memory seems slow in comparison to the reference
figures, but this is simply due to the test PC being fitted
with relatively slow memory

Points to remember

Prevention is better than cure, so always give the finished PC at least a cursory check before switching on and testing it. Ideally you should check that all the cables are present and correct.

Again, prevention is better than cure, so do not be tempted to ignore anti-static handling precautions. It will be time consuming and costly to replace components that were unnecessarily "zapped" by a static charge.

Check for the obvious, such as a lead that has become disconnected at one end, or drive power cable you have forgotten to plug in. In the vast majority of cases where a newly constructed PC fails to work it is something as simple as this.

If the motherboard uses configuration jumpers or switches, check that it is configured properly for the processor you are using. The configuration charts in motherboard instruction manuals are sometimes a bit ambiguous, so check them with a "fine-tooth comb" to ensure you are interpreting them correctly.

Check that the expansion cards are all properly seated in their holders. It only needs one of the cards to be slightly out of position to render the PC completely inoperative.

Try reducing the computer to one that is as basic as possible. Disconnect the hard disc drive, CD-ROM drive, and any non-essential expansion cards so that the PC is just a basic single floppy machine. If this works, reinstate the drives, etc., one by one until the PC fails to work. The last device added is then the one that is causing the problem.

Never open up a faulty monitor as there is little chance of fixing it and a good chance of killing yourself. Monitors operate at very high and extremely dangerous voltages, and these voltages can remain present even after the monitor has been unplugged from the mains supply and switched off.

Check that the memory modules are fitted into their holders properly. DIMMs are reasonably foolproof, and are certainly much better than SIMMs in this respect. However, DIMMs can still give problems unless you are very careful when fitting them.

Never connect or disconnect anything while the PC is switched on. Altering the cabling while a PC is switched on could easily cause costly damage. Definitely do not add or remove an expansion card or a memory module while the PC is switched on. This virtually guarantees that something will be damaged.

If an expansion card is suspected of being faulty, the easiest way to test it is to use it in another PC. Alternatively, try another expansion card in the PC that is giving problems. Keep old video cards, hard disc drives, etc. They are useful for substituting in a faulty PC to help track down the duff component. It is obviously not worthwhile keeping anything that is totally obsolete and not usable in a modern PC, but anything else is potentially useful.

Faulty components in new PCs are actually quite rare. If you get everything put together properly it is highly unlikely that your new PC will fail to work.

Never be tempted to open up the power supply unit. It is not the sort of thing that can be sorted by the average handyman, or even those with some knowledge of electronics. The power supply connects to the mains supply and is potentially lethal. If a power supply unit is found to be faulty, either the power supply or the complete case and power supply should be replaced.

There are plenty of programs available that can be used to check the speed and reliability of the finished PC, and some will help to diagnose faults. It is a good idea to give a newly completed PC a check with one of these programs in order to determine whether everything is functioning as it should.

7 Troubleshooting

Index

Symbols

168-pin	49
2D graphics	59, 61
3.5-inch	9
3.5-inch floppy	119
34-way	110
3D graphics	59
4x AGP	60
5.25-inch	9
8x AGP	60

A

Accounts icon	239
Activate Windows	251
activation	218
active speakers	63
activity light	16
Add Hardware Wizard	232
Add New Harware	196
Add/Remove Programs	167
additional connectors	116
addresses	160
administrator	223
Administrator account	239
Advanced Chipset Setup	146
Advanced Settings	229
AGP	41, 194
AGP Aperture Size	148
AGP cards	124
AGP slot	18
alarms	97
aluminium	71
AMD	27
AMD approved	267
AMI BIOS	138
anomalies	279
anti-piracy	247
anti-static equipment	71
anti-static packaging	19
anti-static packing	73
applications software	232

approved	267
AT	17
AT motherboard	37, 287
AT power supply	117
ATAPI	53, 66
Athlon	27, 32
ATX case	17
ATX motherboard	17, 38
ATX power connector	116
ATX power supply	39
audio cable	126
auto-only	144
automatic detection	82
automatic switching	10
Award BIOS	139
awkward hardware	195

B

Backup	260
backup	21, 84
bandwidth	49
bargraph	210
base	145
basic	257
battery	21
bay	104
bays	8, 42
big fonts	61
BIOS	15, 135
BIOS data	167
BIOS Features Setup	160
BIOS Setup	20, 81
blanking plate	16, 100, 114
Block Mode	162
blower program	164
boot disc	23, 130, 166
boot failure	273
Boot Up Floppy Seek	163
bootable	161, 205
breakdown	2
bus frequency	283

C

cable select	107
cables	16
cabling	104, 110
cache	28, 149
card	224
cards	17, 122, 268
CAS Latency	50, 148
case	74
cases	42
Clock rates	82
CD-ROM	53, 205
CD-RW	5
Celeron	30
CGA	61, 145
chart	36
cheap motherboards	6
check-up	293
checking process	250
chipset features	146
chipsets	45
CL2.5	49
CL3	49
clear CMOS	84
clock frequency	132
clock rate	31
clock speed	81
clock/calendar	21
CMOS RAM	21
colour depth	200, 228
COM2	157
Compact option	184
compatibility chart	36
compatible	127, 212
components	2
compression	260
Computer Management	255
conductive material	19
configuration	81
conflicts	156
connector	65
connector block	120, 291

connectors	105
continuity checker	277
continuity tester	288
Control Panel	167, 238
core voltage	83
correct channels	233
corrupted BIOS	165
cost saving	3
cover	100
CPU	151
CPU settings	153
Create Password	242
crocodile clip	71
cross-point	1
CRT	274
CS	107
Custom option	184
Customise button	213
Cut and Paste	261
Cyrix	82

D

D connector	65
data cable	56, 112
DDR	281
DDR memory	48
deactivate	114
default settings	147
delay times	150
desktop	241
Device Manager	194, 231, 287
dialling information	223
DIMM capacities	281
DIMMs	47, 97
DIN	41, 52, 65
DIP-switches	15, 84
disc cloning	253
disc-free ME	202
discs	283
Disk Management	260
Display icon	201

Display Properties   200, 227
Display Troubleshooter   229
DIY approach   3
DMA   54
DOS partition   173
dot pitch   62
downtime   3
doze   150
DRAM timing   146
drive access   102
drive bay   100, 104
drive bays   42, 44
drive letter   258
drive letters   143
drive modes   54
drive settings   141
drivers   24, 222
drivers disc   199
drives   99
dummy modules   280
Duron   27, 33
DVD   5, 56
dynamic   257

E

earth   288
earthing   71
ECP   157
EDIT program   172
EGA   145
EGA/VGA type   145
EPP   157
error   273
error messages   278
error trapping   146
Escape key   176
exclamation marks   286
existing installation   206
Exit   163
expansion card   123

expansion cards   17
expansion slot   17, 270
experience   4
extended DOS partition   174
extended memory   145

F

F1   140
fan   14, 35, 45, 92, 96
FAT   259
FAT32   173, 210, 259
faulty   3
faulty driver   214
FC-PGA   32
FDISK   172, 205
fixing screws   101
Flash BIOS   163
Flash upgrade   163
flickers   61
flip chip   32
floppy   119
floppy cabling   110
floppy disc   5, 9, 52
floppy drive   108
floppy drives   144
floppy problems   284
Floppy Seek   163
floppyless   163
FM   63
FM synthesis   65
foil   71
folder   252
FORMAT   172
formatting   22, 172, 177, 211, 259
frequency   132
frequency modulation   63
full-size tower   43
future proof   35

G

generic drivers	24
getting started	5
graphics	59
guarantees	3
guide-rail	13, 104

H

hard drive	9, 53
hardware	12, 195, 222
hardware conflict	156
hardware drivers	193, 222
Have Disk option	236
HDD-0	162
health monitoring	152
heatsink	14, 35, 92
heatsink compound	93
help screen	140
hertz	231
home-made PC	1

I

IBM compatible	145
IBM/Cyrix	82
icon	201
IDC connector	110
IDE	53, 141
IDE activity LED	121
IDE connectors	105
IDE HDD Auto Detection	142
IDE HDD Block Mode	162
identification number	248
IEC plug	75
installation	183
installation CD-ROM	22
installation discs	193
installer	22
installing Windows	171
instruction manual	38, 81, 193
insulate	19

integrated audio	7
integrated functions	41
Integrated Peripherals	156
Intel	91
IrDA	158
IRQ Resources	156
IRQ setting	160
ISA slots	59
Installing Windows XP	205

J

joystick	65
jumperless	15
jumpers	15, 84

K

keyboard	41, 51
keylock	121
knockout panels	76

L

LAN	76
language problems	237
language settings	213
language version	238
Large	143
large drives	172
late problems	285
Latency	50
LBA	143
lead checking	274
leads	10, 266
LED	122, 288
level 1	29
level 2	29
lever	87, 125
licence conditions	182
Linux	22
Load Setup Defaults	168
locking lever	125
logical drive	178

login 220
loudspeaker 121
low-level formatting 22
LS120 57

M

main installation 190
mains outlet 10
maintenance agreement 2
Make Private 243
malicious programs 164
manual 81
master 107, 142
Master mode 54
maximum size 173
MDA 61
megabits 49
megabytes 46
memory 7, 34, 46, 97, 280
memory module 47
memory settings 145
memory sockets 14
menu level 161
meter 275
MIDI 41, 65
MIDI port 160
midi tower case 43
mini tower 42
Minimal Boot 168
minor problems 290
mismatch 250
MMX 27
mode 54
modem 7, 194, 223
monitor 10, 61, 274
monitoring 151
mono adapters 145
motherboard 10, 37
mounting holes 101
mouse 51
MPU-401 65
MS-DOS 130, 172

MSCDEX.EXE 180
multiplier 81

N

network 186
New Partition Wizard 255
non-standard IDE 143
normal 150
NTFS 210, 259

O

OEM 36, 107
off 85
on 85
on/off switch 12
Onboard Device 159
Onboard IDE Function 158
onscreen controls 201
operating system 22, 171
operating temperature
44, 152
output powers 63
over-clocking 81, 131
over-temperature 151

P

pad 93
Page Down 144
Page Up 144
parallel port 289
parallel ports 157
parameter 49
partial failure 273
partition
143, 174, 208, 255
partition information 176
partitioning 22
password 192, 218, 243
Paste 261
PC100 47
PC1066 50

PC133 47
PC2700 49
PC3200 49
PC66 47
PC800 50
PCI 18
PCI slots 194
Pentium 27
Pentium 4 30
Pentium II 28
Pentium III 29
Pentium Pro 29
performance 1
Phoenix-Award BIOS 139
pin 1 106, 115
PIO mode 54
plastic cover 100
plate 100
plates 16, 75
play back 64
plug 75
Plug and Play 196
Plug N Play 154
PNP/PCI 154
polarised 105, 118
Portable option 184
ports 40, 114, 286
POST 48, 136
pound 237
power connector 116
power connectors 284
power consumption 132
power failure 165
power LED 120
power management 149
power supply 10, 116, 266
power switch 121
precautions 69
primary IDE 162
primary master 141
printer 7

private 244
processor 27, 87
processors 33
prods 275
Product Activation 244
product key 183, 214
progress bar 189
PS/2 41, 51
PSU 42

R

RAID controller 108
RAID interface 159
RAM 46
reboot 58, 190
record 64
red mark 106
region 216
Regional settings 238
registering 243
repairing 206
reset 268
reset switch 121
resistor 71
resolution 61, 200, 228
ribbon cable 106
RIMMs 50, 97, 280
risk factor 165
Roland MPU-401 65
ROM 64, 135
ROM BIOS 20
Rover 252

S

Sandra 294
Save 163
scan rate 61, 230
Scandisk 180
screen adjustments 62
screen resolution 228
screen settings 201

screwdriver	1, 91
screws	12, 100
scrolled	161
SCSI	57
SDRAM	148
Search facility	252
second drive	254
secondary IDE	56
secondary master	142
self test	136
setting up	20, 85
settings	221
Setup	15, 181
Setup program	
	81, 136, 206
shadowing	149
SIMD	29
SIMMs	47
single partition	208
Sisoftware	294
slave	107
slot	17, 270
Slot 1	32
Slot A	32
socket	87
Socket 370	29
Socket 4	27
Socket 478	36, 88, 94
Socket 7	28
Socket A	40
"soft" modems	200
software	232
SoundBlaster	127
soundcard	127
soundcards	63
specification	4
SPP	157
stand-offs	16, 77
Standard Defaults	84
Standard mode	157
standby	150

Startup disc	167, 173, 187
static	69
static electricity	18
static precautions	19
stereo	64
substitution	271
Super IO	157
supply	96
support chips	45
suspend switch	122
switch	12, 15
switches	84, 168
synthesiser	65
System Information	293
system memory	7
System Properties	234
System Tools	293

T

tabs	213
telephone support	4
temperature	44, 152
temperature warning	122
termination resistors	113
test meter	275
test prods	275
testing	130
Text Services	239
three-pin connector	97
tidying up	129
time format	215
time zone	187, 224
timing	146
tool	1
tower	42
trapping	146
Troubleshooter	229
Troubleshooting	265
twist	111
Typical installation	184

Index

U

UDMA33	105
UDMA33, etc.	55
unallocated	255
uninstalled	214
upgrade	164, 189
US English	237
USB	41
USB ports	17, 290
user accounts	239
using FDISK	174

V

VGA	61, 194
video	7
video card	224, 274
video cards	59
video settings	226
viruses	164
voltage	12, 83
voltage monitoring	151

W

wavetable	64
web site	38, 213
Welcome screen	218
WIMP	138
Windows	178
Windows 98 SE	171
Windows Explorer	166, 252
Windows ME	171
Windows modem	194
Windows Product Activation	244
Windows Setup	181
Windows XP	22, 205
Wizard	255
work surface	70
WPA	244
WPA centre	250
WPA file	251
WPA problems	249

wpa.dbl	252
wristband	71
write protection	164

X

XP	205
XP compatible	212
XP processors	33
XP repair	208

Z

ZIF socket	87
Zip drive	57